Defeat the Enemy Within

Defeat the Enemy Within

◆

Free Yourself of the Inner Shadows That Sabotage and Cripple Your Life

Charles Wm. Skillas, PhD, MBA, DD, BCH, CI, FNGH

Doctor of Philosophy in Engineering

Master of Business Administration

Doctor of Divinity in Spiritual Healing Arts

Board Certified Hypnotherapist, National Guild of Hypnotists

Certified Instructor, National Guild of Hypnotists

Fellow, National Guild of Hypnotists

iUniverse, Inc.

New York Lincoln Shanghai

Defeat the Enemy Within
Free Yourself of the Inner Shadows That Sabotage and Cripple Your Life

iUniverse, Inc.

For information address:
iUniverse, Inc.
2021 Pine Lake Road, Suite 100
Lincoln, NE 68512
www.iuniverse.com

ISBN: 0-595-32777-X

Printed in the United States of America

*This book is lovingly dedicated
to the memory of my mother, Margaret Nagy Skillas,
who gave me the courage to live,
and to my father, Charles Wm. Skillas, Sr.*

*It is also dedicated
to the National Guild of Hypnotists,
Dr. Dwight F. Damon, President,
who taught me how to heal myself so I could live well.*

Contents

PART 2: Healing with Hypnotherapy

PART 3: Articles from my Practice

Acknowledgements

My fervent thanks to the following without whose help this book would never have been written:

Laura, my wife, for her love and steadfast trust in me; LaVonne McBride, whose courage always motivated me; Jerry Kein of the Omni Hypnosis Center in Deland, FL, one of the greatest teachers on earth; Dr. Ed. Martin and Cheryl, who taught me Cell Command Therapy; Dr. Bill Baldwin who taught me much of what I learned about Spirit Releasement Therapy; Dr. Irene Hickman, who taught me how to do remote work; Dr. Edith Fiore, whose work and teaching inspired me; Dr. Arthur Winkler who taught me Past Life Regression Therapy; Brian Wilkes and B. J. Lackey, my editors; Darlene Haas Skillas Caskey, whose love and care in so many dark times kept me going; William L. Skillas and Kristy Skillas, my nephew and niece, who were always there for me; My brother Bill Skillas who I loved so much; My sisters Jean and Sylvia, who shared our early life of hardship and helped me so much; My children, Kathleen, Michelle and Charles Martin who gave me a reason to live when it was the darkest; My Grandchildren, who now give me reason to live in the light; and to Abercrombie, Beauregard, Sweetsiepootsy, and Daisy, my dogs who taught me about unconditional love.

The Truth

After God created the world and settled man and woman there, He wanted to place the Truth somewhere in the world where humans would eventually find it, but not before they had attempted to figure it out for themselves.

He asked the Archangels for advice.

One Archangel suggested that the Truth be placed at the top of the highest mountain, but a second Archangel cautioned that man would quickly crown the highest mountain peak.

Another Archangel suggested placing the Truth at the bottom of the sea, but the second Archangel again cautioned that man would soon fathom the deepest ocean.

Suddenly inspired, a third Archangel said, "Let's place the Truth deep inside every person. They won't look there for a long, long time."

And that is exactly what God did!

"Remember to live."

—*Goethe*

Prologue

I didn't want to die.

I still don't, but it has always felt like it was going to happen to me any minute.

My illness was FEAR, and it grew from the inside out. It was already there when I took my first breath, and the circumstances of my life and the times exacerbated and fed the terror that was within me. At age 10, when my father died, fear completely took over and ruled my life.

In all the years of thinking that I was on the brink of death, I never got used to it. It always terrorized me. I read all the books on death and dying, talked to the priests and nuns, prayed, and desperately kept going back to the doctors, but I was still sick and terrified.

A little background on me will give you an idea of the forces that shaped my life and caused the difficulties which I had to overcome in order to live, prosper and help others. These difficulties shaped my personality, and even though they caused me to be sick, they made me strong and taught me much. Just your reading about my problems and what I did, could cause you to reclassify your life and find respite in how I solved my problems.

Born in the Great Depression of the 1930's of parents who were uneducated and poor, I was fortunate that my parents, particularly my mother, saw education as the way out of poverty and nothingness. Even though my parents didn't have much schooling, they saw the value of it in America. Because they couldn't give me material things, they instilled in me the desire to go to school.

I owe a lot to traditional Western allopathic medicine and psychiatry. Without the help of these doctors, I probably wouldn't have made it. However, allopathic medicine prescribed drugs to alleviate the terror I was feeling but didn't do much to eliminate the source. Traditional psychotherapy didn't do much either, but provided me with a paid listener whom I could talk to about how miserable I felt. Psychiatrists gave me medicines to relieve my anxiety, and I ended up becoming addicted and going through countless wretched withdrawals. I even had to go into hospital detoxification wards to help me get off some of the prescribed medications. The resulting dark abyss of hell I found myself in was as bad as or worse than the addiction. Clinical psychologists cost me a lot of time and

1

money without helping me, and in some cases made my problems worse. The basic problem source of my stark terror eluded my doctors. I had to find help outside of traditional western medicine or I was going to die. Finally, I found release from my hell in holistic or alternative medicine—specifically, hypnotherapy. It is truly sad that in the USA, insurance won't cover the therapies that really help, but does cover the ones that don't.

This is the story of what happened to me, how I was able to continue to live with the great terror, how I was finally able to rid myself of that terror and, eventually how I was able to help others using what I had learned.

I write this book to give hope to others who suffer as I did.

PART 1

My Life

1

Family Values

I was born on March 22, 1930, in Youngstown, Mahoning County, Ohio. I was given my father's entire name, Charles William Skillas, but was not a junior. My dad called me Sonny Boy.

My mother, Margaret Mary Nagy, was born in Toledo, Ohio on January 24, 1909. Her parents were Louis and Janka Nagy. Grandmother Janka Nagy came to the United States from Hungary in 1906. My father was born in Thessalonica, Greece on October 7, 1898 into a farm family, one of many children.

I saw a picture of my father's father once. He was very impressive, with a long white beard, white hair, tall and slender with a strong, erect bearing. The picture was supposed to have been taken on his 90th birthday. He fell and broke his neck sometime thereafter—in a mountain climbing accident I heard!

My earliest memories are of living in Youngstown, Warren and Newton Falls, Ohio. It was fun living with my Aunt Rose and Uncle Chris Mahinas in Youngstown. They were sweet people and I really liked them. They tried unsuccessfully to get my sister Jean and me to speak Greek. They also cooked sheep a lot. I remember that the mutton stank, and I didn't like it.

My mother worked at a bakery and cleaned houses. My father wasn't home much; he was in Tarpon Springs, Florida, diving for sponges in the Gulf of Mexico. He was a hardhat diver, the main diver on a small sponge boat that he and a few of his Greek friends worked. They didn't own the boat, but worked for another Greek who did and who paid them in shares of the sponge harvest. I have a picture of my dad on the sponge boat as the Greek Orthodox priest was blessing it before sailing. When he was in Youngstown, he worked for Republic Steel Company as a roller operator in the rolling mill. Although my mother said he was very good at it, he still lost his job in the Great Depression.

My dad went by Bill Skillas. He was about 5'5", slender and slight, about 140 pounds. He couldn't speak much English, but everybody loved him. He was soft and somewhat quiet. He had no formal education, but had learned to write his name for his U.S. citizenship papers. He was so proud of becoming an American citizen. Over the years, the only things I have been able to hold onto are his citizenship papers and smoke stand. Because he loved his smoke stand so much, I also treasure it and keep my cigars stashed in it.

Because my dad was uneducated, he was often the butt of good-natured jokes by my better-educated Hungarian uncles. It was easy to see, though, that they all liked him, even though he wasn't smart like them. They all loved it when he would cook, and he loved to cook. My uncles' favorite dish was dad's salmon, prepared Greek style.

Dad used to take me out to meet his Greek friends who were always very nice to me. I remember in particular Jimmy Poulas. There were never the deep dismal negatives of my Hungarian relatives. The Greeks always saw things as wonderful or with some humor, even the bad things. It used to tick off my mother that my dad was like this. She would be, rightfully, deep in despair, but he acted as if it didn't matter. It wasn't that he ignored problems; it was that if he couldn't do anything about them, then he shrugged them off. My mother could not do that. I cannot either. This difference in attitude led to many disagreements between my parents.

I've been asked if it was the difference between Hungarian Catholicism and Greek Orthodoxy that made them so different. I think it is the difference between the Hungarian culture, which is Middle European and Teutonic in nature, and the more relaxed, fun-loving Greek culture of the Mediterranean area. My Hungarian family was, typically, rather dour and always worried about everything, while the Greeks, who had the same problems, took an easier attitude towards adversity. During festivals, holidays, and family get-togethers, the Hungarians always enjoyed themselves with wine, song and dance, while the Greeks tended to do this more of the time as part of regular life, not just during special occasions.

Perhaps because they didn't have much education, both my parents were determined that we kids should have a good education. My dad used to say that an education was the way to get ahead and "they couldn't take it away from you once you had it". My mother totally agreed. Unfortunately, my dad didn't really participate in my getting an education because he died on January 6, 1941, when I was only 10. It was to my mother that the responsibility for my education fell. She met the responsibility full force, and it was only because of her that I ever became educated. Lovingly, I dedicated my engineering doctoral thesis to her.

Mom continually urged me to study hard and to keep on going when things really got tough. And they did get tough! I had many problems with panic attacks and fainting spells from the time of my dad's death on. I wanted to quit school many times, but she was always there to help me. Getting the money to go even to high school, let alone college, was a major task, but she did it. When I was about 16, my Hungarian uncles said that she should have me quit school and go to work in the factories in Toledo to help support the family. Instead, she encouraged me to go to school and she took on all the fiscal responsibilities by herself. We had help from my sweet old maternal grandma, Grandmuschka Janka Nagy, but she didn't have any money. She gave us all she could, and much of what she got was from her good friend Andy Molnar and his mother. Andy was a butcher, who provided us with meat,

After my father died, my mother went to work at the Electric Autolite Company on Stickney Avenue in Toledo at night. During the day, when I was in college, she worked as a cook at the White Tower cafe on Superior Street to make extra money to help me. Mom always worked hard. She believed that if you weren't working and doing something constructive, that you were wasting your time, and time was critical because there was so much to do. We never had much money so working to make money was very important. On weekends, when she wasn't working at the Autolite, or cooking hamburgers, she was cleaning houses. Anything to make a buck!

I inherited that work ethic from her. I always had a job doing something to make money. I scrubbed floors, cut grass, raked yards, and worked in greenhouses. I sold newspapers, greased cars, repaired tires, and worked in gas stations. I worked as an usher and janitor in movie theaters, worked on farms weeding and skinning onions, worked in construction digging ditches, laying asphalt, and painting houses. I worked in the Libby Owens Ford Glass Factory on East Broadway as a glass handler and general laborer. One day, while working in the glass factory, I was lifting a 400-pound piece of glass with another glass worker, we dropped it, and it cut off my right thumb. I picked my severed thumb up out of the dirt and ran to the first aid station. They wrapped it and took me to St. Vincent's Hospital where they sewed it back on. They then took me back to the glass factory and I had to work out the rest of my shift under the influence of painkillers. They didn't pamper you much back then.

Because they cut into my time to work after school and we had to pay for the doctors and medicine, I really resented being sick with the panic attacks. Since the severe panic attacks started when I was about 12 years old, it really was hard to work around the feelings of impending death and still get something done. I felt cursed. Only when I finally found alternative medicine and hypnotherapy and started to heal did I realize that all this garbage I had to put up with, especially the fear of death, had been given me to make me strong and empathic so I could eventually help others. At least that's how I rationalized it to make me feel better about it.

Must be how God works!

2

Childhood Values

We moved from Youngstown, Ohio to Newton Falls, Ohio before I was five years old. I know this because I remember falling in the dining room and knocking out one of my front teeth on the old buffet's leg on my fifth birthday in the house in Newton Falls,

It was in Newton Falls that I first thought about the nature of life and death one day on my tricycle at about age three. I distinctly remember thinking that I was playing a part again, that I had done this many times before and would do it again many times. It was strange that in recalling that incident, I remember that as a child I considered it perfectly natural and somewhat ho-hum. No fear, no anxiety, just the remembering, "This is how it is." I know now that this was my first experience in this life with the reality of reincarnation.

Newton Falls was just a little town. There was one dirt main street downtown and they had parades there. My dad put me on his shoulders to watch. There was a covered bridge over a river where my dad and I would sit on the riverbank and fish for bullheads using dough balls for bait. I went to Sunday school in a church there, which wasn't Catholic.

We used to walk down a dirt road to Gubranski's store and buy on credit. Mr. Gubranski kept track of your purchases by writing them in a little book. Sometimes he wouldn't let us get anything because we hadn't paid our bill for quite a while.

Mrs. Zeilek lived on a farm down the dirt road to the store. She had magical powers and could inflict curses on cows and people. She always wore a black dress and always spoke of the devil like she knew him.

My dad had access to a car—from whom, I never knew. Occasionally we would go to Lake Milton and Milton Dam to swim and picnic. Dad was an expert swimmer—he had been a sponge diver—but I wasn't.

When I was five years old, I fell in love with Delma Lou Jenkins, the girl next door. She had long red hair and was the most beautiful girl in the world. When I told her I liked her, she hit me with a milk bottle. Ever since, whenever I fell in love, which I did frequently, I expected the milk bottle treatment. It didn't happen often.

My father lost his job at the steel mill during the depression and we had to move to Toledo and live with Grandmushka, Janka Nagy in her old shut up grocery store at 1301 Girard Street. The store was closed because of the depression. All the roads were cinder, and the store stood on the corner like a Y, across from the railroad tracks. We stole coal from the railroad cars whenever we could so we could keep warm in the winter. The railway guards chased us, but seldom caught anyone. On the few occasions they did, they would beat us up and let us go without pressing charges.

The Kovaks lived across the street. Mr. Kovak was reputed to be a gangster, so I regarded him with childish awe. I played with Steve Kovak, who was about my age. He taught me how to hop the freight trains without getting my leg caught. Most of the rest of the neighborhood was black. I liked the blacks. I loved to hear them singing in the black church on the corner on Sunday mornings and listen to the preacher rant and rage, and froth at the mouth and tell everyone they were going to burn in hell.

3

Life Experiences

Down Girard Street towards White Street was Grandma's old house. Blacks lived there and paid Grandma $10/month. Sometimes she sent me to collect it. The blacks were very poor so I hated asking them for money. Many times, they couldn't pay, but Grandma let them live there anyway. She was like that even though she didn't have much. I surely did love.

This was the same old house where Grandma and her family had lived earlier. That was before she got the store and she was married to Louis Nagy, my mother's natural father. My mother had a favorite little brother named Sammy. One day, in front, of my mom, Louis Nagy in a drunken rage shot and killed Sammy and then himself. My mother never forgot that. She talked about it to me many times over the years. She really loved Sammy. We used to go to put flowers on his grave at Calvary Catholic Cemetery in West Toledo. Mom and Grandma would cry whenever we went there. As a suicide, Grandfather Louis Nagy wasn't buried in the consecrated ground of Calvary Cemetery.

My Hungarian uncles were all bootleggers during prohibition, so they knew all the local gangsters. One in particular, Arpy Fargo, was my favorite, because he was supposed to have killed at least 10 men. My uncles drove cars to bring the hooch to Toledo from Detroit after it was smuggled in from Windsor, Ontario, Canada. I found out later that my father-in-law, John Martin, used to supply the Detroit bootleggers with beer. He had an underwater pipeline from Riverside Drive in Windsor to Belle Isle in Detroit. I was very impressed by this. He was just a little guy, but he had big balls.

I liked living in the closed up grocery store. Mom, Dad, Jean, and I lived in the basement. Uncle Steve and his family lived upstairs in the closed store. Uncle Julius and his family lived upstairs on the second floor. The upstairs second floor was very grand, but I liked the basement better. My bed was in the coal bin. When they bought coal, I had to move all my stuff out of the coal bin so it wouldn't be covered in coal dust. My mother and father slept in a bed and my sister Jean slept on a bench in the corner near the cast iron cooking stove that used wood for fuel. We had a toilet near the sewer with a drape for a door and a sink that hung on the wall. A big old coal fired furnace separated the back part of the basement from the front where we lived and where the stove was. It was very cozy warm in the winter when we had coal.

On Saturday night, about ten of us bathed in a big old washtub that was kept outside. They would heat the water on the wood stove and pour it into the tub. We would all bathe, one at a time, but we all used the same water. Grandma made the soap out of fat and lye that stung like hot acid. When mom and the women washed clothes, they boiled them in a copper kettle because they didn't have bleach then. All the women in our family washed clothes not only for their own family but also for neighbors to earn a little money.

Mom and my aunts also made Hungarian noodles, which they put into little bags, and we would sell for a nickel a bag. The women would make the dough, roll it out on the big *tabla*, and then fine cut it by hand with a knife, which looked like it would shear their fingers off because they went so fast! I loved to watch them cut the dough; it was hypnotic. There is nothing so good as home made Hungarian noodles that melt in your mouth and leave that delicious soft flavor of fresh bread on your tongue.

Grandma stored all kinds of vegetables from the garden in a root cellar behind the grocery store. I liked the root cellar; it smelled like fresh earth. My grandfather, Somogyi Bochi, hid his store of wine in the root cellar so my Grandmuschka couldn't find it. We made our own wine from grapes grown in our own *lugash* (grape arbor) in the back yard. Grandma also made wine out of strawberries, cherries and dandelions. It was all very good and we all, including the kids, drank wine every day. Grandma said it was good for the blood.

On special occasions like holidays, weddings and birthdays, we kids would all line up and get a shot of Schenley's whiskey, followed by a beer chaser. Not until I grew up did I learn that this was called a boilermaker. We also got whiskey when we were sick. And, plenty of garlic! When we had a cold, Grandma put liquor into tea and fed us garlic toast *(fughudgma kennaid)*. We always got better.

Every now and again, the family would get a pig and Uncle Johnny would lead the butchering in the basement. In the morning when we woke up, there would be *kolbasz, hruca* (blood sausage) and *cuchona* all over the place. It was like magic. *Cuchona* was jelled pigs feet sprinkled with paprika. It looked like dishes of frozen soup with red snow on it—and it was delicious!

We ate a lot of things that today would be considered terrible for you. For instance, I would watch the old Hungarian men eat raw pig fat with paprika on it. I ate it too and it was very good with wine. The old guys used to butter their bread with one-half inch of lard, sprinkle it with paprika and garlic and gobble it down. Hungarian soup always had one-quarter inch of grease floating on the top. I think the paprika took all of the bad stuff out of the fat because these old guys all lived to be 90 to100 years old. We had *naschel,* which is now called "Hungarian Turkey". You cut up bread, cover it with raw onions, tomatoes, fresh Hungarian peppers, and drip grease onto the concoction from jowl bacon *(shutne solona)* burned over an open fire. It is delectable! I still enjoy this Hungarian delicacy whenever I can. So much for a diet low in saturated fat!

We had a little radio, which was a big thing then. I remember listening the night they executed Bruno Hauptman for the Lindbergh kidnapping. That night my uncles were all sitting around the table drinking whiskey and betting that he wouldn't be executed. But they did it!

I remember the doctor coming to be with my mother in grandma's store. Like most kids back then, I didn't know anything about sex. I thought the doctor brought my sister Sylvia in the black bag he carried into the store. That is what the family told me, but I remember wondering how she could breathe in the bag. I also wondered why it was necessary for people to be married to have children. Why not just order what you wanted from the doctor? This greatly perturbed me. There had to be something else going on.

Sundays with Grandma

A high point of my week was delivering the Sunday paper to Grandma's store where she would be waiting for me with breakfast after finishing my route. We would eat together and listen to the Hungarian hour on the radio featuring Gulumbush, the pride of the Toledo and Detroit Magyars. The broadcasts were in Hungarian and the music was beautiful Hungarian Gypsy music. I loved it!

Grandma spoke to me in Hungarian, but I understood everything she said. In my memory, these breakfasts with my dear Grandmushka were some of the sweetest moments of my life. She would call me *"adesh fium",* which in Hungarian meant "sweet boy". I would call her *"adesh anyum"* (sweet mother). Later, she got a canary, which would sing to the Hungarian music.

Childhood Work

I had a paper route for the Toledo Blade with 75 customers each morning and evening and on Sundays. The paper cost three cents and I got one cent per copy.

After delivering my papers on Sunday and after breakfast at Grandma's I would hawk Sunday papers at the corner of Woodville and White Street. It was fun on Sundays because I didn't have to get up so early like during the week. I didn't make much money, if any at all. Many of my customers would let their bills accumulate at 18 cents a week for four or five weeks and then refuse to pay me, saying they didn't owe the money. I was too dumb to realize that this was a losing proposition.

I was never a very good businessman, even later in life. I was always far too trusting of people, and got hosed regularly. Curiously, even when I grew up and learned something about life, I still got hosed. I could never do business very well. I liked the technology and the art, but I wasn't good at negotiating or being tough. I'm still not and guess I will never be.

I also worked on farms in the summer. I worked for Mr. Bushen on his farm for one summer. He paid me 10 cents per row that I weeded on my hands and knees. The rows were about a quarter mile long, so I could only do two per day. This was 20 cents for eight hours' work. It took one hour to bike the 15 miles to the farm in the morning after I delivered my papers. I got up at 3:30 AM everyday to deliver the papers and be at the farm by 7:30 AM.

Bushen was also a crook. At the end of the week, when I would tell him that I had weeded twelve rows (six days work) which I had done, he would say that I couldn't have weeded that many rows so he would give me a quarter. This was also not a good way to get rich, and further evidence that I was not a gifted businessman.

My cousins Bob and Steve Nagy were working at Heini Klotz's about 2 miles further down Brown Road from Bushen, and they were making big money (50 cents per day) skinning onions. They helped me get on with Heini Klotz who said he would give me a trial period…so I went to work skinning onions. I loved to skin onions and loved the big money. At the end of each week, I expected Heini to review my performance and tell me if I was a permanent hire, but he didn't. He would just pay me and I would come back to work on Monday. This went on for about 3 weeks. The suspense was killing me, so after a particularly good day of skinning onions and after being paid because it was Saturday, I asked Mr. Klotz if he was going to keep me on permanent. He said no, that I didn't have to come back anymore. I was so embarrassed. Here I was, fired from my first job, because I was so insecure about my job and couldn't keep my mouth shut. If I hadn't said anything, I'd probably still be there skinning onions. This action on my part provides additional evidence regarding my lack of business acumen!

Training to be a Crook

Once a month we went to the Eastwood Theater on Saturday. They had good adventure movies and a running serial. I remember Flash Gordon, Dick Tracy and Capt. Marvel. It cost 10 cents to get into the theater and we got 5 cents for a bag of popcorn. Even though it was only once a month, it was great. The only problem was that we would miss three of the four weekly serial episodes and so we didn't know what was going on most of the time, but it was still fun.

I remember that I liked gum, but couldn't afford to buy any, so the theater was my supply. You could scrape gum off the seat bottoms and chew it. Sometimes it was very hard, so you had to suck it for a while before you could chew it. It always tasted good although it was often gritty. Sometimes I got canker sores in my mouth.

When I reached 14 years old, I worked for the Eastwood Theater as an usher, and was soon promoted to head usher. I also helped the janitor clean the theater after the shows; they ended about 11:30 PM, and the official janitor and I would clean the theater. We swept the floors, scrubbed the lobby and I had the distinctive honor of cleaning the toilets. I would finish up about 3:00 AM and then walk the four miles to home. It was hard work, but it was worth it since I made exorbitant money…forty cents per hour! I had to give up the janitor job when I was in school because I needed the sleep. However, I still kept the usher job.

To augment my income, I used to "fix" the Treasure Chest game on Friday night. I was on the stage with the treasure chests and would palm the winning ticket. When a person from the audience drew the winning ticket and handed it to me, I would have an accomplice from the audience receive the $5.00 treasure chest. Then after the show, we would split the money. I was in training to be a crook.

I used to steal a lot of stuff regularly from all kinds of places. I stole candy from drug stores, soda pop from delivery trucks, ice from the ice trucks, baseballs and such stuff from sports stores. I figured that as long as I was going to hell, prison couldn't be much worse. A lot of the guys in my neighborhood did go to jail and one was executed for murder. I was lucky, however, and only got caught twice, once for stealing penny candy from a drug store. The owner let me off with a warning. Another time I stole a baseball mitt from a sports store. They caught me and accused me of stealing many items over a considerable period of time, which I hadn't. But because they caught me, they said I had to reimburse them for all the stuff that had been stolen that winter which amounted to about $350 or they would send me to jail. Not wanting to go to jail yet…I was only 15, I had to work all summer and give them the $350 I made for working three months laying hot asphalt in the hot weather. I never stole again, not because of hell, but because if you got caught, it was too damn expensive. I decided then that stealing wasn't worth it and I stopped. If hell really is the penalty for stealing, I've already done part of my sentence laying hot asphalt in the summer.

Early Fear

My sister Jean and I were in my Uncle Julius' car with Aunt Edna when I was seven years old. A lashing rainstorm came up and we had to stop because Uncle Julius couldn't see the road.

I was terrified. My fear was so great that I was paralyzed, and began to cry. From as far back as I can remember, I had always felt fear. This time I thought I was going to die, and I was scared stiff. The terror was so overwhelming that it possessed me totally. All I sensed was fear. After it was all over, I was ashamed of myself for acting like a baby, but it was so devastating, I was powerless to combat it. I recognized the fear...I knew it well...I had had it forever.

It wasn't until after I was released from the demons who were attracted to my fear, and in **regression therapy** as an older adult, that I found out what the fear was. My mother was terrified before and while giving birth to me. She was scared because of her financial insecurities and great fear of death. This fear went into me, became a part of me, and was the source of my panic attacks, which began to possess me after a bus hit me at age eleven. This accident was the trigger for the panic attacks, which possessed me from then on.

Monroe, Michigan

Dad found a job in Monroe, Michigan and so we lived there in 1937-1938. We lived in an apartment above a Salvation Army meeting hall. It got noisy when they beat the drums. The Majestic Movie Theater was across the street and my mother with my cousin Madge would go there on Friday nights to get free dishes. You paid your ten cents for the show and you got an entire place setting of dishes or glassware. It's now called "Depression Glass" and can be expensive.

I remember New Years Eve of 1938. Downstairs in the Salvation Army, they were blowing horns, screaming out in the streets, and beating the drums. My dad got very sick one night with quinsy, a throat infection, and the doctor had to come and lance his throat. To makes matters worse, I got the chicken pox in

Monroe, Michigan. Man, was I ever sick! I had pox all over my body, even in my mouth. I thought I was going to die, but I finally recovered.

I got to know my cousins Madge and Hazel who worked at the paper mill in Monroe. Madge married Dominic Natario, an Italian guy who worked for Nick Costell's market as a butcher. I liked Dominick but he drank himself to death. I didn't understand about needs then. I didn't understand why he kept drinking when his doctors said he had cirrhosis of the liver and that he would die if he didn't stop drinking. I couldn't understand why he kept on doing something that was hurting him so much.

Ironwood Street in Toledo, Ohio

Uncle Johnny got my dad and uncle, Joe Kives Sr. jobs at the Jenison Wright Creosote plant off Anthony Wayne Trail in South Toledo. After Dad got the job, at $25.00 per week, we were able to move back to Toledo and into a rented house on Myrtle Street, not far from where Uncle Howard and Aunt Barbara were living. We didn't stay there long but moved not far away to 1623 Ironwood Street. This was a nice house. Aunt Barbara and Uncle Howard lived at 1601 Ironwood just down the street.

My cousin, Joe Kives, Jr., came to live with us and stayed several years. We shared a bedroom together. Sylvia and Jean shared a bedroom, and mom and dad had the front bedroom. Uncle Johnny and Aunt Irma also came to live with us for a while, so Jean, Joe and I slept in the basement then. We had an icebox for storing food, and in the winter, a galvanized metal box hung from the kitchen window to keep things cool. A coal-fired furnace kept the house very comfortable once the furnace was stoked in the morning. Before the furnace was stoked, it was icy. We always had money problems, but $25.00 per week seemed to get us by. We still went to the Eastwood Theater on Saturdays, once per month—still 10 cents for the show and 5 cents for popcorn.

My Ersatz Grandfather

The only Grandfather I ever knew was Somogyi Bochi. My Grandma married him before I was born. He was a little man who was a good carpenter and he loved to drink wine. His main job was delivering milk. Somogyi carried the milk in a basket. Even in the snow of winter, he was always there with the milk. Everyone liked him because he was kind of a nice old guy, but he could get very mean when he was drunk, which he was whenever he could. He didn't speak any

English at all, only Hungarian, and he sang Hungarian songs when he was drunk. Grandmuschka said they were evil songs so she wouldn't translate them for me. I heard that after he came to America from Hungary, he moved to Chicago and lived in a brothel cleaning up the place because he couldn't find work as a carpenter. How he and my Grandmuschka ever got together, I never knew. He hanged himself in the closet on Wright Avenue in South Toledo when Grandma and he lived there while I was in college.

4

Dad's Death

My mother and dad were in an automobile accident that shoved the steering wheel into my dad's chest. My mother was okay. Dad complained about chest pains for quite some time and his doctor had him drink mineral oil.

Because of Dad's chest pains and fatigue, my cousin Joe Kives and I would go with him to help him with his work at the Jennison Wright Company. We didn't go together; sometimes Joe would go and sometimes I would go. I was a strong kid for 10 years old. At the creosote plant, my dad's job was to haul the wood shavings in a big wheelbarrow from a bunker and then shovel them into the furnaces. His job title was "fireman's helper". He really assisted the fireman who was responsible for firing the furnaces to produce steam pressure for the creosoting operation. We helped Dad for about six months.

On January 6, 1941, Dad died at the creosote plant from a heart attack. Neither Joe nor I were with him that night. It turned out that Dad had aortic stenosis; a hereditary disease, which doesn't allow the three leaves of the aortic valve to fully open at birth. Apparently, the auto accident caused a blood clot to form and when it reached his heart, it killed him. He was 43. My baby brother Bill was born exactly one week after my father died on January 13, 1941. It was very tough on my poor mother.

5

Perils of Poverty

I had a lot of trouble with bad teeth when I was little. I never heard of brushing teeth, let alone flossing. One night I had an abscess and Mom had to take me to a dentist on Oak Street in East Toledo. Apparently, my dad had gone there before and still owed the dentist some money. The dentist said he had to pull my abscessed tooth and wanted to know if Mom had the $10.00 to pay for it. She said she had her social security checks. Mom received $14.00/month for each of us kids from social security. The dentist grabbed her purse and took all the checks. He said if she didn't sign all of them over to him then, that he wouldn't pull my tooth. She had to do it. I was embarrassed and so enraged that I could have killed him right there. I could see the fear and embarrassment on my mother's face. I have never liked dentists since then.

After Dad's death, we couldn't live in the house on Ironwood on our remaining income so we moved back to Grandma's store. This time, we lived in the grand upstairs. It was okay, but I liked the basement better. We got a refrigerator. We never had one before, always ice boxes. Mom bought it out of the $1500.00 insurance she got from dad's death. Dad never had any insurance until the year before he died. He smoked a lot, Bugler during the week and Pall Malls on payday. We kids liked to roll his Bugler cigarettes. Dad smoked a couple of packs per day and Uncle Johnny kidded him that the cigarettes had ruined his lungs and he could never get life insurance. Dad got mad and applied for insurance, passed the physical and got the $1500.00 policy. They only paid on it for about a year. That was the first time I ever saw an insurance company come out on the bottom. Hell of a way to win, though.

My tonsils were badly infected, and Doctor Beckwith said they absolutely had to come out. The only way we could do this was to have it done through the "mother's pension", a charity for widowed mothers with kids. So, on the appointed morning, Mom and I rode the bus to the Toledo Medical Building on

Michigan Avenue downtown, and dropped me off to have the surgery while she went to work.

I was nervous, being only 11 years old, so I took a drink of water. The Doctor came out and said that I was next and he hoped that I hadn't eaten or drank that morning. I said no. So, they took me into the back room and I put on my pajamas and lay on the table. They put an inverted funnel over my nose and mouth, and poured ether onto the gauze covering the funnel sieve. Soon I passed out and they started to remove my tonsils and adenoids. I soon awakened throwing up from drinking the water. They had to re-sedate me to sleep three times because I kept getting sick from the water.

Finally, the surgery was over. I woke up laying on a pew in the waiting room. The nurse was shaking me and telling me I had to get up, get dressed and get out of there because they were going to close. So I did, but it was really hard. I can't ever remember being so tired. I got dressed, walked down two flights of stairs and out to the street to hail a taxi. Mom had given me money for a taxi because she didn't think I would be able to ride the bus after the surgery. The taxi was $1.50; the bus would have been only 5 cents. I was glad to be in the taxi since I was so tired and I would have had to transfer if I had ridden the bus. I returned to the empty house and got into bed. There wasn't anybody home until later that evening.

6

Vinal Street

Mom had about $800 left from dad's insurance after paying for his funeral, so she used it for a down payment on a house at 1623 Vinal Street. Before, we lived in Grandma's closed store for quite a while, and I went to Oakdale School. She had gotten a job working for families, cleaning and such and also had good prospects for a job at the Electric Autolite Company over on Stickney Avenue in West Toledo. After we moved to Vinal St., she finally got the job at Autolite, but it was on the 3-11 PM shift. She would take care of my baby brother Bill all day, and then Jean and I would take care of him, if you could call it that, at night. My Aunt Mary and Uncle Steve and their son Billy Nagy also came to live with us. People were always coming to live with us and we were the poorest part of the whole family. I liked having the other people around, except for Uncle Steve because he was mean and would beat Jean and me for nothing.

Raising Baby Bill & Beatings

Jean and I would feed Baby Bill as we saw fit, although we were under plenty of admonition from Mom not to feed him junk, like chocolate covered French fries. We did, and he survived. Aunt Mary was sick all the time so she wasn't any help with Little Bill. Uncle Steve was gone all the time except for Saturday night, when he would come home and beat the hell out of Jean and me...especially me. There was a belief, in those days amongst the Hungarians, except for my Grandmushka, that kids had to be beaten regularly or they wouldn't grow up correctly. I never told Grandmushka about the beating because I was ashamed to tell her that her son was a brutal man. Every Saturday night Uncle Steve would give us a dose of castor oil and whip us with his leather belt. I was the one who got most of it, because Jean was much littler than I. One day I told Uncle Steve that if he hit me again, I would kill him. And I meant it. He never beat Jean or me after that.

22

Mom said I should not have spoken that way to Uncle Steve, because it was disrespectful.

Shotgun Security

Mom got off work at 11 PM, so by the time she rode the bus to east Toledo, it was about 12:30 AM. The bus would let her off at the corner of East Broadway and Vinal Street. That was about four long blocks from our house. It was a dangerous neighborhood, filled with bars and hoodlums, so I used to meet her at the bus stop with a 12-gauge shotgun, fully loaded, and escort her home. Even though I was only 12 years old, nobody ever gave us any trouble.

I used to have to make that same trip many times at night to Collins and Parker Drug Store, near the bus stop, to pick up a new pacifier for my little sister Sylvia. If it got lost, Sylvia wouldn't sleep, so I would have to go out and get her another one at 11:00 PM. I was always scared having to navigate through that neighborhood with all the bars at that time of night. I would carry the shotgun, hide it outside the drug store before I went in, and retrieve it again after I came out. I used to practice shooting the gun in a vacant field and I got fairly good at hitting what I aimed at. It kicked like the devil however, and I would sport a sore shoulder for a few days every time I practiced. I didn't have money to buy any shells, so I would steal the shotgun shells from my Uncle Johnny, a deputy sheriff. I felt guilty stealing but did it anyway. It was a means to an end, I told myself. I had to have shells to protect my mother and I couldn't afford to buy any so I stole them. If I go to hell for that, then so be it. I was going to hell anyway, according to Father Hebbeler, our parish priest.

7

Catholic School

After Dad died and we moved back to Grandma's store, my mother was put under a lot of pressure by my Hungarian Catholic relatives to send us kids to Catholic school. We switched from Oakdale School to St. Thomas Aquinas.

St. Thomas was on Raymer Street away past Navarre Park. Oakdale was only a short walk, but St. Thomas' was almost 5 miles away. And at St. Thomas, you had to go to Mass every morning before school. Father Hebbler was the pastor and Sister Eleanor was the principal. I liked Sister Eleanor; I didn't like Father Hebbler. He expelled me from school because I accidentally kicked Paul White in the backside one day while standing in line. Father Hebbler said I was a pagan and would probably go to hell when I died. I already knew that I was bad and so what he said made real sense. I figured that the panic attacks I was having was God's punishment on me for all the bad thoughts I had, especially about girls—after all, they threw milk bottles at me!

I mostly liked the Sisters. Sister Teresita, my seventh grade teacher, was my favorite. I had to learn to serve Mass and become an altar boy. I studied the Latin Mass, and it was a great achievement when I was finally selected to serve. I loved to serve mass because you were up in front of everybody like you were something special. I served mass from the sixth grade on. I was also in the Chancel Choir. I liked the singing and most of it was Gregorian chant, especially the Litany of the Saints. It really got to me.

The trouble with serving Mass was that I would get assigned the 5:00 AM mass. This means I would have to be at the church at 4:30 AM. It was too early to deliver papers when I got up and left home on my bike for St. Thomas. When I had to walk the 5 miles, it took about 2 hours. When I finally saved the $5.00 needed to buy a used bike and could ride, it took about 25 minutes. It was especially bad in the wintertime because it was dark at 2:30 AM when I had to leave the house. Moreover, it was cold. After Mass, I had to go back home, deliver my papers, and then go back to school to be there for the 8:00 AM bell. One good thing about serving Mass was that you didn't have to go to church with the rest of the class at 7:00 AM, since you had already been to Mass at 5:00 AM.

I didn't really want to go to Catholic School and I didn't really like it, but I had no choice since the Hungarian Catholic side of my family took over after my father died. I liked Oakdale School better. Father Hebbler insisted that Jean and I be baptized Catholic. I had already been baptized Greek Orthodox when I was born. Uncle Julius, my mother's brother and Aunt Edna, were our godparents. For my confirmation, my Uncle Joe Kives Sr., husband of Elizabeth, my mother's sister, was my confirmation godfather.

Joe Kives, Sr., like my dad, worked at the Jenison Wright Company. He had the same kind of job as my father, but on a different shift. One day Uncle Joe was in the boiler cleaning it when someone accidentally turned the live steam on and cooked him. He died in terrible agony at St. Vincent's Hospital on Cherry Street.

When I was baptized Roman Catholic, I knew that you couldn't be baptized twice. I had already been baptized, at birth, in the Greek Orthodox Church. This didn't seem to make any difference to Father Hebbler, who taught me that you can't be baptized twice. When I asked him about it, he said the first baptism didn't take. I think it did. When I was in Greece I wanted to visit a little church on a hill in Athens and was told I couldn't enter unless I was baptized in the Greek Orthodox faith. I didn't have any trouble telling them that I was Greek Orthodox. Therefore, I visited the church without any problem.

One of the things I liked about St. Thomas was that I got to play on the school basketball team. I was a good Center. One of the things I hated about St. Thomas was that if you didn't have any money, you did not get milk and graham crackers everyday after Mass. Every morning after Mass, they would serve chocolate milk and graham crackers to everyone. Everyone except me. The milk cost seven cents, and naturally, I couldn't afford it, so I would sit there every morning and drool while all the rich kids (everyone else in the class) got their milk and crackers. I never got any. Not only was I hungry, but embarrassed that I couldn't get any milk. To add insult to injury, I would often be chosen to pick up the empty bottles and haul them to the school basement after everyone else had their milk. I hated this and I hated all the rich kids who got milk and graham crackers, while I got none. If I had known about Communism then, I probably would have become a Communist.

8

War

In 1938, Orson Wells put his story of the attack on our world by Martians on the radio. It was called *The War of the Worlds*. It was great excitement. Everybody listened to the Mercury Theater shows that Wells put on, but this one was the best. People actually believed that we were under attack by the Martians. People moved to the mountains and barricaded their homes from the Martians. I was only eight years old and I knew that it was a radio show. It amazed me that grown ups could act so foolish. In contrast to this fantasy, *The War of the Worlds* became a reality when Hitler invaded Poland in September 1939.

People were very afraid of the war raging in Europe. When the Germans attacked Poland in September of 1939, it seemed the Germans were invincible. Everybody talked about the war, and we kids had little colored pictures of the war in China showing civilians being tortured and killed. The pictures were very vivid showing people being beheaded with their arms and legs cut off and burned alive. It was very scary. We thought that if we went to war, that's what would happen here.

I was in the Eastwood Theater when the management stopped the show and said that the Japanese had bombed Pearl Harbor and we were at war. It was a terrifying time. People thought that German and Japanese bombers would begin to bomb our houses at any time. All the lights everywhere went out at night and we all had blackout curtains so that light didn't show through the windows. The air raid wardens patrolled the streets to enforce the lights out rule. You could go to jail and be considered a saboteur for letting the enemy know where we were. We kids were told that the penalty for this was hanging or at least 100 years in prison without parole.

With the war came rationing of many things like gasoline and food. No new cars were made during the war, so everyone had to get by with what they had. The speed limit for all traffic everywhere was set at 35 MPH to save gas and tires. You couldn't buy new tires; you had to get recaps made from synthetic rubber.

They were almost worthless as they kept coming off the tire base if they got very warm. An "A" card got you four gallons of gas per week. Gas was 16 cents per gallon. Sugar, meat, gum and cigarettes were severely rationed.

Pork Chops

My grandmother's friend Andy Molnar was a butcher who provided meat to our family, so we ate well. I was a strapping adolescent and could eat six pork chops at a sitting with no problem. My mother would cook the chops and put them in front of me and I would eat them. I was in love at the time with Jeannie Hatfield, a beautiful redhead, and she invited me to dinner at her home. Including me, there were six people at the dinner table. Mrs. Hatfield put six pork chops down on the table in front of me and I proceeded to put all of them on my plate and eat them. It wasn't until later that I realized that no one else was eating any pork chops. I couldn't understand why no one but me liked pork chops. It was strange, but our love seemed to cool after that dinner and I noticed that they never invited me back to eat again.

World War Two Ends

I was working at a Standard Oil gas station, pumping gas, changing tires, greasing cars and changing oil and trying to learn how to do tune-ups. I remember the day the newspaper extras came out and said we had dropped an atomic bomb on Hiroshima. No one knew what an atomic bomb was, and then we atomic-bombed Nagasaki a couple of days later and the papers said that the war was over. Everyone was very happy. It meant that Joe Kives, my cousin, would be coming home from the war. I really liked Joe. He sent me a German helmet and a German 22 caliber rifle in the mail from Germany.

9

The Bus Accident

After my father's death, I had to assume the responsibilities of the man of the house, since I was the oldest. This meant that I had to take care of the furnace in the wintertime and do things like cutting the grass in the summertime.

When I was 12, I was mowing the grass in front of the house and a Toledo Transit bus hit me on the right hip and threw me up onto the porch, a distance of about 20 feet. I remember feeling the pain in my hip and not being able to talk. I was able to limp into the house and tried to tell my mother, who was in the kitchen what had happened. I couldn't talk for about ten minutes from the shock, I guess. Finally, I was able to communicate to Mom what had happened and she became hysterical. While I was incommunicado, she was desperately trying to find out what had happened to me. She called the bus company and they said for her to take me to the emergency room at St. Vincent's hospital, which she did. They examined me and said that I was badly bruised and had some severe skin abrasions on my ankle and hip where the bus had hit me, but that there was nothing serious. So, we went home. Mom didn't believe the doctors that I was all right. She said "that's what they said about your father after the auto accident, and look, he died from a heart attack not too long after". Later I would learn that the seeds she planted with that statement had affected me greatly.

About 6 months later while working in the front yard, I began to have some chest pain. I told my mother about it and she became hysterical and berated me for not having told the doctors at the hospital after the bus accident about all my pain. I didn't remember having chest pain from the bus accident but I was having them now. I got very scared that the same thing that happened to my dad was happening to me. Soon I began having fainting spells and panic attacks. The panic had lain somewhat dormant within me from birth, although I always knew it was there. Now this bus accident, the connection with my father's death reinforced by my mother's fear opened up the floodgate of terror. I suddenly knew that I was mortal and could, would, die. I could die right now. I waited for it to happen at any moment, vulnerable and horrified. Thus began the panic attacks and terror that ruled my life from then on.

Before the bus hit me, I played on the St. Thomas basketball team, served Mass and sang in the Chancel Choir. I loved doing all of these things because it put me in front of people and I felt good. The panic attack I suffered after the bus accident now appeared to be indelibly fixed in my brain. All of a sudden, I became aware that I could faint and die at any time and in front of people and I would be so ashamed. I couldn't play basketball, I couldn't serve Mass, although I really tried to serve Mass because I liked it so much…but it became hell for me every time I got out onto the altar. The panic would build inside of me, I would start to hyperventilate and get faint, and I thought I would die. I tried for a long time to continue to serve Mass, but it got to the point that after surviving to the end of Mass, I was wringing wet with perspiration and white faced from the fear. I had the same problem with singing in the choir. I continued to do both, but it was torture.

I thought that if I just faced the fear, that eventually it would go away, but it didn't. It just got worse. I simply endured it…it didn't get any better, only worse. I found it was difficult now to even walk anyplace outside of my house. I would start to get the panic feeling…it would develop into a full-fledged panic attack, and I thought I was going to die. I got so I didn't want to leave the house, I was so scared that I would have an attack and no one would be there to help me and I would die. I finally graduated from St. Thomas' but I wasn't able to go on the stage with the other kids to get my diploma, I was too terrified. They just gave it to me.

10

Panic Attacks

People who have never experienced a panic attack cannot imagine what it feels like. You think you are dying. The fear becomes so overwhelming that you revert to being a baby and want to cry out for someone to help you. It is terrible. I had my first panic attack shortly after my dad's death. After the first one, they came often. Just having experienced the first one opened my mind to subsequent ones and they came easier. It was like after the first one, the skids were greased and you slid into them so easily.

A panic attack is an amplification of the body's usual response to fear. The chemical, adrenaline, which is normally produced when we need action to run from danger or to fight, is overproduced. Because you don't run or fight and use up the adrenaline, you feel the effects of it and it terrorizes you. You breathe fast and shallow, your heart beats rapidly, you can feel numbness in your body and you think you are about to die. I think the generalized high level of fear, which produces terrible anxiety is the precursor to the attacks. At least in my case it was.

My high level of fear was with me from birth, having gotten the fear from my mother. After my dad died, I was faced with the fact that I too was going to die. I didn't know how to handle it and so, when I had the bus accident, I related that event subconsciously to my father's car accident before he died. I also thought I was going to die immediately.

My first panic attack was as an altar boy at St. Thomas Church. Suddenly, I realized on the altar that I was in front of people, and that they could see my fear and see me die. This caused me to focus on my bodily sensations, looking for something that would indicate that I was about to die. The mere act of intense focusing on myself brought on heightened sensitivity to all my bodily processes, and the sensations, however small, became magnified and developed into symptoms. After that first panic attack, they came faster and easier every time. The skids were greased and I fell deeper into the pit of terror with every subsequent attack. I was now captive to this unspeakable horror and I was locked into the prison of myself with no way out. I was dead…I was just not buried and I was so afraid. I was also just 12 years old.

This panic was with me all through school, forcing me to sit in the back of the classroom so I could escape easily if I started to die. I didn't want anybody to see me acting like a baby…I was so ashamed of the weakness that was with me in every waking moment. I lived with imminent death every minute. I remember lying in bed on Vinal Street counting my heartbeats and wondering when my heart would stop. My terror was compounded by my fear of what would happen to me *after* I died. Catholic School had impressed me with guilt and hell, and I was sure I was going there.

I had a particularly difficult time with flying, which I had to do a lot of in my professional life. Being locked in the plane and unable to get out when I started to panic was sheer torture. I devised all sorts of ways to bear the agony of flying. I carried a paper bag into which I could breath to restore the carbon dioxide balance of over-breathing, as well as Xanax and Ativan drugs to help me. I also found that if I wrote about how I was feeling when I was feeling it, that it tended to relieve the anxiety somewhat. When I got off the plane at my destination, I was usually soaking wet from sweat. This also happened when I had to do public speaking or any activity when I would have to stand out in front of people.

High School Fear

High school was awful. I had to take a bus downtown and transfer to the Cherry Street streetcar to go out Cherry Street to Central Catholic High School (CCHS). This was and is today a great school. The teachers understood my problem, even though I never told them about it. They let me sit in the row near the door so I could get out if I started to feel faint.

Scholastically, I was smart, so I did very well in my grades and I liked learning, but the panic attacks ruined high school for me. I got to know a priest, Reverend Dr. Dunn, who taught mechanical drawing and who was very kind to me—he even let me drive his car. I continued to work at the Eastwood Theater during high school to earn a little money, but I could no longer get onto the stage and run—or rig—the "Treasure Chest Show".

Shock Treatments

While I was in high school, my mother took me to some psychiatrists and to the Lucas County Hospital, under the county charities for kids without fathers, to see if I could get some help. The medical doctors always said I was healthy and the problem was my nerves. The psychiatrists put me into Mercy Hospital and did twelve electro-shock therapy treatments on me to try and help me. All it accomplished was to make me lose my memory for a while. Nothing helped, and I was getting worse instead of better.

In my senior year, I was out for the entire second semester, but, because I had such good grades, CCHS allowed me to graduate. They sent me my diploma in the mail. I had finally made it through high school, but it was miserable!

11

University

The legacy from my parents and my own desire made it imperative that I go to college. Even with the wretchedness I was suffering, I had to go to college. There was no way around it. However, I had two problems: I had no money and I was sick. Other than that, every thing was great. What to do?

I had known that I wanted to study engineering since I was nine years old. My dad had no education or training of any kind except that of sponge diving and what he learned working in the steel mills. When we lived on Ironwood Street before he died, he and I were in the garage with his old 1933 Ford, which wouldn't run. The garage floor was cinder ash from the furnace. Dad didn't have any money to get the car fixed, so he decided to take the engine apart and see if he could see anything that looked broken and fix it. He lost lots of parts and screws in the cinders and couldn't get the engine back together again. When my Hungarian uncles heard about it, they laughed at him and called him stupid, even though they liked him. I was very upset and ashamed that my father was so stupid and uneducated.

After dad died, I went out into that garage with that old Ford still all disassembled and cried my eyes out. I loved him, even though he was uneducated and stupid as my uncles said. I vowed then that I would avenge my dad, that I would become whatever it was that knew all about things like cars and machinery and show my uncles that Bill Skillas' son wasn't stupid and uneducated. I asked the parish priest who it was that knew about such things and he said engineers. That's when I decided to become one.

Getting Through the University

I decided to attend the University of Detroit (U of D), which was a Jesuit school and had a good engineering reputation. One of the overriding considerations was that U of D had a work-study program called "Co-Op" which after the first two

years you could go to school three months and work three months until graduation. This lengthened the time until graduation to five years instead of four, but
that was all right. My cousin, Steve Nagy, was also going to U of D for Electrical
Engineering, but his parents could afford to pay for his tuition, books and living
expenses. I didn't have these luxuries.

My mother and I talked about how to get me through the first two years at U
of D. We figured that once I got onto the Co-Op work-study program, I could
earn enough to pay my way. Mom had an insurance policy on me for a few hundred dollars, which she had been paying on with Prudential since I was born. It
was about fifteen cents per week. The Prudential man would come every week
and collect the money and mark it in a big fat book. We gave U of D the few
hundred dollars and Mom continued to work at the Autolite from 3:00 PM to
11:00 PM and then cooked at the White Tower Restaurant from 12:00 AM to
4:00AM in downtown Toledo. I worked after school in Detroit sanding cars for a
paint and body shop.

The University gave me a job as night watchman in GESU School, which was
across the street from U of D and allowed me to live in a little room in the basement. I also had the task of killing pigeons around the U of D; they bought me a
Crossman air rifle for this. I also cleaned a restaurant after it closed at night and
they allowed me to eat all the mustard and ketchup sandwiches I could hold.
Between what my mother could send me from her work in Toledo and what I
could earn working and living in the basement of GESU School and working at
the restaurant, I got through the first two years at U of D. I was tired a lot, but I
got through it.

All the while going to school, I had panic attacks at least twice a day. I always
sat near the door in class and stayed out of any public limelight. It was very difficult in English debating class when I had to stand up in front of the class and
debate. I got to know the U of D doctor quite well, as I saw him at least three
times per week when I thought I was dying.

I got through the first two years and was able to go to work on the U of D
work-study Co-Op Program. You would go to school for three months and work
for three months. You did this for three years. My first two work periods were for
Bohn Aluminum & Brass Company in downtown Hamtramick, a Polish part of
Detroit. It was an interesting neighborhood, but it was hard to find anyone who
spoke English. It was like Birmingham in Toledo, where everyone spoke Hungarian. I worked as a draftsman for Bohn and didn't like it, so I thought I'd get
something different for the next work period.

I had been working at nights for the U of D Mechanical Engineering Department as a handyman. They liked my work and were building a new dynamometer laboratory, and they asked me if I would like to work there during my work periods. Of course, I said yes. I loved this job! I soon became the boss of all the Mechanical Engineering Laboratories and had four people working for me. This was a pattern that manifested in all my future jobs. I would start out in a low position and end up the boss.

Early TV

Whenever I could, I would go home from the University. I would go over to my Aunt Barb & Uncle Howard's house because they had an 8-inch Admiral Black & White TV. Most of the time, all you saw was the test pattern but we were able to see a lot of Kukla, Fran and Ollie program. We also watched local wrestling from the Toledo Sports Arena. This was the best! Gorgeous George, Nature Boy Buddy Rogers and the Zebra Kid. There was also Farmer Brown, who came into the ring with a pig. My uncle Howard had a porch and 25-30 people would gather on the porch to look through the window when we watched wrestling. It was a wonderful time. We ate popcorn while watching the wrestling matches.

Patricia

I met my first wife, Patricia Martin, in my junior year in college. She went to Marygrove College, a private girl's school a short distance from my school, the University of Detroit. She was the daughter of John and Marie Martin of Windsor, Ontario, Canada. I liked the Martins very much. They were very kind people and treated me extremely well. I never let any of them know that I had the panic attacks, not even Pat. I was so ashamed. It was a great deception and played a large roll in our eventual divorce. Patricia and I married on June 13, 1953 right after graduation and headed for California, where I had a job working for the Navy.

12

Guided Missile Research & Development

After graduation from University of Detroit with a Bachelor of Science Degree in Mechanical Engineering, I took a job with the US Navy Air Missile Test Center (USNAMTC) at the Point Mugu Missile Test Range in California. I was a project engineer in the Missile Launcher Evaluation Branch as a GS-5 making $284.00 per month. I liked the job and learned much, although we didn't eat very well on that income.

While at USNAMTC, I received two Navy Superior Accomplishment Awards for my work on an Induced Pitch Launcher for launching Regulus Missiles off submarines at sea, and for designing an air gun for simulating air launched missile-launching forces.

I worked directly for Dr. Willy Fiedler, one of the German Scientists who came to the USA after WW-II with Werner Von Braun. Fiedler was with Von Braun at Peenemunde in Germany during WW-II working on the V-1 and V-2 Rockets, which devastated England during the "Blitz". Fiedler had actually flown a V-1 Buzz Bomb to check out the guidance system. With Fiedler, I was among those who participated in the launch of the first missile from a submarine at sea…the launch of the Regulus missile from the submarine *Tunney*. I also helped install the first steam catapult system aboard the aircraft carrier *Hancock*.

I once asked Dr. Von Braun what made the German scientists so valuable to the USA and Russians after the war. He replied that to develop a successful rocket system, you first had to make 60,000 mistakes; the Germans had already made 30,000 so the job was half done.

I had a hard time in this job with the panic attacks, although I enjoyed the excitement of the job and I learned so much. I had to go to sea often in Navy vessels, submarines, destroyers, cruisers and aircraft carriers and fly in Navy fighter jets, so it was scary for me with my fear of dying. I used to come home shaking with fear from the experiences.

It was interesting that with all my fears, when I had to face a genuine fear situation, I could often do it with relative calm. A case in point: One time we were temperature cycling two rocket boosters for Sparrow Missile booster rocket tests for which I was the test conductor. The rockets were brought from the conditioning chambers about a quarter mile away and put onto the launchers on the launch pad. The boosters had to be mated with the Sparrow Missiles on the launch pad, and I had to put an igniter into each of the boosters before leaving the launch pad.

Everyone but me had left the launch pad. I put the igniters into the boosters, mated the boosters with the missiles, and walked off the pad, down the steps and into the control bunker. I pulled the steel door shut behind me and turned to look at the TV monitors and the missiles exploded on the launch pad, destroying everything on the pad surface. I had left the missiles about 20 seconds before they blew up.

Subsequent investigation revealed that the booster rocket solid propellant grain had cracked during the temperature cycling and exothermic decomposition began in the grain of the rocket propellant. The temperature in the boosters reached ignition temperature 20 seconds after I put the igniters into them. Somehow, I had picked up 20 seconds during the two days of temperature cycling, which saved my life. For some reason, I accepted this occurrence calmly, without panic. I went back to work and did the same job repeatedly after that.

I taught courses in physics, calculus, and differential equations at the Navy Base under the UCLA extension program while studying for my MS in Mechanical Engineering. I finally had to quit teaching because I just couldn't stand up in front of the class with the panic. I also had great difficulty driving to and from work, having to stop many times when I thought I was going to die.

My two beautiful daughters, Kathleen and Michelle were born in Oxnard at St. John's Hospital. I was so proud of them and loved them so much. I was always afraid they might have inherited my panic problem, but they had not. Thank God!

While working at the Navy base, I re-injured my back, which had been damaged from an old wrestling injury and had to have disc surgery. That surgery left me with scar tissue, which to this day affects me. Back in those days, the Navy didn't provide health insurance so I had to pay for my children's births and for my surgery. It took me seven years to pay off that debt.

13

Bendix Missiles

With a growing family, I had to make more money and we wanted to be closer to home, so I began looking around for a new job back East. I wrote a paper on "How a Mechanical Engineer Looks at the Design of Electronics in High Stress Missile Environments" and presented it at the American Institute of Aeronautics and Astronautics Conference in Los Angeles. Somehow, I got through the presentation, which was very well received, and the chief engineer for the Bendix Missile Division in Mishawaka, Indiana offered me a job packaging the electronics for the TALOS Nuclear Fleet Defense Missile, which they were building for the Navy. I accepted, and we moved to South Bend, Indiana, which was closer to our homes and families in Toledo and Windsor.

My new job was head of the Mechanics Laboratory at Bendix Missiles and I soon established a reputation as someone who could solve the reliability problems of the missile. What I learned working for the Navy and my mechanical engineering education made it possible for me to bring a fresh approach to packaging the missile electronics, which had been failing miserably. The TALOS missile electronics were packaged around the diffuser of the ram jet engine where they were subjected to the terrible environment of heat, shock, and vibration, which the missile imparted to the electronics causing the missile reliability to be less than 40%. Bendix liked my work so well that they made me Chief Mechanical Engineer for Electronics with about 150 people working for me. The reliability of the missile rose to 95% with our new electronics packaging concepts.

My son Charles Martin was born in South Bend. He had a congenital heart defect called aortic stenosis, which was what my father had. My nephew, Timmy, son of my sister Jean also had aortic stenosis and he died from it at 11 years of age. We took Charles Martin to Chicago where the doctors confirmed the condition. They said there was only one place in the country that could help him, Children's Hospital in Boston, because they had a heart-lung machine modified to handle small children. As soon as I could arrange it, I got a job with Sanders Associates in Nashua, New Hampshire, which was close to Boston.

My son Charles Martin had his first open-heart surgery at Children's Hospital Medical Center in Boston. That was a very hard time for Patricia and me. We both loved him very much and felt so powerless in combating his affliction. I knew I had to keep myself together so that I could help him. This is one of the ways I found to cope with my terrible fear: I had to focus my mind on something very big outside of myself. Focusing on my love and concern for Charles Martin helped me bear the fear.

I remember when he came out of surgery and was in intensive care, I asked the doctors if I could hold him and they said yes. It was the best medicine I could give him. Charles Martin had open-heart surgery again as a grown up in Atlanta in 1990. Patricia, my brother Bill and I were there. I went in after the surgery and held him again.

Before I went to the Boston area, however, I was asked to lead a crew of six Bendix engineers to the Applied Physics Laboratory of Johns Hopkins University in Silver Spring, Maryland, just outside of Washington, DC, to design and build the electronics system for the Transit-1 Navigational Satellite System. The Transit-1 was to be used for guiding US Navy Submarines, particularly for launching ballistic missiles against the Soviet Union. The Transit Satellites were the forerunners to the Global Positioning System (GPS) Satellites used today for navigation. We moved from South Bend to Silver Spring for the next 7 months and when the job was successfully completed, we went to Nashua where I began work for Sanders.

14

Sanders Associates

We arrived in Nashua in late summer of 1960 and lived for about three months at Robinson's Pond, until we found a house to buy at 6 Dover Street. At Sanders, my job was to head up a Mechanical Engineering Branch responsible for packaging the electronics of Electronic Countermeasures Systems (ECM) and Anti Submarine Warfare Systems (ASW). The ECM systems were used to spoof enemy missiles aimed at US military aircraft and ships and the ASW systems were used by the Navy to detect and track Soviet Submarines.

In spite of the great struggle I had with my fears, I enjoyed the challenge of the job and learned much. When work got slow, I went out to other companies and began looking for tasks my group could do to fill contract gaps and developed a flair for technical marketing. I began to do more and more of this and eventually found myself being transferred out of engineering and into marketing.

I had a lot of trepidation about getting into marketing, because it required lots of travel, being away from home and standing up in front of the customer to talk. All these things scared me because of the panic attack fear. Flying was especially hard for me. I felt closed in and I knew that if I had an attack, I couldn't get out of the plane. Many times, I arrived at my destination sopping wet from fear. I developed many psychological coping mechanisms so I could continue with this marketing job because I really liked the challenge and creativity of it. I carried paper bags to breath into when I began to hyperventilate and always had with me instructions as to what to do with me if I died.

Sanders decided to revamp the Marketing Division, so I went to work for Norm Stone as Director of Marketing for Ocean Systems. Norm headed up the Ocean Systems Division for Sanders. Under Norm, we went after oceanographic research programs as well as ASW programs and won them. We were a great team and a great success.

We would conduct tests throughout the Caribbean, including the Bahamas and the US Virgin Islands. We also worked off Bermuda, off Hawaii, in the Mediterranean Sea and off other exotic places around the world. I traveled on conventional and nuclear submarines, aircraft carriers, destroyers, P-3 and S-3 ASW aircraft and even rode out a horrific Category 5 hurricane in Bermuda where the wind speed exceeded 165 MPH. This work was very challenging and creative, and we felt we were doing something quite important during the Cold War.

I had gone to Bermuda about two days before the hurricane hit and was staying in the Princess Hotel in downtown Hamilton. I had been on a Navy destroyer and transferred to an Office of Naval Research Texas Tower, which had been converted into an oceanographic research station called Argus Island. This old Texas Tower had many oceanographic instruments attached to it and was located on Plantagenet Bank about 25 miles off Bermuda.

In order to get aboard Argus Island, I went by destroyer and transferred to a small boat that maneuvered underneath a landing net, which in turn was attached to a 40 foot I beam which swung out from Argus Island. To board Argus Island, you had to leap out of the small boat and grab the landing net, and people aboard Argus Island would swing you onto the island. This method of boarding was used when it was not safe to land a helicopter.

Because the wind was coming up so strong, I had to board this way. I stayed aboard Argus Island about 3 hours and leaving had to disembark using the landing net. A Navy commander and I both got onto the landing net and were swung out over a raging sea to get into the small boat. The boat had difficulty staying under the net, and the bowsprit was heaving up and down about ten feet because of the rough water. The bowsprit hit the commander, stove in his back, and he fell thirty feet into the ocean. They then spent about twenty minutes trying to rescue him, while I held onto the landing net hung out over the roiling sea. I felt the fear grabbing me and had a panic attack out there, but was able to hang on until they could get the commander into the boat and take me aboard.

The destroyer took me into Hamilton Harbor and I disembarked for the Princess Hotel, where I buttoned up for the hurricane. The wind speed indicator at the airport broke at 165 MPH, so we didn't know how fast the wind was. We saw cars tumbling down the main street and palm trees flattened against the sidewalks. The rain, driven by the wind was so intense that it came through locked windows and doors, and flooded the hotel. The storm fascinated me. I had never experienced anything like this before, and I tried to open the back door of the hotel to look outside but was unable because of the vacuum created on the hotel's lee side. The storm blew out all the water in the swimming pool.

I had worked quite a bit in Bermuda over the past four years because I was the Corporate Oceanographic Engineer for Sanders Associates. In this position, I was responsible for working with the Woods Hole Oceanographic Institute (WHOI) in Falmouth, Massachusetts to develop ocean technology for Sanders. I would go to sea on the Atlantis II Oceanographic research vessel with WHOI scientists and work with them laying buoy lines to measure ocean currents and other oceanographic parameters. WHOI did much work for the Office of Naval Research and because Sanders had Navy contracts and I had the necessary security clearances, I was able to work with WHOI. They were a fine bunch of people and I enjoyed being with them as well as learning a great deal about ocean engineering and instrumentation.

One particular scientist, Dr. Nicholas Foffanoff gave me my start working with WHOI. He allowed me to accompany them to Bermuda to lay buoy instrumentation moorings and conduct ocean current measurement tests. We stayed in Bermuda at the Marine Biological Station in St. Georges. One night, it was my turn to operate an observation post tracking lighted surface buoys at sea. I had to ride my motorbike in the pitch-black night over the little Bermuda roads to the post. I kept hearing squishing sounds as I rode my bike and walked to my post. In the morning, I saw that the squishing sounds had come from my riding and walking over thousands of tiny frogs which came out at night. Ugh!

While in Nassau, Bahamas on a Difar test, I was staying at the British Colonial Hotel when I saw an announcement on the lobby bulletin board for experienced scuba divers to serve as movie extras. I thought this might be exciting, and since I was a certified diver, I applied. It turns out that the movie was *Thunderball*, a James Bond thriller starring Sean Connery. I signed up and was in a couple of scenes for an underwater fight between the "good guys in orange" and the "bad guys in black". I met Sean Connery, and had great fun!

Another time off Hawaii, we were on a barge doing Oceanographic Research for the Difar Program and the instrumentation barge started to sink. We all had to abandon ship, and swam in the shark-infested water until the rescue boats could reach us. Scared the hell out of me!

I often went to Hawaii during my Sanders Associates years, not only to do technical work, but also to brief the Commander of the Pacific Fleet about ASW technology particularly relating to sonobuoys and acoustic signal processing. Later on, when I was with Sparton and as a Private Consultant, I also went to Hawaii to brief and to solicit fleet support for programs in which I was interested. I would also reenter the USA in Hawaii on my return trips back home from visiting Japan. I liked going to Hawaii, but it was so darn far from everything. Fortunately, I was a Sparton vice president so I could ride first class on the plane.

15

Politics

I had deceived Pat. She thought I was a normal grown up male, but I wasn't. I was a scared little kid no matter what my age or size. She never knew how I was feeling, not because she didn't want to, but because I was too ashamed to admit to her that I was so scared all the time. Instead, I tried to act macho to hide my shame. It didn't work. I just wasn't macho enough to lose the fear that was so much a part of me. I continued over the years of our marriage to sink deeper and deeper into fear and depression. It wasn't her fault…I never admitted to her that I had the problem.

I felt so badly that I went to the Lahey Clinic in Boston and had a complete physical. They said there was nothing physically wrong with me; it was my nerves. Where had I heard that before? The medical people sent me to another psychiatrist, in addition to the one I had been seeing in Framingham, Massachusetts, and his recommendation to me was to separate from Pat for a while until I could get my emotions under control. Pat couldn't handle this, so I moved out and into a dilapidated hotel near my work. The night I moved out and moved into that fleabag has to be the saddest night of my life. I thought I would die. We then proceeded to get divorced. I was now not only in panic, but also entirely alone. I lost my home, my beautiful children that I loved so very much and now I had nothing. I thought my life was over.

What saved my life was that I was doing so well in marketing at Sanders Associates that I got heavily involved with politics in 1964 shortly after Patricia and I divorced. Since I had a lot of time, not having a home to go to and seeking to assuage my depression, I eagerly accepted this new challenge. It wasn't politics, per se, but rather with the New Hampshire Congressional Delegation who was trying to save the Portsmouth Naval Shipyard from closing with a program called the "Seacoast Regional Plan". I got to know US Senators Tom McIntyre and Norris Cotton as well as Governor John King during my efforts to drum up support for keeping the Shipyard open. I became the Sanders Corporate Oceanographic Engineer and gave speeches all over the state about oceanography, ocean engineering and Anti Submarine Warfare (ASW). Because Sanders expected that there would be an ocean equivalent of NASA formed because of the great interest in underwater exploration for both military and commercial applications, Sanders paid my expenses as a public service in hope of getting in on the ground floor of this exciting new technology business area.

Under direction from the New Hampshire Congressional Delegation, I helped write the bill that created the National Oceanographic and Atmospheric Agency (NOAA). This was valuable experience for me as I learned about the congressional process and lobbying the federal government. This acumen helped me greatly when I later had to deal with the US Senate and House Of Representatives Armed Services Committees and Defense Appropriations Committees in connection with funding programs I was pursuing in my marketing role for other companies.

I think I had an effect on the Vietnam War because of my relationship with Senator McIntyre, who was on the Senate Armed Services Committee. One day while talking to him in his office in Washington, I mentioned that I thought it stupid that we were sending a $35-million dollar strike aircraft in to bomb mud huts when the planes were very vulnerable to enemy fire. Since Vietnam was such a narrow country and exposed to the ocean, I suggested that it would be much better to have battleships stand offshore and fire the big guns at the enemy…a lot cheaper, and the ships were essentially invulnerable to attack. He listened quite intently and shortly thereafter, the US Navy decided to do just that.

16

Ski Accident

I wanted to learn to ski, so I went to a hill near Hollis, New Hampshire, close to where I was living before our divorce. I quickly broke my right leg, and I was in the hospital for three weeks. On release, I went and stayed with Norm and Audrey Stone in Hollis, who treated me like one of their family. What great people! But it became obvious that my leg wasn't healing, so I would need to have it surgically set in Sacred Heart Hospital in Manchester. I had a good doctor, but he didn't believe in painkillers. He wouldn't let me have any drugs but aspirin after the surgery and I about went out of my mind with the pain. He had cut my leg open and inserted three stainless steel screws into my leg.

Fortunately, before the surgery, I called my brother Bill in Toledo and told him what was coming down. The second day, as I lay screaming in the hospital room, in walks Bill. He had flown to Boston from Toledo, rented a car and drove up to Manchester. I told Bill to get me out of there. I checked out of the hospital, against the doctor's advice, got some codeine pills from a doctor in Nashua, and Bill drove me to Boston in a raging snowstorm to catch a plane for Detroit. We flew to Detroit where my brother-in-law Hank Koepfer picked us up and drove us to Toledo. When I arrived at Bill's home, I collapsed with some black licorice twists my sister-in-law Darlene had waiting for me.

I spent the next month there at home with Bill, Dar, and my mother. I was home with people who loved me, and I felt safe for the first time in a long while. I didn't have any panic attacks while there.

When I recovered enough to travel, Sanders wanted me to work in Washington as corporate marketing representative to the Navy, developing programs and interfacing with Congress. I lived at the Sanders Corporate Apartment on New Hampshire Avenue in Foggy Bottom, near the State Department. For quite a while, I had a suite of rooms at the Watergate Hotel with a great balcony overlooking the Potomac River. Later, my fiancée Laura and her mother stayed with me and we had picnics on the floor with wine, pepperoni, good Italian bread and pickles. In those days, the Watergate cost $22 a night for a deluxe room. I liked the Watergate and was disappointed when the Navy moved from Constitution Avenue to Arlington across the river to Crystal City. There, we stayed at the Crystal City Marriott or the Hyatt, which were expensive—$26 a night and nice, but not the Watergate. Meanwhile, the panic attacks resumed in force because I didn't have the safety of my family around me.

After a year in Washington, I returned to Nashua and resumed my work on the Seacoast Regional Plan, developing programs in Ocean Systems for the states of New Hampshire and Maine. New Hampshire Governor John King appointed me the NH Co-chairman of the ME/NH Bi State Commission on Oceanography with the task of keeping the Portsmouth Naval Shipyard open. We succeeded. It was during this time that I had the pleasure of meeting and working with many wonderful people in the Ocean Community, such as Dr. Jacques Cousteau and Dr. Nicholas Foffanoff of Woods Hole Oceanographic Institute. I accompanied Dr. Foffanoff on several expeditions to Bermuda to learn how to set up and launch large oceanographic arrays at sea. This knowledge was invaluable in my work at Sanders where we were developing systems using arrays for Anti Submarine Warfare (ASW). I worked with Cousteau on habitats in the Mediterranean Sea and in the Gulf of Maine.

17

Sparton Electronics

In March of 1968, Sanders asked me to go to Key West, Florida to help on the Difar Test Program. Difar was a passive directional acoustic system using air launched sonobuoy sensors to detect and track Soviet submarines. On my way to Key West, I met Laura James in Miami, who was to become my future wife. Laura was a flight attendant for National Airlines. She was very beautiful and I wanted to see more of her.

While in Key West, the vice president of Sparton Electronics invited me to be their new Director of Marketing. Sparton was very big in the ASW Sonobuoy Business. I had considered leaving Sanders because I was so unhappy there, now bereft of family, having daily panic attacks, and remembering how good I had felt in Toledo. Jackson, Michigan was only 90 minutes from Toledo. I accepted the job, and joined Sparton in August of 1968.

My ex-wife Patricia said she couldn't handle the kids and sent them to me. I was so happy to have them. I thought that being close to my family in Toledo would be a great asset with the kids. Since I had to travel extensively in my new job, I thought I would put the kids into private boarding schools during the school year. Patricia had attended such a school herself. I registered the girls at St. Mary's in Adrian, Michigan, and I was looking for a good school for Charles Martin, when Patricia suddenly reappeared and took the kids back. I was devastated. I then learned that Patricia hated the boarding school she attended. I went through a long period of depression when the kids left, snatched from me when I was getting it together again as a family.

St. Croix

Just as I was settling in at Sparton, the Navy asked me if I would like to run the new Sonobuoy Test Range in St. Croix in the US Virgin Islands. An outfit called Vocaline Air Sea Technology (VAST) had the Navy contract for managing the

47

range and the Navy wanted me to go to work for VAST and direct operations at the St. Croix range. Since it was the Navy asking, and I had never been to St. Croix, I agreed to go down there for a week and check it out. I didn't tell Sparton that I was going there to check out the range for a job, only that I was going there to check it out because Sparton would be testing sonobuoys there.

I flew from Detroit to St. Croix by way of Miami and Puerto Rico. An Atlantic hurricane made it one of the worst flights of my life. The DeHaviland Dove, which was illegal to fly in the USA, bounced around all over the sky between San Juan and St. Croix. The pilot, whom I was certain was drunk, finally turned the plane around after 2 hours of this and headed back to San Juan. I was so grateful, because I was having severe panic attacks and desperately wanted to get out of there. But, no—the pilot, I think, drank more whiskey, refueled the plane and we set off again. After two more hours of insane flying, we finally landed in St. Croix at about 2:00 AM during a lull in the storm. I was numb all over and trembling as if I had the palsy from hyperventilating during the panic attacks. I was certain that I was going to die and I cursed having made the decision to go to St. Croix. Besides the pilot and me, there was only one other person on the plane—a drunk who threw up all over his seat, eight chickens and a pig. It brought a new meaning to the expression, "when pigs can fly."

A broken-down taxi took me to the Estate Carlton Hotel, a beautiful place that charged exorbitant rates. For $56 a day, they gave you a villa with three meals. There was a fine pool with a waterfall and a bar in the middle of it so you could sit in the water and drink pina coladas. The Carlton was a fine place to headquarter when testing sonobuoys in St. Croix. Over the next ten years, I spent a lot of time at the Carlton and at the range, but I didn't take the job. I didn't want to live in the Islands, especially with my continuing panic attacks and the lack of good medical facilities there. It was also the time of the Black Power Movement race riots in America, and many of the native blacks of St. Croix made it plain that they didn't like us. One time in a supermarket, a black woman deliberately ran her cart into me and cursed me. I hadn't done anything to her. That upset me because I always liked blacks, but it was just the time. I also noticed that many of the North Americans who did live there drank an awful lot of rum, and many of them became alcoholics. Rum was very cheap. You could buy a fifth of Cruzan rum at the super market for thirty cents and Stolichnaya Russian vodka for sixty cents. A Coke cost three dollars. I liked to visit there but I didn't want to live there, so I turned down the job.

Marketing Genius

Sparton was a wonderful opportunity for me to learn and I loved the people there. I never thought I would find a better company than Sanders, but Sparton was the best. The management, from the President on down supported me completely, allowing me to flex my creative muscles, and we scored very big in successful new programs. I led Sparton to new heights in sonobuoy technology and procurement. The marketing strategy I devised was to get the company to invest in advanced technology, build a prototype, and take it to sea under the Navy's auspices using submarines, aircraft and surface ships to demonstrate effectiveness. Then we would write a report on what had been accomplished, give it to the Navy and get them to allow us to bid on the next procurement using the report as technical substance. I needed strong relationships within the Navy to make this strategy work. My team at Sparton accomplished the task brilliantly. We did so well, that Sparton made me a Vice President. This marketing approach worked because the Navy had a great need during the Cold War for innovative fresh new approaches to the Soviet submarine threat. We at Sparton helped protect our country by our pioneering actions.

My co-chairmanship of a two-year major study on Sonobuoy Mobilization Readiness for the National Security Industrial Association (NSIA) prompted them to make me an NSIA Vice President. It was my honor and terror to present the study results before the entire NSIA (1600 people) at the State Department. It was very hard for me to do, but the admiration and respect I had for the NSIA made the agony acceptable and bearable. As an NSIA Vice President, I would sit on the dais during dinner functions and rub shoulders with admirals, generals, senators, congressmen and leaders of the United States defense industry. In addition, I also headed up several other studies on Airborne ASW for the NSIA. The Navy and the ASW community liked my work and treated me with respect. This served me well when I became a consultant advising the Navy and American aerospace companies on technology and programs to counter the Soviet threat.

18

Foreign Business

I also intensively promoted Sparton's foreign business. Their sonobuoy designs were the envy of the rest of the world. Sparton engineers had a simplistic approach to the design of sonobuoys. Inexpensive materials and production processes kept the cost of the devices low, since they were throwaways. The US Navy liked Sparton's approach, and so did many of the other Western countries that wanted to participate in Airborne ASW but also wanted the most inexpensive expendable devices.

I figured that if we could sell license agreements to other countries to build sonobuoys to Sparton design, Sparton could make money off the designs and sell parts to the licensees. This was a fine way to make additional money, since Sparton already had the designs and was building the parts for the sonobuoys we supplied to the US Navy. Sparton already had some preliminary arrangements with some foreign countries, but I decided to expand the business considerably.

I contacted the Germans, French, Italians, Greeks, Norwegians and the Japanese, and got them interested in Sparton's sonobuoy designs. We began to enter into very lucrative deals with these governments and the private companies they selected to be their indigenous producers. I visited all of these countries and worked out licensing agreements with them for various Sparton sonobuoys. I enjoyed working with these governments and their contractors, and was able to keep them from discerning my panic problems. In business, foreigners look with extreme disfavor on people who had problems like mine. They seem to equate mental and emotional problems with unsound business and engineering. Actually, this is also the perception in the USA. In business, you cannot betray these kinds of weaknesses; the customer gets uneasy and unconsciously transfers your problems to the company, and they don't want to be involved with you. I had to fight this at every level of my job and life in order to continue.

While visiting Amsterdam to speak with Dutch authorities about sonobuoy licenses, I had an experience that opened my eyes to the "gay world". I was stay-

ing at a small inexpensive walk-up apartment near the opera house that had no
bathing or shower facilities. I opted for this cheap place so that I could stay on a
few extra days in Amsterdam and enjoy its sights. Paying less for the apartment
than living in an expensive hotel room made it possible. After about a week in
Amsterdam, I was badly in need of a bath. I walked about a lot and was sweaty,
rancid and fragrant. I thought I might find a public bath nearby so I began asking
people where the nearest one was located. I happened to ask the clerk in a men's
trouser store. I was hoping for a public swimming pool or bath where I could get
clean and "unstunk." The clerk didn't know of one nearby, so he asked another
gentleman where I should go and he wrote an address down for me that was quite
close. I was very grateful.

Immediately on leaving the trouser store, I headed for the public bath, found
it where it was supposed to be and ran up the long stairway. I went to the recep-
tion desk and told the man behind the counter that I wanted to bathe. He said it
would cost five guilders to take a shower, so I paid it and looked forward to my
cleansing. Just as I was leaving the desk with my towel and soap in my hand, the
clerk said, "Do you realize that this is a gay bath?" I said I didn't care how happy
the people were; that I just wanted to get clean and strolled into the changing
room.

I kept thinking about why the attendant was interested in telling me how the
people using the bath felt. Maybe it was a resort of some kind, and everybody
who went became happy and gay. Putting the thought aside, I went into the
dimly lit interior, preceded to disrobe putting my clothes into a locker, and grate-
fully went into the empty shower. I let the water run over my body and felt the
delicious feeling of cleanliness begin to cover me as I soaped up from head to toe
and soaped my hair, languishing in the purification. It felt so good!

Just as I had completed soaping down my whole body, about fifteen buck-
naked guys came into the shower and just stood around looking at me. Every one
of them had an erection. I didn't know what to think about this. Why were they
all just standing there naked, looking at me, and all with erect penises? What kind
of place was this? Then it slowly began to dawn on me that these guys were
homosexual and I was the object of their intended affection.

Once this realization sunk into my hard head, I got mad and told them all to
screw themselves as I had paid five guilders for this shower and was going to finish. I don't know if they understood my English, but no one attempted to get
close to me. If they had, I was angry enough that I think I could have beaten the
hell out of all of them. I ignored them and they shortly began to leave the shower
room. I finished my shower, got dressed and left the "gay" bath, a little bit wiser

about the term "gay" and a lot cleaner than when I arrived. No longer was "gay" to me a simple expression of emotional feeling. It now had a completely new connotation. I noticed that the desk attendant to whom I paid the five guilders smiled broadly at me as I left and I think I was red-faced. I thought about going back to the trouser store and chewing out the clerk who gave me the address, but I didn't. After that, I found a public swimming pool about two blocks away in the opposite direction and stayed clean there. Even though I now bathed regularly, I never sold any sonobuoys to the Dutch government.

The Norwegians used sonobuoys and set up a plant in a small town on the Skagerrak off the North Sea, about two hours train ride south of Oslo. Sparton sold the Norwegians a design package on a sonobuoy and I would periodically go over there to help them.

When visiting the plant I was amazed at the lunch break taken by the employees of the sonobuoy plant. They were primarily young Norwegian girls between the ages of 18 and 28 who assembled the sonobuoys in the plant. I was visiting the managing director of the plant and he took me out to view the lunch break, which took place on large rocks sitting in the river next to the plant. About 100 beautiful Norwegian girls were sunbathing on the rocks, very nude. The managing director told me that one of his biggest problems was providing comfort to the girls sitting at the assembly lines who had gotten their buttocks sunburned. The other problem he mentioned was that there were not many men in the village and the girls were extremely lonely. I felt very sorry for him that he should have such problems.

The company selected by the Norwegian government to build the sonobuoys in Norway hired a gentleman in Alexandria to represent them in the USA and to deal with me. His name was Colonel St. John. He was a very proper gentleman, retired from the US Air Force. Col. St. John and his very elegant wife lived in a beautiful town house in Olde Towne Alexandria, a suburb of Washington. Mrs. St. John was a graduate of the Cordon Bleu cooking school in Paris, France. She had gone to learn French cooking because the colonel loved good French food. They also owned a farm in Normandy, France to which they retired for several months each year.

Colonel St. John invited me to dinner at his home in Olde Towne Alexandria and since my wife Laura and sister-in-law Jennifer were with me, they, too, were invited. Since Jennifer was unattached, Col. St. John also asked a US Navy captain to be Jennifer's escort at dinner. It was a beautiful six-course dinner with a different wine for every course. A splendid Waterford crystal chandelier hung over the table and Belgian lace covered the table.

The evening's conversation centered on the colonel's porcelain collection. The Navy captain was also an avid collector, so the conversation stayed with this subject interminably, at least to me. I only had a passing fancy with porcelain, and in a whimsical effort to open the conversation to other avenues, I suggested that we talk about the jails we had all ever been in. It turns out that I was the only one who had ever been in jail and the conversation never did go anywhere. For some strange reason, even though I continued to do business with the Norwegians, I never again received an invitation to Col. St. John's home for dinner, or for that matter, any other purpose. I always wondered why.

19

Jails

Since I've mentioned jails, let me tell you of my three experiences with them. First off, none of them was any fun. The old images of singing "Old Man River" and "Birmingham Jail" just don't cut it. I do not like jails, no matter where they are. Once you have been in jail for any reason in any place, even for a short time makes you want to be very law abiding. Since my jail experiences, I have always bent over backward to obey the law. Actually, only one of my jail experiences had to do with violating the law and that was in Canada for speeding. The other two times in Mexico and Greece were misunderstandings.

In Canada, my crime was simply speeding on my way back to Detroit after visiting my first wife's family when I was in college. I was an American, so instead of just giving me a ticket, they threw me in the Windsor, Ontario jail. I called John Martin, Pat's dad and he came down and bailed me out after I was there for about three hours. It wasn't a bad jail, but I felt very claustrophobic in there. I was very happy to get out of my first lock-up at about 4 AM. When I got back to Detroit, a car slipped in the snowy January streets and slammed into my car broadside. Man, what a time!—First jail, and then car accident. What next?

My second sojourn in jail was in Juarez, Mexico. When I worked for Bendix Missiles in Mishawaka, Indiana, our missile was test fired at the White Sands Missile Range near Alamogordo, New Mexico. I had been working there for about three days, and decided to go to Juarez, just across the border from El Paso, Texas and not too far from White Sands. I had about $400 in my pocket because I was to be in New Mexico for about two weeks and this was my expense money. I enjoyed dinner and had a few drinks in Juarez, but someone nefarious slipped a drug into my drink, and I passed out on the street. I woke up about 4 AM in the Juarez Jail without pants or shoes and socks and very sick. All my money and identification were gone.

Because I didn't have any ID, the Mexican authorities kept me in jail for two days, believing me to be just a drunk who passed out in the streets. My protesta-

54

tions to the contrary, that I had been drugged and robbed, were ignored. I heard later that the Mexican cops never believed "gringos". I only had my shirt and underwear on, since my pants and shoes and socks had been stolen. I received bacon and some beans with corn bread during the two days and three nights I was in the Mexican jail. The food was sparse but good, and the jail really stank of vomit, feces and urine. I did not care that I didn't get much to eat, since I felt pretty rotten from the knock out drug and the stink.

When they finally decided to let me out, I called the White Sands Missile Range and one of my friends came down with clothing for me, and $200 for my drunk-and-disorderly fine. That jail had no redeeming features at all. There were about a dozen of us in the cell, and everybody—including me—reeked. There was no place to wash or sleep except on the hard concrete floor, and there were so many of us in there with the rats that there was hardly any room to lie down. A hole was a cut into the concrete where you could relieve yourself. I didn't use the toilet all the time I was there, preferring constipation. In addition, I was still too sick. When I returned to the Missile Range, I had to live out the remaining six days of my stay there borrowing money for food and lodging and my return airline ticket to Indiana, since my ticket was stolen along with my wallet and clothes.

In Greece, I visited their Defense Ministry to try to sell them sonobuoy licenses. Greece is a member of NATO, so they used sonobuoys with their P-3 ASW Aircraft.

I had flown to Athens from Zurich on an Olympic Airways Comet-4 jet. The Comet aircraft were to put the British into a commanding lead in jet travel and were the first jet aircraft to fly commercially. Structural fatigue problems caused it to crash several times, killing a large number of people. After that, the Comets lost out to the Boeing 707, which became the dominant jet aircraft for travel. I was very excited about visiting Greece, the land of my father's birth, and had many relatives there even though I didn't know any of them. I had the strange feeling of coming home, even though I had never been there.

I checked into a hotel off Constitution Square and went to a tavern in the Plaka, the old section of Athens around the Acropolis. I was sitting there having a 30-drachma (about $1.50) bottle of good Greek wine. Two lovely young girls were sitting on either side of me. They began talking to me and after about 40 minutes, I finished my wine and was about to go eat dinner. I asked for my bill, and was shocked when it totaled $250. I told the bartender there was a mistake. He said "No mistake," that I had been buying the two girls champagne at $125 a bottle, and they had drunk two bottles. I knew this was a setup, and told the bartender that there was no way that I would pay that exorbitant bill and started to walk out leaving the equivalent of $5 on the bar for my $1.50 bottle of wine. The bartender jumped over the bar, brandished a knife against my chest and wouldn't let me go.

Fortunately, there was a guy down at the end of the bar from Olympic Airlines who remembered me from check-in at the downtown terminal earlier. He called the police, who took all of us to jail. It was about 7:00 PM on Monday. At the jail, I explained in English what had happened. The bartender and the girls explained their version to the captain of police in Greek. The captain let them all go, but threw me into a classic dungeon near the Acropolis, to live on bread and water. I imagined who might have been there before me, and my mind danced with the thoughts of romantic and fascinating intrigues.

In reality, this was a miserable place. The stone walls and floor were covered with a kind of fungus navigated by rats and worms. There were things moving all the time in my cell, and I was afraid to close my eyes for fear that I would be devoured by some hungry Greek denizen of that dungeon. The bed hung on the wall from chains and there was no mattress, only a section of chain link fence supporting me. This jail also stank, not with vomit and feces like the Mexican jail, but with a dank earthy stench laced with urine. I found it faintly reminiscent of my Grandma's root cellar! One faint light bulb burned constantly in the middle of the cell. I was told that this cell usually held about ten people, and that I was lucky because an amnesty had released all the prisoners the day before I got there. If I had been arrested two days before, I also would have been released.

The next day, Tuesday, the captain twice interviewed me with the two girls and the bartender who spent the night at home while I was in the dungeon. We would all tell our stories again, I in English and they in Greek. Then they would go home, and I would go back to the dungeon. The same thing happened on Wednesday and Thursday. By Thursday, I was ready to pay whatever it cost to get out of there. The conditions were terrible, but I must say that the loaf of dark bread and the fresh water they gave me twice each day was excellent. I still like Greek bread, but it brings back unpleasant memories.

On Friday during the morning interview, I was told that I had hired an attorney, that he had gotten me off and that I could leave the jail after I paid him. His fee was $400. I paid it readily and left.

The rest of my time in Greece was wonderful, and I met many excellent people who more than made up for the bad start to my visit. One of the things I learned in Greece was that Greeks don't particularly like Turks. The movie *Zorba The Greek* was playing in the USA and I had mentioned to my friends there that

I loved the movie, but they said the movie was not about Greeks, but rather about Turks. In the movie, the Greek townspeople take all of Boobolina's possessions after she dies. My Greek friends said that the movie could not have been about Greeks, because Greeks don't steal—only Turks steal.

An interesting corollary: I went to the American Embassy in Athens to complain about my treatment and having to spend all that time in a dungeon. After explaining in detail what had happened to me, the Foreign Service Officer, who kindly listened with great patience, advised me not to go back to that tavern again. I thought that was good advice, so I didn't.

20

Sparton's Programs

While at Sparton, I led them to a monumental win on the Difar Sonobuoy Program. We were able to arrange Sparton's participation in Navy tests off Bermuda and Key West. In Key West, we were able to get a P-3 aircraft and a submarine to work with us under the auspices of the Naval Air Development Center's Key West office. In this test, Sparton demonstrated a directional hydrophone, which tracked the submarine and made Sparton a contender for the Difar Sonobuoy Procurements. Over the years, these procurements netted Sparton more than $200 million dollars, and they are still building them today.

Sparton's corporate headquarters and engineering facility were in Jackson, Michigan, and that is where I lived. The air launched acoustic sensors used to locate and track Soviet submarines called sonobuoys were built in a plant in DeLeon Springs, Florida, about 20 miles west of Daytona Beach. Besides being famous for the beach, Daytona Beach was also the home of the world famous Daytona Speedway. A premier event every year was the 24 Hours of Daytona Race, where racing cars from all over the world competed in an endurance race for 24 consecutive hours. The Navy Program Manager for the Difar Program was a wonderful gentleman named Walt Edwards. Over the years, I was privileged to know him and his wife Margie who became our close friends. Walt was an avid devotee of racing. He himself had raced and wrote articles for racing magazines, so whenever possible we would schedule Difar Program reviews at DeLeon Springs to be held either before or after the race weekend so we could attend the race.

On race weekends, I would rent a large recreational vehicle (RV) and Walt and I plus several guests, including: my brother Bill; his son Smort, Bill's brother in law, Mark Haas; my future wife Laura, my son Charles Martin and others at various times, would camp on the infield at the speedway to enjoy the race. We would pull the RV onto the infield on Friday morning and remove it the following Monday evening, so we were there all four days. Once in the infield, we were stuck there until Monday. You couldn't leave. The men never slept, bathed, shaved or changed clothes during the entire period. In addition, we would usually run out of drinking water and food by Sunday. We would bathe in vodka on the roof of the RV, causing quite a sensation for onlookers. We ate Kentucky Fried Chicken until pinfeathers started to grow on our bodies, and then we switched to hamburgers. Vodka, fried chicken and hamburgers with potato chips were our diet for four days, and we wondered why our stomachs were a bit queasy the following week. Flying back to Atlanta, where Bill lived, we usually commanded an empty part of the plane because of our odor and when we arrived at Bill's house, Darlene would hose us down before she let us into the house. Overall, Difar Program Reviews at Sparton were a huge success.

I also got Sparton involved with the Advanced Difar Program in the Mediterranean. I interfaced with the NATO ASW center at La Spezia, Italy and spent time at the US Navy Air ASW Base in Signonella, Sicily. I lived in Catania, Sicily working out of Signonella. We successfully experimented with advanced Difar sonic arrays in the Mediterranean and Sparton was given contracts to develop these new systems.

While in Sicily, I climbed Mt. Etna and got a spectacular view of the inside of the active volcano. It was a windy day and I was alone. I took the funicular overhead tram three-fourths the way up the mountain, then took a jeep within 100 yards of the volcano's edge and walked through the ash the rest of the way. As I walked to the edge and looked into the volcano, it looked and smelled the way the priests had described hell to me so many years ago.

Through a college friend who was with the CIA, I caused Sparton to become involved with the Agency. Sparton was to build an underwater system to house sonic listening devices and recorders, which could be surreptitiously dropped into a Soviet anchorage off Greece to listen for underwater communication between Soviet warships. The Soviets did this to avoid Electromagnetic Intelligence (ELINT) interception of their communications. The Sparton system was to listen and record the Soviet signals and then, at night, broadcast what it heard to a satellite, to be relayed to an American receptor post. We tested the system off Panama City, Florida, and the system imploded and sank to the bottom. I had to go into the CIA in Langley and explain this failure. I wasn't too happy to do so. The agency put me into a big room with combination locks on the door and made me wait for about one hour before they joined me. They scared the hell out of me.

21

Medical Fallacies

Several times, I had to go into the Chelmsford Hospital near Jackson because I was so torn up with the fear from the panic attacks. I never told Sparton or any one else why I was going to the hospital. They thought it was because of a back problem, when actually it was to take strong psychotropic drugs to help me get by for a while longer. My psychiatrist used this hospital to fill his patients full of strong drugs. The psychiatrist never talked to me very much; he just gave me drugs all the time. One time, I passed out from all the drugs, fell, and hit my head causing it to bleed extensively. This caused a headache for the next two days. At first, I think the drugs helped me a bit with my fear, but not for long. It would come right back in a short time. My wife, Laura, would come to see me every few days, but I was embarrassed that she should see me there.

Because the psychiatrist hadn't helped me, I saw a Clinical Psychologist in Ann Arbor, for about 4 years and got nowhere with him so he sent me to the Neuro-Psychiatric Institute at the University of Michigan Hospital for five weeks. They put me on MAO Inhibitors for depression, even though I wasn't depressed. I was scared. I told them I was scared and couldn't sleep because of my Restless Leg Syndrome problems and the U of M doctors said it was depression and the MAO Inhibitor was for depression. The medicine didn't help the fear and it didn't help the sleep problem, so after 5 weeks, I checked out.

I finally got out of there, and when I went home, I really began having trouble. In my Sparton office, I began to have a panic attack. I was feeling so unreal, faint and couldn't breathe from the MAO Inhibitors, so Larry Staszak drove me to the emergency room in Jackson. Once again, I thought I was going to die. Actually, I always thought I was going to die when I had the panic attacks, but this one was so much more intense, I really thought it was over.

I was terrified. I lay there in the Emergency Room for over 3 hours having skipping heartbeats, full body tetanus and unable to breathe freely. Finally, the attack subsided and I was able to go home. The doctors in the ER said that the

MAO Inhibitor I was taking could intensify panic attacks, so I decided to discontinue them.

Another time shortly thereafter, while the MAO Inhibitors were still in my blood, I dropped a bottle of pickles in a grocery store, severely lacerating my hand. I had to go to the ER again, but because the MAO's were still in me, they said I couldn't take any kind of tranquilizer, pain medication or numbing medicine while they stitched my hand up. I had to go cold turkey. When you are on MAO's, if you take the wrong kind of medicine, drink red wine or eat certain kinds of cheeses, you could have a cerebral hemorrhage and die because of the extremely high blood pressure the drug causes under these circumstances.

What a crazy world! What crazy medicine! I had to get off these medicines and away from these particular people of the medical people or they would surely kill me.

I was very angry with the University of Michigan Hospital. They never told me that this could happen to me. I also stopped seeing the clinical psychologist who sent me there. These people didn't know what in the hell they were doing with me and just used me as a guinea pig. The second day I was in the UM Hospital, they had me stand up in front of the whole staff and tell them about my problem. They wisely scratched their chins, rolled their eyes and then put me on this terrible stuff without even telling me what to expect or how dangerous it was.

Man, this is bad! What kind of medicine is this? In addition to all this trouble, it cost me an arm and a leg in money to have them mistreat me like they did. I could have bought two new Corvettes for what they charged me. At least I would have had something of value. These damn doctors didn't give me anything except more fear, and I already had plenty of that.

Shortly after this experience, I began having severe headaches, so I went to a general practitioner who said I now had high blood pressure. He put me on hypertensive medication.

22

Christian Science Philosophy

We had some friends at Gillette's Lake who were Christian Scientists and I wondered if this could be the key to my being healed from the terrible fear, which affected me, and so I began to investigate this religion. I had heard of Mary Baker Eddy when I lived in New Hampshire because she was from Concord. I also had visited the famous First Church of Christ Scientist in Boston as a tourist.

To my understanding, Christian Science says that we are perfect and all illness is error. By knowing and declaring illness as error…illness, because it is not real, loses its power over us and we are healed. I am very much drawn to this philosophy. It rings true to me. I began to study Christian Science. I read Mary Baker Eddy's book "Science and Health with Keys To The Scriptures", subscribed to the Christian Science Monitor, read voraciously at Christian Science Reading rooms and began attending Christian Science services at the local church. I was very impressed.

I contacted a Christian Science Practitioner and saw her regularly for about a year. I learned much about this wonderful religion, but try as I could, I couldn't get it to work for me. My panic attacks continued unabated, I couldn't sleep and my blood pressure continued to increase. I don't consider this to be the fault of Christian Science. I firmly believe the basic tenets of this religion, but no matter how I tried, I just couldn't apply it successfully to solve my problems. To this day, I confidently believe the basics of Christian Science.

23

AA Aaabanbaben

On March 11, 1972, I married Laura James at the home of our good friends Jerry and Lavonne McBride. Larry and Gloria Staszak were there. Lloyd Demco, my new blind psychotherapist and an ordained minister married us. Laura knew I had some problems, but she didn't know how deeply seated and pervasive they were. Over the years, she found out, but stuck with me anyhow. I was always too ashamed to tell anyone about the fear and panic attacks—even my wife.

Laura and I lived at Gillette's Lake just outside of Jackson, MI. The lake was about one mile long and one-half mile wide. Most of the homes were little inexpensive places. I bought ours for $12,000 on a land contract, paying $78 per month with a 3% interest rate. After a couple of years, I just paid off the contract. The place had 800 square feet of living space with two bedrooms and one bath, a septic tank, a pump for well water, an oil fired space heater and big picture windows that looked out onto the lake. We had a dock and a 22-foot catamaran sailboat. One thing I didn't like was that it didn't have a garage, so I had to park my new Corvette Stingray in the driveway. Laura didn't much like the place, but I did. It felt very cozy to me and I liked the people around us. We made many good friends there.

We had a dog, a beagle mutt, who came to live with us as a birthday gift to Laura from our friends, the Campbell's. This dog was exceptionally smart and could swim like a fish. He had the ability to dive to the bottom of the lake and pick up rocks, which he deposited on the shore. If the rock was too heavy, he would surface and get someone to help him. He was known everywhere for this rock retrieving ability, and I showed him off to all who came to observe his great skill. His swimming ability was awesome. When people asked me what breed of dog he was, I always said he was half beagle and half chicken-weasel. He loved chicken, swam like a weasel and kind of looked like one.

When I moved to Jackson, I thought it would be nice to have the first name in the phonebook, since Jackson wasn't a very big place, around 50,000 people. I signed up with the phone company as AA Aaabanbabben and did become the first in the phonebook. Since my name was not actually AA Aaabanbabben, I thought that some being ought to exist that in fact had that name, in case the phone company came calling, so I gave the name to our dog and he became AA Aaabanbabben. After a while, people began to ask me what the AA stood for and I said, Abercrombie Aardvark, Thus his name became Abercrombie Aardvark Aaabanbabben. Over the years, other names were added signifying some occasion or special capability in his life, or just because I liked the name. So his name grew. His name finally ended up as: Abercrombie Aardvark Abernathy Algonquin Arbutus Archibald Alipesarus-ferrox Argoogle Aaabanbabben, Esquire-I, the Paraclete of Kaborka, Sans Accoutrements, Ashley, Beauregard Buford Longworth Skillas, the First. The name of Alipesarus-ferrox was added because he could swim like a fish and I encountered a fish by that name on one of my Oceanographic expeditions. He got Sans Accoutrements after Laura had him castrated. We ended up calling him Babber for short.

Not only was this dog remarkable for his swimming and rock retrieving capability, but he was also a great lover, both before and after his castration. Laura had him castrated because he would moan, groan, and climb the fence to get out of our yard. Castration was supposed to control this behavior. I asked our vet, Dr. Chapel, about this and he said Babber could still perform as a great lover because he didn't know that the castration would stop his ability. Right then and there, I realized that impotence was mostly in the head and not in the accoutrements. A great lesson!

Because of his great ability to swim and retrieve rocks, Babber was much in demand around the lake to clean up beaches. So, I rented him out to beach owners and he made considerable money cleaning up beaches. He got paid for the total weight of rocks that he brought up at 10 cents a pound. He wanted me to invest his money for him so I obtained power of attorney for him and invested his money in return of capital utility stocks, as that is what he favored. I didn't mind doing this for him, but it was a chore having to write out his full name for all the transactions.

As Sparton Electronics' Vice President and Director of Marketing, I had to host conferences with high-ranking USA and foreign government officials and with foreign private company technical people. I would visit France, Norway, Sweden, Holland, Denmark, Germany, Italy, Spain, Greece, Switzerland, and Japan with whom I had either license agreements in place or pending on Sparton's sonobuoy technology. When these officials visited Jackson, Michigan, they would come to my home at Gillette's Lake for a cookout and relaxation. That little house in that little plebian neighborhood would often have grand limos pulling up in front with impressive people disembarking. It used to raise many eyebrows amongst my blue-collar neighbors. Many of them, I found out later, thought I was Mafia. I always warned my distinguished guests however, that they should be wary of moaning, groaning, and attempting to climb our fence because they risked being taken to Dr. Chapel's veterinary clinic by Laura. None of them ever did it.

24

Spinal Surgery

I used to run around the lake with Babber pulling me with a rope and noticed that my back started to bother me again. Pains started shooting down my left leg and I would get a peculiar tingling sensation in my legs. It really started to affect my sleep. This was new for me. Even though I had other problems, I could always sleep very well, falling asleep within minutes of my head hitting the pillow. Now that wasn't happening any more. Now, I could be up half the night without sleeping. I tried several different over-the-counter sleep aids, but they were useless. I consulted a neurologist, and he said the disk at L5 had degenerated from the spinal surgery back in 1954 when I worked for the Navy and that I probably would need additional surgery with a spinal fusion to fix it.

I was very busy with the Advanced Difar Program and put off the surgery. While in St. Croix in the US Virgin Islands, where we tested sonobuoy air ASW acoustic sensors, I suddenly found myself in terrible pain after lifting a sonobuoy. Not only was I in pain, but I could hardly walk. In addition, the panic attacks worsened. I didn't want to go into the hospital in St. Croix, so I flew to Washington, DC where I had to talk to the Navy about the Difar program, because I knew I would be laid up for a while if I had surgery. When I arrived in Washington, I couldn't walk and the pain was intense, so I went to a neurosurgeon. He said I needed immediate surgery or I might never walk again. Because of the seriousness of the condition, I was forced to have the surgery at Fairfax Hospital in Fairfax, Virginia.

After the surgery, I had to lie flat on my back in bed for 12 days while they made a special back support for me. During that time, I was very sick. Lying flat on my back all that time caused bowel problems and nausea. I had to have a blood transfusion, which my daughter Michelle supplied for me. The panic was with me all the time I lay in the bed because I couldn't leave. I felt like I was trapped and sometimes it almost overwhelmed me. At night, when nobody could see me, I cried because of the fear.

When I finally could leave the hospital, my friends Walt and Margie Edwards, who lived in Fairfax, invited me to stay with them until I could travel again. Walt was the Navy Project Manager for the Difar program and I knew him for a good twelve years. Laura joined me in Fairfax at the Edward's and finally I recovered enough to begin interfacing with the Navy again at Crystal City in Arlington, Virginia. I moved into the Holiday Inn across from the JP-1 building, the NAVAIR HQ, and was able to get back into the Difar Program.

Finally, I was able to travel and I went back to Jackson and returned to work. It was tough trying to work with the brace on. It was made of steel and supported my entire back from my shoulders to my coccyx. Straps held it to me very tight. I had to wear the brace for six months, and during that time, the skin under the brace broke down and I had ulcers on my skin, which hurt like hell. Laura had to wash me in the bed because I couldn't move when the brace was removed.

The Navy had a special briefing in Washington on all the Air ASW Programs and Sparton had to present their programs. I had the engineers from Sparton come to my home at Gillette's Lake, and we prepared the presentation while I lay in bed. However, there was no one to make the presentation, so I had to go and do it. The Sparton guys picked me up at Gillettes Lake and took me to Washington, where I made the presentation, and then brought me back to Jackson. It was a very difficult trip. I passed out several times from the pain both going and coming. You just have to do these things when it is your responsibility.

25

Sleep Agony

After I recovered from the back surgery, I noticed that the tingling in my legs at night seemed to worsen, and I was finding it increasingly difficult to get any sleep at all. I consulted with several neurosurgeons who said I had Restless Leg Syndrome (RLS) brought on by the surgery, and they put me on sleep medication so I could rest. The principal medication was Xanax, a benzodiazapine drug. It not only helped me to sleep, but it ameliorated the panic attacks somewhat. Without it, I wouldn't have been able to work.

After a while, it took increasingly larger amounts of Xanax to help me but it didn't work so well anymore. I had to go through withdrawal several times each month in order to get the drug to work for me. Withdrawal was very hard. It meant going without sleep for 3 to 4 nights before I could take the drug again. All this time, however, I had to continue to work, which included making presentations to the Navy and conducting meetings with my staff and with the Sparton management.

The Sparton people were very kind to me and gave me every consideration, but they still didn't know about my panic attack problem. They thought that the problems I was having were all due to the surgery. I tried several times to get off the Xanax, but couldn't do it. Several times, I went 5 days without sleep and almost became psychotic. I was hooked. The only good things about Xanax were that it significantly decreased the incidence and severity of the panic attacks and I was able to get some sleep, when it worked. But, what a penalty to pay!

In addition to the RLS, I also began having stabbing and needle prick sensations in my feet. I could handle it during the day, but at night, it almost drove me crazy and added to my difficulty in sleeping. My doctors said it was peripheral neuropathy and there was nothing that could be done about it, except to take lots of medication and put up with the side effects.

My mother was living in Atlanta with my brother Bill and his wife Darlene. I was still working for Sparton and was spending a lot of time in Washington. I often went to Atlanta to visit Mom, Bill and Darlene. Bill and Darlene had two children, Billy (Smort) and Kristi (Firkin Lerken), and they loved Mom (Nana). Darlene and Bill took good care of Mom. Darlene treated Mom like she was her own mother. Darlene is like that. I always loved Darlene. Bill and I took Mom out to dinner once and when she heard what the bill was ($50.00 for five people), she had a fit and said we were idiots to spend that kind of money to eat. She said she could have fed the whole family back in Toledo for a month on what that one meal cost. She would never ever let us take her out to eat again. Mom always said that Bill was a good boy and had his head on right except when I came around him. She said that whenever I got close to Bill, we both became half-wits. She was right.

Mom was failing in health and one day I got a call from Darlene when I was in Washington. She said that Mom was very sick, so I flew to Atlanta to be with her. I spent a few days with her, but illness had advanced to the point that she didn't know me. It wasn't long after that they called me in Washington again and said that she had died. Even though I knew that she was going to die, it was a great shock. I always considered her immortal. She was a great woman and I loved her. I dedicated my PhD thesis to her.

The panic attacks and sleeplessness worsened so much that I found it increasingly difficult to do my job at Sparton and so I took stock of my options. I had saved a large sum of money during my years at Sparton and had a good investment income stream. Since my brother lived in Atlanta, I thought that I might go there and become a consultant. I figured that if I was a consultant, I could set my own hours and if I didn't sleep, I could sleep in. So, I told Sparton that I had always wanted to be in my own business and resigned my position. I didn't tell Sparton the real reason for quitting. I was so ashamed of my weakness.

I really hated to leave Sparton. I liked it there, the people were wonderful and I had accomplished great things, but I just couldn't hack it any longer. Having to be up for meetings at 8 AM when I hadn't slept for several days had become impossible for me. Sparton never did know the real reason why I resigned. They thought I was crazy to leave a great position like I had. They even suggested that I see a psychiatrist. They didn't know that I had been seeing psychiatrists for years. No Sparton vice president had ever resigned before in the history of this grand old company. You could be fired or die, but *resign?* You had to be nuts to give up such a great job. I didn't tell them that I would probably lose my mind if I didn't do something to resolve the panic attacks and sleep problems. I was too ashamed. I had to do something else than what I was doing, or die.

26

Consulting

The US Navy hired me to be a consultant to the Sonobuoy Program Office. My boss was Cdr. Chuck Wicker, Program Manager for the Navy's Sonobuoy Program. I loved doing this work. Cdr. Wicker was a great boss and we worked well together. I made some significant contributions to Mobilization Readiness by developing a Mobilization Plan for Sonobuoys, which was adopted by the Navy and is still in use today.

As a consultant, I had to have a Washington DC office, so I rented an apartment near Crystal City, and lived and worked there when in Washington. I started doing this work for the Navy in December 1980, when I left Sparton and felt a little better; although, I was still having the panic attacks, sleep and blood pressure problems. I didn't feel all that good, but I was getting by. I was really enjoying my role as a consultant and thought that maybe I had turned the corner on at least some of my problems.

Just before Christmas 1981, my stockbroker called me in Washington to inform me that I was broke. He had sold me out to pay for uncovered calls he was making on my account. He had been churning my account to make big commissions for himself, and had ruined me financially.

I almost had a stroke! I couldn't talk or even move. It was like I was paralyzed. I stayed in the apartment for a whole day before I could function. For a poor child of the depression, this was catastrophe! With all my financial security gone, I was very sick again.

The next day I went back to Atlanta, but didn't tell my wife what had happened. We were going to Florida to be with her family over Christmas, and I didn't want to spoil it for her. Somehow, we got through Christmas and I returned to Atlanta to see what could be done. I contacted an attorney and finally recovered about 5% of my assets. But I still had to pay capital gains taxes on the profits my stock had made before the broker sold me out. Therefore, there wasn't much left.

I had to start over again. Now the consulting was vital for me; it was not something that I could do just for fun. I now felt under pressure because I knew that now I had to do it. It was much different. I was very afraid. So, here I was: my financial security was gone, still sick, in debt to pay the IRS for profits I had never received, and no stable job.

I continued to work for the Navy as a consultant. Because of my reputation in the sonobuoy business, Raytheon, Honeywell, General Radio, Hermes Electronics, Bell Labs and several other companies asked me to work for them. GTE asked me to do a study, which led to a substantial contract to lead them into the sonobuoy battery business. Then the Navy changed directions in air ASW sensors, so the battery program didn't go anywhere. Meanwhile, my consultant job with the Navy terminated as new people came into power in NAVAIR.

Fred Brehm and Chuck Furciniti, vice presidents of Hazeltine Corporation and old friends of mine, wanted me to work for them. I consulted for Hazeltine and covered the Naval Coastal Systems Center in Panama City, Florida in an attempt to get business for them in the field of Acoustic Deception Devices (ADC) for Submarine Torpedo Defense. I also marketed their Microwave Landing System to the airport community. I liked working for Hazeltine and learned much about the aviation business.

Hazeltine soon wanted me to work full time for them. I took the new position because it afforded me full company benefits, including medical insurance, and I felt reasonably secure again. I led Hazeltine to a major win on an important submarine torpedo defense program. After a brilliant marketing and engineering campaign, we won the engineering development program for the Acoustic Deception Device, ADC/MK-4. During the campaign leading to the ADC/MK-4 contract, Emerson Electric bought out Hazeltine, and both Brehm and Furciniti left the company. The day after we won the ADC-MK-4 contract, I was fired. So, here I was again—no job, no security, and still suffering from both the physical health problems and the panic attacks.

27

Drug Addiction

I was able to keep working as a consultant for various companies, with the help of Xanax for the panic attacks, Neurontin for the RLS, and hypertension medication for the high blood pressure. I was able to prevent the people I worked with from detecting my problems. I was still ashamed of my weaknesses, particularly of the panic attacks.

I developed a tolerance for Xannax which made it no longer effective. Even though it wasn't working to help me sleep, it still lessened the panic attacks and prevented them from becoming full-blown crises. I tried to get off the Xanax several times by myself with no success. I could go five days without sleep and instead of getting sleepy and tired, I would become hyper. My doctor decided that I needed to go into detox at Northside Hospital to get off the Xanax.

I stayed there for a week with the alcoholics and drug users. The doctors gave me drugs to help me while the Xanax was expelled from my system. In addition to the detox drugs, the therapy included participation in group therapy.

All the others were there because of addictions to alcohol, recreational drugs, or both; I was the only one who was getting off prescription drugs. It amazed me to see so many young people from the teens into their early twenties who were hooked on heroin, cocaine, crack, and alcohol. I asked many of them how they got on the drugs. Most of them said it was just to experience the high. I was using prescription drugs because of my panic attacks, but these people did it just for fun? What a terrible price to pay for a little high! At night you could hear them screaming in their misery, in spite of the drugs used to help them. Some had spent the last five to ten years of their lives in and out of detox and rehab centers. What wasted lives of despair that might have been happy and constructive!

I got to know several alcoholics fairly well, and after we got out of detox, I attended Alcoholics Anonymous (AA) meetings with them in the hope that I could get help with my terrible panic attacks. The attacks had grown more severe

72

now that I was off the Xanax. My voice became very low and I acted like a very old man. Just clinging to life, I found myself looking for any avenue of respite.

I liked the people I met at the AA meetings and marveled at their camaraderie, but the meetings didn't help me. Actually, it depressed me to hear people get up in front of the group while smoking and drinking coffee like fiends, and say with conviction bordering on pride that they were alcoholics. They kept repeating that they were powerless over alcohol, that they could never be cured, that the best they could do was control their alcoholism. I know that this works for some of them, but they were constantly acknowledging and imbedding into their subconscious mind that they were alcoholics and there was no hope of cure. It seemed to me a self-defeating tactic. They spoke about a biological predisposition, a gene in them that made them drink, and there was no way to correct it. Some of these people went to AA meetings seven days a week!

When I learned about hypnotherapy, I developed my own understanding of alcoholism. I believe that the source of their alcohol problem is buried in their subconscious, and if it can be found and the source energy released, they could be cured. Years later in my practice, I would release demons on some of these people and help them. In these cases, the old cliché "demon rum" was true.

I left the detox center a shaking mess. We were going to Panama City with my brother Bill and his family to spend a week on the beach and sail our 33-foot Hunter sailboat. The panic attacks worsened in Panama City, and I had to stay in the condominium waiting to die while they all went sailing. It was miserable. Now I was no longer taking the Xanax, so the panic attacks intensified and I was in terror all the time.

For the next year, I was like a dead man. I would go to Washington or to Panama City, or wherever I had to go to work, but it was like going into death. I would get on the bus to the airport and be soaked with sweat before I even got on the plane. I found it hard to talk, and for the first time in my life, I didn't think I would make it. I thought many times of suicide, and actually pulled out my gun several times and looked at it for hours on end. But I really wanted to live. In spite of all the miserable cards I have been dealt, I still love life…but I was at the end of my rope.

I knew I had to get help, but where? The allopathic doctors couldn't help me, the psychiatrists couldn't help me, the clinical psychologists couldn't help me, God couldn't or wouldn't help me, nothing could help me. **God had abandoned me.** Then, as if to punctuate God's disdain for me, my brother Bill died from colon cancer. Bill and Darlene, along with my wife, Laura, and friend, LaVonne

McBride, were the only ones who knew the extent of my problems. I really loved Bill. He was my strength, and now he was gone. What could I do?

28

Bill's Cancer

For my consulting practice in Atlanta, I was renting an office from my brother Bill's company, Webb Skillas & Associates (WSA). WSA was in the fire alarm business and I was in the defense consulting business, so I didn't participate in WSA. Bill had the office in front with the big windows and I rented a back office. He was 11 years younger than I and very healthy. Bill was never sick; he never had a panic attack in his life, and his blood pressure was always normal. *I* was the one with all the problems. Whenever I felt like I was dying, which was often, I would call Bill or Darlene and talk about my illness, and they would help me by reassuring me that they were always there for me. I had named Bill as executor of my estate and knew that he would handle everything when I died, which it always felt like it would be in the next day or two.

One day in the office, Bill threw up. We all thought it was the stomach flu, but I wondered. Bill never got the flu or any sickness. The next day he threw up again. I had gone to Washington on business and was visiting my friend, patent attorney Nick Aquilino, when Laura called to tell me that Bill had been diagnosed with colon cancer.

It couldn't be—not Bill! He never got sick. I remembered that my cousin Betty Jane died from colon cancer, and so had Uncle Steve, and Aunt Elizabeth. Now I was very afraid for Bill. I was numb with shock, and I went into even more sever panic attacks for the next two days.

Bill and Darlene decided on chemotherapy. I was against it, but didn't have anything better to offer them. I had heard that the chemo would destroy his immune system, leaving him without any defenses. His body would not be able to fight the disease, or any other that took advantage of the weakness. Chemo only worked about 5% of the time. I was so against it, but what else could he do? I asked my gastroenterologist how this could happen. Bill had passed the Hemocult test and sigmoid tests the previous year during his annual physical. The doctor said that Bill's cancer was so far up his colon at the intersection of the small and large intestines that those tests didn't pick it up. Only a colonoscopy would have found it. By the time Bill had symptoms, the cancer had already metastasized to the peritoneum, and on to the liver where it was lethal.

I had just finished reading Bernie Siegel's book in which he said God talks to us in dreams if we ask. I asked God to help me help Bill, and I soon had a dream. Bill and I were in a western town with a huge jar of stuff in the town square. Everyone was pointing at it and holding their noses. I interpreted the dream as God telling me to go west for Bills healing, and that the jar of stuff in the square was chemo. I asked everyone I knew about cancer treatments and one of my doctor friends, an osteopath, said he had heard of an Indian out west who worked on cancer and also about a Dr. Burton in the Bahamas. I researched the Indian and came up with Kote Lotah of the Chumash tribe in Ventura, California. I felt that this Indian represented the west I saw in the dream and so I got in touch with Kote Lotah and arranged for Bill and me to come to him for healing.

He worked on both of us. The treatment was mystical and interesting, involving incense, chanting and drawing an eagle's claw over the body. Kote said that I was in much worse shape than Bill was. I told Kote about my sleep problem, and he gave me some ground up herbs that he said would knock out a horse. After the treatment, Bill and I felt good so we decided to rent a car, go to San Diego, and see the Americas Cup trials in San Diego before we returned to Atlanta. That night in San Diego, Bill slept like a baby. But I was up all night with panic attacks in spite of taking the Chumash herbs for sleep that would "knock out a horse." It might work on horses, but it didn't have any effect on me.

After returning to Atlanta from the west coast, we waited for Bill's healing, but it didn't happen. The cancer worsened. We researched Dr. Lawrence Burton's clinic in Freeport on Grand Bahamas Island, contacted them, and arranged to take Bill there. Darlene and I flew with Bill to Freeport and got him into the clinic. The Burton Immuno-Augmentive Therapy treatment consisted of injecting yourself 10 to12 times a day with serum made from your own blood to enhance the immune system. Bill was very squeamish about the needles, but he learned to do it very well. The first time was the hardest. We found a condo in Freeport, rented it and rented an old junk car for an exorbitant amount of money so Bill could go to the clinic every couple of days to get his blood drawn and new stocks of filled needles for the injections.

Bill and Rufus Webb, his business partner, owned a 42-foot sailboat. We decided to bring it to Freeport and dock it at Port Lucaya so Bill could live on it and save money. I would stay with Bill for a week, and then Darlene would stay with him for a week. We did this for three months, after which the clinic said he could go home and simply come back every three months or so for a tune-up.

We got to know about a dozen cancer patients like Bill who were also patients at the Burton Clinic. When I went to Freeport for my week, I would energetically work on several of the cancer patients who were in severe pain, and it seemed to help them temporarily. The energy work I did on the cancer patients in the Bahamas was based on what I had learned from my grandmother as a kid.

They looked forward to my visits for the relief from pain that I brought them. However, it was strange that I never seemed to be able to help Bill no matter how hard I tried.

After Bill was back in Atlanta for a few weeks, he got another CAT scan which showed that his liver tumor had grown alarmingly. The Bahamas clinic hadn't helped him. We had to do something else. I began looking for another treatment for him and had two faith healers work on him and a naturopath. None of them had any discernable positive effect on Bill. I also heard about Orgone treatments, which were supposed to develop and amplify Chi energy for healing, so I bought one of the Orgone generators and we used it with visualization on Bill without any noticeable success.

About this time, I came up with the name of Dr. Stanley Burzynski in Houston, Texas, who had a treatment for colon cancer. I also heard about an experimental treatment for colon cancer at the M. D. Anderson Hospital in Houston, TX. I called the developer of the treatment in South Dakota who gave me the name of the principal investigator in charge of the experimental program at M.D. Anderson. When I called him, he invited us to Houston, so we flew Bill there—with some difficulty, as he was in great pain. I rented a big Cadillac so he would have room to lie down in the back of the car and then checked into a hotel near the hospital.

After examining Bill, the doctors said there was nothing they could do for him because he had the chemo treatments, which destroyed his immune system. The experimental program was based on enhancing the immune system, like the Bahamas program. I tried in vain to get them to change their minds, but they were adamant that Bill was not a candidate for their program because of his previous chemotherapy treatments. I even appealed to the developer of the treatment in South Dakota to no avail. They simply said that Bill had a disease for which there was no known treatment and they were sorry. I hated them! Since we were in Houston, I asked Bill if he would let me take him to see Dr. Burzynski. Bill said he wanted to go home, back to Atlanta, so we checked out of Houston and flew back.

Back in Atlanta, Bill's condition and pain worsened. We continued to use the Orgone generator on him, but it didn't seem to have any effect. He was now taking heavy doses of morphine for the pain and didn't want to eat anything. I talked to him and begged him to let us take him back to Houston to see Burzynski. He agreed, so I set it up with Burzynski. We had to take him to Hartsfield Airport in a van because the pain was so bad he couldn't sit up much. It was a long trip to Houston because he was so miserable. Once again, I rented a big car and we took him to see Dr. Burzynski.

We rented an apartment near Dr. Burzynski's treatment center and took Bill in to see Burzynski. After paying the $5000 initial fee, we were told that he had to have a shunt installed into an artery in his chest, and Burzynski referred his patients out for this part of the treatment. The shunt was for a pump that would pump anti-neoplasms into him to dissolve the cancer. So, we had to travel half way across Houston in the heavy traffic with Bill in terrible pain to find the doctor who would install the shunt. This took several hours. The next day, the pump was installed, and we looked forward to Bill feeling better.

Darlene had to clean the shunt regularly so it wouldn't block up, and we had to make sure that it didn't come out during the night. After two days on the pump, we thought Bill was feeling better and we were greatly heartened. Bill seemed to be doing better, the pain was much less, but he still wouldn't eat anything and he told me that he was seeing two of me…double vision. I thought this was from the medication.

Bill Dies

We took Bill back to Burzynski the next day and, since Bill hadn't been able to urinate, they wanted to catherize him, but he wouldn't let them. He agreed that I could do it, so I had the nurse teach me how and I did it. But he didn't urinate; his kidneys had shut down. Dr. Burzynski said we had to get him to defecate to get the dead cancer cells out of his body, so Burzynski gave us a prescription for a heavy laxative, which we gave to Bill. We got Bill back to the apartment and he wasn't able to help us get him out of the car and into the apartment. Darlene and I literally had to carry him in. We got him on the bed and we could see he was very uncomfortable so I called Burzynski and asked if we could get him onto some kind of dialysis machine to detoxify his liver and Burzynski said there was no way to do so. Shortly after, Bill said he had to use the bathroom and so Darlene and I tried to help him. But his eyes blinked out and I knew he was in a coma, so I called 911.

The Houston fire department responded and confirmed that Bill was in a coma. They immediately took him to a local hospital, not far from where we were staying. When I got to the hospital, Bill was laying on the table in the emergency room. The staff asked me what I wanted them to do for Bill and I said, "save his life". They said I should call Dr. Burzynski, who was Bill's doctor, and ask him what to do. The medical people in the hospital regarded Burzynski as a charlatan, so they wouldn't call him.

I called Burzynski and told him what was happening to Bill. He told me that Bill's tests that morning showed that his liver was destroyed by the cancer, and that there was no way to save him. There was nothing to be done for him, and putting him on life support would have only prolonged his agony. I told the hospital staff to let him go.

Darlene was freaking out so I comforted her and she left the emergency room to be with the nurse while I stayed with Bill. The doctor asked me if she should give Bill something for his pain. I said yes.

She gave him a shot, and shortly after I watched the monitors as his blood pressure kept dropping and his heart stopped beating. I held him in my arms as he died, telling him to not be afraid because I was there.

He died in my arms, and I remembered holding him in my arms when he was born. I was 10 years old then.

After Bill died, Darlene and I sat outside the emergency room and held each other in shock. She asked me to go back in to get his watch, so I went back into the emergency room and took his Rolex watch off his wrist to give to his son. I kissed his hand and his forehead. Bill wasn't there—only his body was. Bill had gone and he wouldn't be back.

Bill's kids, Kristi and Billy flew to Houston and we brought Bill back to Atlanta to bury him. My little brother on whom I depended for strength was gone, and I was alone with all my misery.

God had abandoned me again!

29

Alternative Medicine

I was educated in technology and business, so I was a very left-brained person. I only believed in things that were scientific and that were demonstrable by the methods of science. I had exhausted the scientific avenues of healing which are the basis of Western allopathic medicine, psychiatry, psychology, chiropractic and many other healing paths without finding anything that could help me. Actually, I was getting worse, not better, because of my dependence on prescription drugs. I had to find something else out there that would help me. I must at least try something else, but what was left? My sister Jean was into metaphysics, and I always thought she was a little nuts, but I had to try something else. Nothing I had been doing would allow me to continue to live.

At a vitamin store, my wife heard about a chiropractor, Dr. Phillip Princetta, who used gemstones for healing. I resisted going to see him, thinking it was crazy. Finally, I went because I had nowhere else to go, and I was dying. Here was my summarized situation in a nutshell:

Summarized Situation in a Nutshell

I thought I was dying. I could not get my breath, and my head spun day in and day out. My heart pounded as if it was going to explode. But worst of all was the cold grip of fear enveloping me. Please, God, help me! This was the panic attack I lived with daily. I couldn't sleep. Often I went sleepless four to five days in a row from a sleep disorder called Restless Leg Syndrome (RLS). My blood pressure soared astronomically (220/120), and I waited for the stroke that was surely coming.

I went to medical doctors, psychiatrists and psychologists, but found little help. Three sleep clinics and countless doctors put me on sleep drugs. I became addicted and had to suffer the agony of withdrawal repeatedly. I took psychotropic drugs for panic attacks, and beta-blockers, ACE inhibitors and calcium channel blockers for hypertension. I wound up in the hospital emergency room on nights when the fear engulfed me beyond my ability to cope. This was how I lived, if you could call it living. With all this, I still had to make a living.

In spite of these problems, I advanced in my jobs, becoming vice president of Sparton Electronics, a major defense electronics firm, and responsible for over three hundred million dollars a year in Anti Submarine Warfare Systems. In this job, I had to conduct meetings, travel extensively, make presentations to high-ranking government officials in Washington, DC and be on my toes in this very competitive business. I was finding it increasingly difficult to cope with my job responsibilities.

The sleep problem ultimately became so bad that I reluctantly quit this job and moved to Atlanta to become a consultant to the government and aerospace companies. I figured a consultant could set his own hours, and I might live with my affliction. I had saved enough money for a good investment income and felt fairly secure, financially.

I had not been in Atlanta a year when a dishonest stock market broker almost cleaned me out and I was in debt. Panic attacks, terrible insomnia, severe hypertension, almost broke and without a job. So much for security! Now, I had to go back to work and to do that I had to improve my health.

After a session in a hospital detoxification center to get off Xanax, which I had taken for sleep and panic attacks, I went for a year with super-intense panic attacks and sleep deprivation. I now realized I had to change things or I could not continue to live, much less work. That's when I discovered Alternative Medicine.

My metaphysically oriented wife, Laura, desperate to help me, found a chiropractor who used gemstones in healing. She wanted me to try him. I certainly wasn't getting anywhere with the treatment I was receiving. I was a conventional left brained businessman and technologist, with a PhD in Engineering and an MBA in business. I thought this "voodoo" treatment was ridiculous and wouldn't have it, preferring to find an accepted solution. However, I just couldn't get there. The problems persisted despite the best efforts of my allopathic doctors, psychiatrists and psychologists.

Despair finally drove me to try the gem stone chiropractor, and for some reason I didn't understand, I felt better and more relaxed. Curious about why I was feeling better from some crazy stones, I continued to see him and began to investigate other alternative therapies.

The change I felt from the gem stone therapy, although positive, was very subtle. So, I looked for stronger therapies. Over the next few years, in addition to chiropractic, I tried homeopathy, energy healing, aromatherapy, herbal therapy, shamanistic soul retrieval, acupuncture, rebirthing, body electronics, massage, yoga, tai chi, Christian Science, and finally, hypnotherapy. All the therapies helped some, but hypnotherapy, eventually, saved me. Yet, I didn't get there easily. Hypnotherapy by itself, helped me to relax, but it didn't seem to get to the source of the problems I was having. The benefits were fleeting.

During this time, I realized I could feel Chi energy flowing in the body and I could sense blockages. I remembered my Grandmother could do this; I must have inherited it from her. I was so impressed with even the small change in my health with alternative medicine that I began to treat others with shiatsu, a technique that opened blockages in the body's energy pathways and was successful in temporarily alleviating some miseries of people I worked on. I read voraciously and realized that I was only working on symptom release and not healing the source problem.

Hypnotherapy & Entities

What I finally came to understand was that the sources of the problems, both in myself and in the people on whom I worked, were in the subconscious. I realized that the only way to achieve permanent healing was to find and eradicate those source problems. I also found that the only way into the subconscious was with hypnosis, so I began to study hypnosis and hypnotherapy.

I studied hypnotherapy, became a certified hypnotherapist, started using it with my shiatsu energy work, and found that I could help a greater number of people and the results lasted longer. But it didn't always work, and the results, although good, were never permanent. This was the same problem with my own therapy: I felt somewhat better for a while, but it never lasted very long. I kept having the panic attacks, although not as often. My blood pressure, even with medication, was still very high. If it was true that the problems were in the subconscious, how could I get to them and release them so I would heal?

I had clients for whom I did everything right and they didn't get better. What was wrong? How about me? I was doing everything, too; forgiveness therapy, gestalt, regression, and I was still having severe problems. What was I missing?

I spoke to many of my colleagues at the National Guild of Hypnotists (NGH) conventions and read everything I could get my hands on regarding hypnotherapy, in hope that I could discover the "hidden ingredient" to healing. At the NGH conventions, I ran across Dr. Fred Leidecker from California, Dr. Bill Baldwin from Enterprise, Florida, and Carl Carpenter from New Hampshire. These therapists told me about spirit, or entity attachment, and the results they were getting with sick people by releasing entities when everything else failed. I remember my old Grandmuschka telling me about people in Hungary who got well when spirits of dead people who had attached to them were released. I also recalled listening to Father Hebbler at St. Thomas in Toledo talking about Jesus casting out demons and healing people.

Could entity attachment be the missing part to the healing equation? I was afraid to believe that it could be because it scared the hell out of me. I really didn't want anything to do with this, as I thought I would be messing with something very dangerous that could destroy me and make things worse for me than they already were.

I began to tell my clients whom I couldn't help that they should go to a priest and get exorcised, but they just looked at me like I was crazy. One particular client, whom I couldn't help, was dieing of anorexia and she did seek out several Catholic priests but was turned down by them. She then went to a protestant church where two women practiced deliverance (exorcism) and got them to try it on her. Both of the women were pregnant and miscarried before the deliverance process was complete. The women subsequently refused to have anything further to do with my anorexic client, and threw her out. I then decided that I had to learn how to do spirit releasement in spite of my fear and trepidation about this whole concept. Something inside of me told me to do it despite my fear.

At that moment, I made the decision to learn at least enough about spirit releasement so that I could have it done on me, as I couldn't seem to make any further progress. My life, although somewhat better, was still very much a mess.

I attended every lecture, every seminar, every course offered on entity release and read every book I could find on the subject. During my studies, I experienced spirit releasement at the hands of my teachers.

I was scared to death the first time. After I was put into an altered state of consciousness, this voice started speaking through me. It cursed, screamed, threatened my therapist, and said it was going to kill me because I was letting the therapist do the releasement. It took over one hour to get it to leave. When I came out of hypnosis, I felt badly shaken, although much relieved and quite a bit calmer. Subsequent releases were also dramatic, but I had an idea of what to expect after the first release, so the fear was diminished. They took eight layers of entities off me, including demons, soul mind fragments of other people, and earthbound spirits.

After being released of the attachments, I began treatment with a competent hypnotherapist and working together, we did more conventional uncovering and releasing of childhood ego states and conflicts that were within me, and I really began to feel better. After a lot of work, my blood pressure dropped drastically, the panic attacks stopped completely, and I began sleeping better at night, in spite of the continuing RLS and peripheral neuropathy problems. My life was saved!

I was so impressed that I began using Spirit Releasement Therapy (SRT) in my practice and the outcomes were awesome. People who I had not been able to help were now getting well in droves and holding onto their healing. My anorexic client was healed. Not only an occasional healing but time after time, I now was able to help people with very severe problems on a consistent basis, and the results were lasting. I had found the "hidden ingredient". Get rid of attached entities first, *then* do traditional hypnotherapy and the outcome is miraculous. This is, I believe, what Jesus did.

Thank You, God!

Channeling

The gemstone chiropractor that my wife took me to was Dr. Philip Princetta. His was very different from any healing work I had ever experienced before. He laid gemstones on my body and used arm mentoring, which I found out later was called kinesiology, to inquire of my subconscious mind what needed to be done for me. When he asked questions, I wondered whom he was talking to. He said, "I am talking to your body". How could this be? My first impulse was to get out of there as quickly as I could. This had to be the "lunatic fringe alternative quack medicine" I had heard about. The problem was that I felt better when I left than when I arrived. I asked myself, "What was going on here"?

Further questioning revealed that the gemstones were actually "harmonics", frequencies programmed into stones and plastic, which corrected undesirable frequencies in my body. Being an engineer, and very familiar with frequencies and vibrational analysis from my work on destructive vibrational frequencies on guided missile components, I wondered how this stuff fit into what I knew to be a mathematically precise science. In my work, I spent much time analyzing destructive modes of resonant frequency behavior on structures and missile guidance and control systems. I asked myself "how did this "airy-fairy" stuff relate to physical systems analysis, and how could it correct illness? Later on, when I formulated my own understanding of healing based on the "Eastern Model of Disease," I came to understand more of how all of this worked.

Dr. Princetta introduced me to Dr. Mel Reese, Ashley, Nicholas Aquilino and a group of chiropractors called the International Systemic Health Organization or ISHO. Dr. Reese headed up ISHO; Ashley was a South African film producer who was also a trance medium and lived in Johannesburg; and Nick Aquilino was a patent attorney in Washington, DC. These people were quite different, to say the least, from the Defense Industry businessmen, engineers and scientists I was used to dealing with. They believed it was possible to correct illness using Chi energy and the mind. They were not big on allopathic medicine or psychiatry, but they did believe in natural medicines such as homeopathy, chiropractic, massage and energy healing.

What really brought my attention to their way of thinking was an incident relating to Ashley, the South African. After I felt somewhat better from Dr. Princetta's work, he called to invite me to a trance medium session by Ashley over in Dunwoody, a suburb of Atlanta. At first I refused because when Dr. Princetta told me what was to happen, I just couldn't buy it…the idea was so far out and foolish to my way of thinking. However, I was also curious and I wanted to experience this crazy stuff and see for myself what it was all about. So, I went.

There were about 15 people gathered around a large table. Ashley sat at the head of the table, went into a trance, and began moving his right hand back and forth to indicate that he was now "channeling" information from some elevated discarnate being. A woman, named Mara, who was down at the other end of the table picked up a pad of paper and began to write what Ashley was channeling. The channeling was all about people I didn't know, and sounded like "mumbo jumbo" to me. After the gathering was all over, I left feeling embarrassed that I had even gone. I couldn't understand how seemingly intelligent, successful people could believe that information was coming through Ashley and being picked up by Mara and written down. Why hadn't Ashley simply written it himself, or simply told us what he was getting, if anything? Why, if he was really getting information, did it have to be retransmitted to Mara for writing? I asked Dr. Princetta about this, and he said that was just the way Ashley did it. I was more convinced than ever that this stuff was just wild, and I was embarrassed that I had participated. I vowed to myself that I would never, ever be taken in again like this.

I continued to see Dr. Princetta occasionally, because it made me feel a bit better even though I didn't know why. Maybe it was all just in my mind that I felt better, and he didn't really do anything. I stayed away from these crazy people, except for my visits to Dr. Princetta.

About three months after this "channeling" session, I received a 3 AM telephone call from Ashley in Johannesburg, South Africa. He told me that he had been talking to the Chief Holy Man of the Zulu Nation, Credo Mutwah, who described me and said that I had channeling for him. My immediate reaction was anger at Ashley. I thought he must be drunk or on drugs. I sputtered to Ashley that I was not interested in this stuff, and not to bother me again with such crap, especially at 3 AM. Ashley, however, persisted and insisted that I channel for Credo Mutwah. I told him I did not know how, didn't believe in it and he should get someone else. He would not be put off however, and preceded to tell me what to do. He was adamant that I get pencil and paper and start to write. Because he would not leave me alone unless I humored him, I did as he asked and sat there in bed for close to 30 minutes, just holding the pencil. Of course, nothing came to me. This was all crap. He kept telling me to write whatever came to me and I kept telling him that nothing was coming to me. Finally, he agreed that this was a mistake and we terminated our conversation. I was mortified that he would think that I would fall for this, and simply shook my head in disbelief that people could be so gullible and weird.

Four months later, I got a call from Dr. Princetta telling me that Ashley was returning to Atlanta and they were going to have another session in Dunwoody during which he was going to channel again and would like me to attend. I told Dr. Princetta that I was not interested. Two weeks later, he called again, saying that Ashley was now here and he earnestly wanted me to attend his channeling session. I again refused. Two days later Dr. Princetta again called me and said that Ashley understood my reluctance but thought it very important that I agree to attend his channeling session. I said that I would consider it. "What the hell," I thought. It would only take an hour or so and I would get Ashley off my back, so I agreed to go.

The scene was much the same as before. About 15 people gathered around the long table with Ashley at the head and Mara again at the other end. I sat across the table from Mara and prepared myself to act interested, so as not to embarrass the others. I felt foolish and somewhat dishonest as I was there with no interest or belief in what they were doing.

I watched as Ashley put himself into a trance with some deep breathing and soon he was waving his right hand again as he had done before to signal that the information was coming. Everyone, including me, looked at Mara and expected her to pick up the pencil and pad and begin writing as she did the last time. However, Mara did not pick up the pencil and pad, she just looked concerned and soon everyone was looking at her and wondering why she wasn't writing. Ashley, in the meantime, began gesturing even more with his right hand and he appeared to be irritated that she wasn't writing, but Mara just looked perplexed.

I began to notice a discomfort coming over me as though I wanted to pick up the pencil and pad and write, but I resisted, thinking how foolish I would look if I did so. My uneasiness continued to increase and before I knew it, I picked up the pencil and pad and feverishly began to write. Thoughts just kept coming to me like a dam had burst and wanted to flow. It was the strangest experience I ever had. I just kept writing and writing, unable to stop. My conscious mind was resisting, but to no avail. I simply kept on writing. After a while, the thoughts stopped and so did the writing. We looked at what I had written and there were 22 pages of information for Credo Mutwah. It had to do with medicines and people I never heard of. This was very weird. I was very discombobulated and confused. What had happened to me, and where did this stuff come from? I excused myself and left, feeling quite strange and bewildered.

It took me several days to recover from this experience. I felt nervous and upset, and it exacerbated my feelings of panic because I had felt possessed when the writing happened. I expressed my fears to Dr. Princetta and told him of my concerns that something evil had happened. He reassured me that it wasn't evil, that instead, it was good and that the channeled information would help many people. Because I trusted him, I believed him, and the fear of evil ameliorated, although my nervousness persisted. Shortly thereafter, I began getting calls from Dr. Reese and others in ISHO asking me to channel information for them. I found that if I just relaxed and let go, I would get thoughts that answered their questions. Over the next year, I channeled volumes of information for ISHO people and Dr. Reese.

To this day, I don't know where this information came from or why it came through me. I did have the feeling, however, that it was good and that I had a role to play in helping others. This experience ultimately led to my healing, as I learned more and more and began to apply what I learned for myself to helping others. Something supernatural was happening to me, and I began to understand why I had all the problems in my life. All the pain had a purpose—it was so I could learn and help others. The whole experience I had been through had been good, and it had to come from God, the source of all good.

God certainly works in mysterious ways.

Epilogue

♦

The Hard Way

Since my healing, I devote myself to healing, teaching, and writing about hypnotherapy. My life is dedicated to helping others through hypnotherapy. I got into this because hypnotherapy saved my life when western medicine and psychotherapy hadn't helped me and I didn't have anywhere else to turn. I was doing fairly well, both physically and emotionally and feeling good about my life, especially being able to help so many people, when all of a sudden, things turned bad.

A lot of things happened to me during the past year of 2003, tragic things which tried my faith, and the return of personal illness that I thought I was rid of forever.

In January 2003, my sweet dog, Sweetsiepootsy had to be put down because of cancer. Pootsie was more than just a pet. She was my Clinical Associate and was featured on my website. She would greet my clients at the door and usher them into my healing room, where she would bring them a toy to relieve their nervousness. When I put the client into hypnosis, Pootsie would also go into hypnosis and then when I brought the client out, Pootsie would greet them as they awakened. She had such a warm heart and I loved her dearly.

In March, my sister Jean died of a heart attack. Jean and I were always close. She was a nanny and loved to take care of little kids. I took care of Jean for the last 20 years of her life because she could not make that much in the nanny business. She was my connection to the past because she and I shared so much growing up. She and I practically raised my brother Bill because my mother had to work.

In April, Richard, my son-in-law committed suicide. Like me, he was depressed from childhood, felt very insecure and linked security to the amount of money he had. Richard was very gifted mechanically and was a US Airways Senior Captain. When the airline went bankrupt, Richard lost most of his retirement, which meant so much to him, and he killed himself.

In May, my only son died after surgery for an aneurysm on his heart's aortic valve. The aneurysm was imbedded into his sternum. When the surgeon opened his chest, he cut the aneurysm and nothing could stop the bleeding. Charlie loved life, was doing very well as a CPA and had a good job and wonderful family.

Suddenly, in three months, six of my eight grandchildren had no father and I had lost my sister, son and son-in-law. This is a lot of stress. Going to three family funerals in three months does not inure you to death. Instead, it brings death right into your face, full force.

I have a past history of high blood pressure and a sleep problem caused by two surgeries that left me with scar tissue. This scar tissue irritated the sciatic nerve going to my feet and caused stabbing pains in my feet at night when I tried to sleep. Hypnotherapy and mild blood pressure medication took care of these problems and allowed me to lead a normal life and do my work.

I was okay with my blood pressure and sleep during and after the family deaths until about mid November when my blood pressure began to rise with increasing speed. With the approval of my allopathic physician, I increased my blood pressure medication to compensate. Two weeks later, I went to the hospital emergency room because my blood pressure was up to 210/105. My blood pressure soon reached 220/120, and I was in the hospital ER five times between December and March. This happened despite taking seven powerful blood pressure medications. I continued with hypnotherapy, allopathic medicine, psychiatry, psychological counseling, herbal medicine and shamanic healing without any success reducing my blood pressure. Here I was again back in the same old trouble as I was before my healing.

I really thought I was going to die from a stroke. Nothing that my doctors suggested had any effect on my blood pressure. It was consistently very high and I was scared that this was it for me. I lived with the Sword of Damocles hanging over my head all the time and could not get out from under it. I began to cancel clients and students and prepared myself for death. How could I help others or teach them about healing when I was about to die? I had no idea of what to do about it.

I asked Sherry Henderson of the Inner Space and Oracle if she would do a reading for me to get some insight into what was happening with me. Sherry did the reading, and also consulted with an Ayurvedic associate. They determined that I was full of rage over what had happened to me during the year. This rage was causing my high blood pressure. But, how could I translate this knowledge into something concrete that would lower my blood pressure? As usual, I didn't know what to do about the problem. But, I didn't have to worry; the Creator (Spirit) did it for me...again.

This is how Spirit works. If we don't get the message from our life lessons, then Spirit will keep creating bigger and bigger lessons for us until we finally do get it. It is the hard way to learn. All my life, I have always been cursed to learn my lessons the hard way. Unfortunately, that's the way I constantly do it. I never learn until it is shoved into my face time after time. It's stupid and really unnecessary, but there are those of us who are too dumb to learn any other way. We, who are dumb, are condemned to learn life's lessons the hard way.

This is how I learned. All my life I had been afraid of death. The fear came to me when I was in my mother's womb and I had never been free of it. The lessons of my family's deaths were Spirit's way of teaching me to accept death as a part of life. But I resisted because I was still so afraid, and so Spirit drove it home to me in this very hard way by making me face death repeatedly. The fear in me combined with the rage I felt towards learning the hard way drove my blood pressure up. I could not get this fear and rage out of me to lower the internal pressure.

After Pootsie died, we got a new little dog whom we named Daisy. We got her when she was eleven weeks old. She really grew on us, especially me. She was a little eleven-pound sixteen months old Shih Tzu. I had grown to love her and she loved me; we had a very special relationship. I loved the way she would cock her little head and growl at me when she wanted something and the way she would put her little head on my shoulder when I was sitting on the floor with my back to the couch eating something. She was very precious to me and occupied an especially warm place in my heart.

We were remodeling parts of the house and the workers had arrived early that morning. Daisy, who had slept with me, was hugging me in bed. I left the door open so she could leave whenever she wanted. I hadn't noticed that she had left until I heard my wife screaming. I leaped out of bed full of foreboding and found out what had happened. Daisy had gone out of the house through her doggie door and had been run over and killed in the driveway by one of the workmen. When I heard this, I felt like I exploded. I shrieked, cried, and screamed for over one hour. I could not control the outpouring of emotion from within me. When I finished, my blood pressure was better. Daisy, in dying, had saved me by providing me with the safety valve that vented my internal pressure. So now, my blood pressure is improved, but I have no Daisy. I have replaced pressure with grief—a hard way to resolve my blood pressure problem.

Is it really necessary that learning be so hard? I think that Spirit works like this if we don't do what it is necessary to learn and correct our lives. If we just go on muddling through life's problems without resolving them, then this is the way we learn. I think that Spirit wants us to use our minds to come up with our own solutions to life's problems because that's a good way to learn. If we don't solve our problems, then they will be solved for us and we may not like how it is done.

Remember the old adage: "Be careful what you wish for, you just might get it". If we just wish that the problem were solved for us without doing it ourselves, then we leave the problem to Spirit and it might be a hard solution. We should not just leave the solution to our problems to the Universe or Spirit; we should solve our problems in the way we want them to be solved. Otherwise, the solutions may be taken out of our hands. This is very elegant because we learn and grow by taking responsibility even though it is much more work. But that's why we have minds.

Our minds can often lead us to a problem's solution that is much easier and acceptable to us than if we just leave it to Spirit. Perhaps this is Spirit's way to get us to get off our duffs and make us learn. Perhaps if we go the hard way a sufficient amount, we finally say "enough" and try to learn an easier way. It's not that Spirit wants us to suffer; it's just that, unfortunately, many of us only learn that way…we have to suffer enough first and then we begin to get a little smart. If we are lucky, this happens when we are fairly young. But then there are those of us who don't get the message until we are pretty far over the hill. It's the story of the jackass who had to be hit over the head with a two-by-four to get his attention.

I am that jackass, and I am telling Spirit now that, yes, I have finally gotten the message.

I will solve my problems. You don't have to do it for me.

In Part Two, I discuss what I have learned about the message and how it has healed me

Amen!

PART 2

Healing with Hypnotherapy

1

Looking for Help

○ ○

Every method of treating illness works. High-tech laboratory-tested therapies of Western medicine work. So do the ancient techniques of Eastern medicine. Laser surgery and chemotherapy, crystals, ginseng root and Echinacea, low-fat diets and vitamin mega doses, as well as the whole armamentarium of New Age medicine—such as aromatherapy, music therapy, Therapeutic Touch, Reiki, macrobiotics-they all work. Every possible decoction of forest and garden, and yes, a rag, a bone, and a hank of hair, has been used to heal and have healed. In the history of the world, there has never been a medicine or treatment that did not heal someone.

How is this possible? What is really going on here? To compound the puzzle, why doesn't a given treatment work on everyone who has the same disease? In addition, if a treatment is effective in Switzerland, why doesn't it work in Swaziland? Moreover, if a treatment worked in 1800, why didn't the identical treatment work in the year 1900? Science always claims to look for the simplest answer, the elegant solution. Is there one that could explain this conundrum?. The truth is that your health is in your mind.

—*Lolette Kuby* **"Faith and the Placebo Effect"**
(Origin Press, 2001)

When you think you are in imminent danger of death, as I always did, you will go for anything that might help you. It was obvious that the doctors and treatments I was using were not helping, so I had to take my life into my own hands

95

and not depend on them anymore to save me. That is when I got into hypnotherapy. But, I could not depend on hypnotherapists to do it for me, I had to take control and learn about it if it was going to help me. That is how my mind works.

This is what I learned about Hypnotherapy and Spirit Releasement in my search to save myself. I finally realized and accepted the fact that my healing was not going to come from my allopathic doctors, psychologists and psychiatrists. My healing had to come from within me, from my own inner self, since I couldn't seem to find it anywhere out there. Maybe, if I could have found a Master like Jesus or Buddha or a Saint to lay their hands on me, it would have been different. But here I was stuck with illness that was ruining my life, and I didn't have anywhere else to go except within myself and so, with lots of help that's where I went.

As I searched for something that would help me to survive, I found this beautiful and powerful modality of hypnotherapy that not only helped me, but also allowed me to help others and I am so grateful. Maybe it is God's purpose that I went through what I did, so I could learn from the experience of my own need to not only help myself, but also help others. If that's all it is...then it's enough. I did learn—I was helped—and I do help others. Thank you God!

And, thank you to all my wonderful teachers, like Dr. Martin Hart, Gerry Kein, Carl Carpenter, George Baranowski, Rev. Dr. Scot Giles, Dr. Irene Hickman, Dr. Edith Fiore, Dr. Ed Martin, Dr. Robert Phillips, Dr. Arthur Winkler, Dr. Richard Harte and Dr. William Baldwin, amongst others who taught me what they knew so I could be saved and to save others. I love the National Guild of Hypnotists (NGH) and all the magnificent people I have met through the Guild and what I have learned from them. Hypnotherapy has to be the most potent healing modality there is. It has allowed me, with the help of other hypnotherapists, to find and pull out the festering problem sources within myself that were destroying me, and reach for the heavens of new knowledge and understanding of how things are and what can be done. I am so grateful!

2

An Engineering Model of Hypnotherapy

This is how I see it. It is most likely not the way other Hypnotherapists see it, but it's how I see it integrating everything that I learned in technology and business with what I was taught about Hypnotherapy and what I learned by being in practice for twenty years. I needed to develop a conceptual model of how all this works that would satisfy my technical analytical mind and yet was relatively consistent with what hypnotherapists believe and teach. The following is my model:

Hypnotherapy heals because it allows the hypnotherapist to enter the subconscious mind wherein is buried the negative energy sources causing the illness and release those energies so they no longer can make us sick. I call these negative energy sources Negative Forcing Functions (NFF). Once the NFF's are released, the subconscious computer's hard drive can be positively reprogrammed and life changes for the better.

The concept of Forcing Functions comes from the mathematics defining the motion of objects in space subject to external forces. In the real world, an object in space not acted upon by any external force will remain at rest until an external force acts upon it. This is called inertia. If an external force is applied and is then removed, the object will eventually come to rest again because of viscous and coulombic damping (friction). If, however, the external force continues to be applied, the object will remain in motion because energy is being added to the physical system overcoming friction.

If we consider a "bad thing" that happened to us as the continuing applied force (energy generator), then this "bad" energy is continuing to reinforce the negative program that the "bad thing" installed on our subconscious mind's computer-like hard drive. Until we get rid of the "bad thing's" continuing supporting energy, it is almost useless to try to put new positive programs on the subconscious hard drive and expect it to work against deeply imbedded and constantly reinforced bad programs.

"Bad things" that happened to us cause Negative Forcing Functions: These bad things can be from:

- This life
- Past lives
- Unresolved internal conflicts
- Negative biological carryovers from our ancestors
- Attached foreign energies

Negative Forcing Functions distort the body's energy field cutting off or reducing the flow of Chi (Life Force Energy) to the body's cell communities and this Chi deprivation causes the body to suffer physically and mentally. The Negative Forcing Functions also install and continuously reinforce negative programs on our subconscious computer's hard drive. The programs in our subconscious computer determine our behavior, how we feel and how we respond to life.

The Negative Forcing Functions can be found under hypnosis and their energy released. If there are attached foreign energies, they must first be removed or you cannot get to the person's own Negative Forcing Functions. Once, you release all the Negative Forcing Functions, the body's energy field is restored to normalcy and physical illness is healed by the restored Chi flow to the cell communities. Now that the Negative Forcing Functions are gone, they no longer support the negative programs they created in the subconscious hard drive and therefore new positive programs can be installed and imbedded under hypnosis, and behavior and response to life are changed positively. This is permanent healing.

3

Our Mind

To comprehend how hypnotherapy heals, it is necessary to understand the functioning of our mind. We actually have **three separate and different minds**, three singular selves. These are:

1. The Super Conscious Mind (High Self)

2. The Conscious Mind (Middle Self)

3. The Subconscious Mind (Low Self or Inner Self), which has, as a part of it, the Unconscious Mind

The Super Conscious Mind (High Self)

Nobody has ever seen the High Self. I think you can talk to it through prayer. Most of what I learned about the High Self comes from the *Huna* (traditional healers) of Polynesia. The *Huna* say that the Super Conscious Mind or High Self is the most elevated Self of our three Selves. It is our connection to Divinity, to God. The *Huna* call it the "Amakua". Carl Jung called it the Super Conscious Mind. High Self knows about both the Conscious and Subconscious Selves. High Self's purpose is to help the other two Selves grow from unawareness to understanding and enlightenment through life experiences.

High Self is genderless, but combines the masculine and feminine within us into one whole. It functions like a wise parent, who is very permissive within limits. High Self doesn't usually get involved in our day-to-day lives unless it is really needed and is directly asked. It can only be accessed through our Subconscious Self. The Conscious Mind cannot directly contact the High Self. The Conscious Mind must go through the Subconscious Mind. This is the same as when we pray to God.

High Self is the source of love within us. Love is a spiritual force and the greatest force in existence because it comes from our link to God, who is Infinite Love and the source of life. In all healing, Love is the healing force, but its healing effect can only be accessed through the Subconscious Self. A healthy body and mind reflect the High Self and since health is supposed to be our natural condition, healing is, simply put, a restoring to our natural healthy condition.

The High Self never perceives us as sick in either body or mind. It always views us as perfect, no matter what is going on with us. The High Self is as unlike your conscious self, as your rational, analytical Conscious Mind is unlike the fundamental, holistic, irrational consciousness of your Subconscious Self.

Wings are the emblems of the High Self in many cultures. The Mexicans symbolize the High Self as the winged serpent; Christians recognize winged Angels, and the Tarot deck shows the High Self as a winged face. Wings are a common archetype symbol and probably are the mind's way of reaching for the High Self. The *Huna* say, "The Subconscious Self is controlled by Nature, and the Conscious Self is ruled by intellect and society, but Hermes, God of Wisdom, controls the High Self".

The Super Conscious Mind or High Self is an element of the Soul. This allows it to access and be a part of the Universal Consciousness or Cosmic Intelligence spoken of by Carl Jung. This admittance is what makes it possible for all of us to tap into infinite knowledge and provides us with our psychic insights. High Self is our connection to the infinite and is the part of us that is godly. It is each of us in our most rapturous raiment, our most sublime expression of being. The High Self fuses us with all living beings, making us a part of the brotherhood of mankind.

The Conscious Mind

The conscious mind is where we live everyday when awake. It speaks, reasons, analyzes and controls all of our voluntary actions. It knows things by intuition. Conscious Mind senses and experiences life and unites us with universal humanity. Conscious Mind separates into two independent functional parts, the right and left hemispheres of the brain. Intuition and creativity are in the right feminine side and analytical rational reasoning is in the male left side.

Our initiative, intention, and range of options are in the conscious mind. Here is where we decide on our life objectives. The conscious mind initiates all action; the subconscious mind's job is to make whatever thoughts, desires and feelings happen that get to it from the conscious mind. What you think and feel creates your reality.

Our conscious mind starts every action in our life. It analyzes, evaluates, judges and ultimately selects what action we take. Conscious Mind orchestrates both sides of the brain to function correctly and simultaneously. However, Conscious Mind is always aware of the distinction between feelings and thought.

Our conscious mind does all of the assessing and judging of situations and either accepts or rejects optional courses of action as well as constantly monitors our subconscious mind and directs its actions. Conscious Mind is always free to select alternatives, but it can allow your subconscious feelings to run your life, often to your detriment, since there is no rational or analytical ability in the subconscious. You can, however, consciously take charge and control your life.

Conscious Mind, because it is digital and serial, always experiences time dichotomously. Rationally, it perceives time as past, present or future. Intuitionally, it knows that it is always just now. "Now" embraces past, present and future as one. It is always just "now".

Gestalt psychology shows us that the two hemispheres of our brain working collaboratively create a moment-by-moment view of our reality that is composed of a foreground and a background. Our conscious mind utilizes both the foreground and the background in perceiving our reality. It is always fully aware of the foreground; but is barely aware of the background. For example, we are usually oblivious of what our body language is saying to others because it remains in the background, although body language is actually our primary means of communication.

When we focus on the foreground of any situation with our left-brain, our right brain holistically is aware of and explores all of the background in its awareness. If something of personal interest stands out in the background, our right brain directs our attention to it. Our right brain always notices and focuses on personal things like desires, which have a lot of "charge" associated with them. If we consciously disregard these "perturbations" to our conscious awareness, the data moves to our subconscious mind for permanent storage and is programmed by every thought or feeling we ever had. We spend most of our time in our conscious mind.

The Critical Factor

The conscious mind has a blocking function called **The Critical Factor** and it is under the subconscious mind's control. To conserve energy, it thwarts any suggestion of positive change because that requires an expenditure of energy and since the subconscious is lazy (inertia), the Critical Factor blocks the suggestion.

The only way to get new programming onto the subconscious hard drive is to bypass the Critical Factor, and hypnosis is the only way to do this because hypnosis bypasses the Critical Factor.

Bypassing the Critical Factor allows suggestions for change to go directly into the subconscious and they are embedded onto the computer hard drive. Moreover, **once in, they change the person's life** because the programs on the person's subconscious hard drive determine his behavior, how he feels, and how he responds to life.

Conscious Mind Characteristics

The following are the principal characteristics of the conscious mind as taught by my teacher, Gerry Kein:

1. **One Thing at a Time:** The Conscious Mind can only do one thing at a time. It is a digital serial information processor. It is not holistic and analog like the subconscious, which is capable of multitasking.

2. **Analysis:** This characteristic analyzes and figures out a way to solve our problems by applying inductive and deductive logic. It calculates and arrives at the hundreds of choices we must make each day. We may believe the decisions are automatic, but they are not. Whether we want to or not, we have to make decisions: Should I open the door? Should I turn the water on? Should I tie my shoes?

3. **Rational:** We must have a reason for every decision we make. If we don't have a reason, we can go insane.

4. **Will Power:** This is an adrenaline-like power function that lasts only a short time. Because of the time limitation and the need for large amounts of energy for it to function, will power does not affect much positive change.

5. **Temporary Working Memory:** This is the memory we utilize every day and it is in the forefront of our consciousness such as: How do I find my way to work? What's my spouse's name? What's my phone number? This memory is not permanent.

6. **Translator.** Because the subconscious cannot understand anything except images and feelings, the conscious mind translates the spoken or

written word into images and feelings that the subconscious mind can understand.

The Subconscious Mind

The subconscious mind is really a holistic parallel processing analog bio-super-computer, and it performs like a computer. Its literal and exact deductions regarding time and space expose this computer mentality. This bio-computer is exact and factual in understanding everything it receives. The subconscious mind doesn't understand words, so the conscious mind has to translate words into images and feelings stored in the subconscious memory banks. The subconscious mind is analog compared to the conscious mind, which is digital. Subconscious Mind processes information analogically, holistically and in parallel rather than serially and digitally like the conscious mind does.

Every sensory input such as sounds, sights, smells, tastes and feelings are recorded in Subconscious Mind, and it cannot tell the difference between what it gets from our thoughts (our imagination) or from the environment. The subconscious marks and classifies all inputs to it and organizes them into an extraordinarily complex network of associations.

It links all received data with what is already there, classifies it, and assembles all of it into recognition patterns, much like signal recognition patterns are used in Anti Submarine Warfare to recognize and classify enemy submarines. In addition to actual sensory data, Subconscious Mind records all of its conditioning, including all the life rules directing our conscious life. Our self-image, which comes from other people's reaction to our actions, is also in our subconscious.

Subconscious Mind operates with sensory data; imagery and memories from experience, thoughts or feelings and really cannot distinguish between them. It has a holistic grasp of reality, which encompasses everything that is there.

Questions to the Subconscious Mind must be asked literally and, because it only understands literal, your answers will also be literal. Indefinite and/or compound questions are not understood. Any answer by the subconscious to an unclear question is just gibberish, because the question was never understood by the subconscious. This is why reprogramming of the subconscious after clearing all the Negative Forcing Functions must be done carefully and with full awareness of literal meanings by the hypnotherapist.

Because rational thinking and analysis exists only in the conscious mind and not in the subconscious mind, it cannot rationalize or analyze like the conscious mind can. **The subconscious mind simply accepts everything.** Every item in awareness is permanently marked in a cataloging procedure. After marking all incoming discernment, Subconscious Mind files this data in permanent memory by the association arrangement. Psychoanalysts use free association to get at subconsciously buried material, and the use of this technique derives from this association arrangement.

The subconscious mind's fundamental consciousness reflects back whatever it receives like a mirror. It does not have the capability to analyze, evaluate, judge or reason. It just accepts all thoughts and ideas that come into it and everlastingly remembers all that it or the conscious mind has ever experienced or perceived. This is our permanent memory.

Protective: Subconscious Mind is very protective and is in charge of our mental, physical, emotional, and personal survival. It must protect us from all danger, real or imagined and it cannot tell the difference. It does not comprehend morality per se; but instead, establishes a moral structure from all the information it gets. In creating this moral structure, it is guided by its dominant need to safeguard us from harm.

This inability to discern real from imaginary is also a powerful aspect that hypnotherapists use to help improve performance by athletes and artists. It is possible to rehearse in the mind, under hypnosis, athletic or artful actions and create programs in the subconscious to perform a desired response to a situation. For instance, a golfer under hypnosis can repeatedly rehearse his golf stroke and perfect it. The same is true for tennis, dancing, or for any endeavor, which takes repetitious practice to achieve perfection. Every time the action is performed in the mind, the programs operation is more deeply imbedded into the subconscious, and if the person gets his intellect out of the way, the subconscious program will take over and the action will be perfect.

Live or Die: The will to physically live or die is at the root of the Subconscious Mind. **Life or death is directly tied to the Subconscious Mind's fundamental need to communicate and create. If this basic need is frustrated for any reason, the Subconscious Mind will kill the body.** This seems like a dichotomy of the survival instinct and the death wish but it is merely a primitive reaction to its denied essential purpose.

The will to live drives the Subconscious to heal the physical body when it is injured or sick, but it only does this because it wants to go on expressing its creative facility. **If this creative expression is thwarted, then the will to live reverses itself and becomes the will to die**. If this happens, the subconscious may assertively destroy the body by making the person accident-prone or by declining to support the body against assaulting pathogens by turning off the immune system or having it attack the body.

Physical Guardian: Our Subconscious Mind looks after our physical life. It generates hunger pangs when food is required and engenders appetite for needed correct foods. Subconscious Mind, in its protective role warns us of survival threats and knows how to keep us strong and healthy—or it can produce situations favorable to illness and injury. Unless we have a strong wish to continue living physically, Subconscious Mind will not try very hard to keep us well. Unless we are positive about life, Subconscious Mind will not provide the necessary energy essential to achieve our goals.

Subconscious Mind directly mirrors our will to live. If you don't like life and are continuously unhappy, subconscious mind will see to it that you don't have to live very long. If you have no dreams for your life, that is tantamount to rejecting life and you will die. Subconscious mind will see to it. It won't keep you around if you really don't want to be here.

Our subconscious mind fully controls our physical body, but we can influence what it does. Consciously, we can command our subconscious to provide the energy we need to realize our goals. We can also consciously command it to heal us immediately. Both of these commands absolutely require that we be passionate about living. Subconscious Mind is crazy about passion. If you have passion about things in life, you will probably get them. Without passion, no matter how much you think you may want things, you won't get them. Passion is the energy that opens the road, pulls down the barriers and sparks the subconscious into accomplishment. To be passionate about life, you must feel good. To feel good, you must be clear. To get clear, therapists must enter that sacred realm of the subconscious, and hypnosis is the only modality that allows direct access to the subconscious mind. That is why we use hypnosis...to go where the problem sources are and deal with them. The problem sources are not in the conscious mind...if they were, we would be able to solve them ourselves, consciously. But, when they are buried in the subconscious, the conscious mind cannot reach them. If you can't reach them, you cannot resolve them.

Only our subconscious mind can heal us. There is no medicine, person or thing outside of us that can do this. Through Subconscious Mind using Hypnotherapy, we can heal by clearing subconscious Negative Forcing Functions and reprogramming positively. Entity attachments (one of the Negative Forcing Functions) must first be released and then the rest of the subconscious mind can be cleared and reprogrammed for life instead of death. Then you feel good instead of rotten, and live long and happily.

4

Subconscious Mind Functionality

The largest part of your reality resides in your subconscious mind. If you could compress your conscious mind into a sphere the size of a golf ball, your subconscious mind would be the size of the Atlanta Georgia Dome. At least ninety percent of our reality is subconscious.

Part of the subconscious is the unconscious mind. This part controls our immune system and our autonomic functions, like heartbeat, respiration, hormone production, regeneration, etc. The Subconscious is tremendously potent. As Gerry Kein says: "It makes us rich or poor, fat or thin, happy or sad, poor or wealthy. **Our Subconscious Self is who we truly are!**"

Our Subconscious Computer

The Subconscious Mind is really a full function analog, parallel processing bio-supercomputer. It sums and integrates all of the programming (conditioning) that it's ever acquired by whatever means and produces a person conforming to the integrated summation. You get what you get. That's what and who we are: the integrated sum of all the programming on our subconscious computer's hard drive.

The programming in a computer tells it what to do and how to do it. If the program is changed, the computer operates on the new program. **However, some deeply imbedded programs that are constantly being reinforced with energy are very difficult, if not impossible, to override.** You can put in new programs that counter deeply imbedded old programs, but they don't affect the output of the computer much...if at all. The old programs have to be severed from their support energy (Negative Forcing Functions) and new positive programs *with* support have to be installed to counter the old bad programs. Then you have a good chance of overriding the old programs. This is precisely how our subconscious mind functions, because it is an extremely powerful analog computer processing data in a holistic fashion.

The analog aspects of our subconscious computer are what make it so powerful. It can do parallel data processing and consider the complete holistic environment at the same time, unlike our conscious mind which is digital and must process data serially. Digital processing can only consider one thing at a time and in order, that is, serially.

Our subconscious computer is always being programmed by our life experiences. Initially, our subconscious computers have no programming except the biological functions inherent in our animal nature. But, every day, through every life, we add programming to our subconscious computer's hard drive. All the programming is integrated and creates the person we are.

Subconscious Mind Characteristics

Gerry Kein, my teacher, lists the characteristics of our subconscious computer as:

1. **Permanent Memory.** Everything since you separated from Source is in there. Nothing is ever forgotten. Everything that ever happened to you is locked permanently into the memory banks of your subconscious mind. In hypnosis, that memory bank can be accessed and we can and actually relive that experience entirely. For example, in regression hypnosis you can travel back and relive your first birthday or your birth. You are not remembering; you're actually there.

2. **Habits:** Habits are deeply imbedded programs. Most habits are just utilitarian habits. When we first face a new situation, like learning to tie our shoelaces, our rational, analytical conscious mind works out the procedure to do it. Then as we perform the task repeatedly, the task program becomes imbedded into the subconscious and it becomes automatic. For example, when the doorbell rings we don't look at it and wonder what it is, we just answer the door.

3. **Emotion:** All emotion is in the subconscious mind, and since the subconscious has no rationality…when we are emotional, we are not rational. When we become emotional, we become irrational, juvenile and literal like the subconscious mind is.

4. **Protection:** Subconscious Mind must protect us against any danger…real OR imagined and **it cannot differentiate between the two.**

An imagined danger is just as real to subconscious mind as if it was actually happening.

5.   **Inertia:** Although the subconscious is very powerful, it's also extremely lazy. It doesn't want to accept positive suggestions for change because that takes work and requires an expenditure of energy. It likes the status quo. Positive suggestions are very difficult to get onto our subconscious hard drive, but if a positive suggestion does get imbedded onto the subconscious hard drive, IT WILL CAUSE CHANGE, because our subconscious computer must respond to the change in programming.

6.   **Creative:** The subconscious is where all of our creative ability lies.

5

Subconscious Mind Programming

We can program or condition our subconscious mind. Every experience we ever had since we separated from Source has installed a program onto our subconscious hard drive. Some of the programs are good and some cause us problems. Programming is the process by which the subconscious mind learns to function in this reality. Through programming, the subconscious mind acquires its sense of morality and learns types of behavior required to live in a civilized society.

The ability to be programmed is one of the subconscious mind's greatest characteristics. This is how it learns physical skills such as walking, driving, bicycling, tying shoestrings, and skiing. A skill is a habit. Habits are programs deeply imbedded in the subconscious hard drive. We acquire habits by repetition. When we first learn a habit, we consciously perform it and then by repetition, the action becomes a habit. Repetition is a powerful way to program the subconscious.

To become competent, we must practice a skill repeatedly, and then it becomes embedded and thus automatic. We don't have to consciously think about performing a habit. Actually, if we consciously try to do something already programmed into the subconscious computer, we will probably mess it up. Think about trying to consciously tie your shoestrings or swing your golf club. Think about it consciously and you will screw it up. I heard the great comedian Joey Bishop say that before he went onto the stage, he had to "get himself out of the way," to keep his conscious mind from interfering with what he knows how to do.

Morality: Our so-called conscience, which is our sense of moral right and wrong, resides in the subconscious mind. We weren't born with a conscience, so where did we get it? The answer is from our culture...from other people's beliefs. The subconscious mind naturally clings to whatever belief or behavior it already owns, whether it is right or wrong and it does not really care if it is right or wrong. It simply does not like change and resists leaving a comfortable rut.

Conscious Mind can sleep and dream, but Subconscious Mind is always awake. It maintains continuous awareness of us, regenerating and rebalancing the entire physical system and doing all the essential things that keep us alive. Subconscious Mind is constantly attentive during sleep, protecting us. It is also aware during anesthesia, so it listens to what surgeons say, and if they say pessimistic things about you, you could die. Under anesthesia, Subconscious Mind doesn't have Conscious Mind's reason to interpret for it. Therefore, whatever the surroundings offer is literally translated and absorbed into Subconscious Mind. **Subconscious Mind takes all suggestions literally as an authoritarian command.**

Authority easily programs the subconscious mind. Authorities are gods to the subconscious mind because authority can give or withhold what Subconscious Mind wants. Parents are our gods at birth and therefore the ultimate authority and, so what parents say are easily accepted as programs by the child. If the parent tells the child that he is worthless, the child accepts that programming and will feel worthless all it's life, no matter what it accomplishes. Later, through persistent life experiences, firm personal outlooks are formed. For instance, if you come to believe that getting cold and wet causes you to catch cold…you will get a cold. However, if you decisively believe that you can refuse any cold causing germ, you will not catch cold, no matter what the weather.

The subconscious mind implements all autonomic behavior such as habits, skills and rituals. All habits and programs are rituals, and so are individual skills, because they are set by a pattern of sequential actions. Subconscious Mind loves habits. It loves to carry out identical set sequences continually. Once Subconscious Mind learns a ritual, it is upset if the sequence is altered or the task is not completed. It loves the status quo because it requires less energy to maintain it.

The subconscious mind clings tightly to everything it has learned and it is not easy to change. **It is particularly hard to change if the learned ritual meets some profound unconscious need.** When you consciously design a new ritual or behavior that you want to put into your subconscious, you must rehearse it in your mind continually. This rehearsal is just like you were actually performing the task or behavior because the subconscious can't tell the difference between imagination and reality. A repeated ritual will become more dominant and deeply embedded if it is executed with intense desire and feeling (passion). Cherokee Indian healers will tell you that intent without intense desire and passion just doesn't accomplish anything—but with passion and intensity, the power is there. Artists and great athletes hone their skills like this. You can become a great golfer or tennis player or artist by mentally rehearsing your activity with intensity and passion.

Divination: The subconscious mind has access to much knowledge because it is directly connected to the Superconscious Self (High Self) and can give highly discerning answers if questions are asked properly. Asking questions of the subconscious mind is an art that must be developed. Subconscious Mind will help you, but you must ask it properly. It is very eager to please you. Seeking verification of answers that you already have decided on is useless. **Subconscious Mind will always give you the answer you want** because it wants to please you.

To get a real answer, you have to hold your own desires and opinions in abeyance, not thinking about the answer—just the question, and you must be neutrally open to whatever comes. This is extremely hard to do. You have to be aware of this when looking for answers from the subconscious when using devices like the pendulum or even muscle testing (kinesiology).

Many people access the subconscious by using the pendulum. Remember that the pendulum response is just the ideo-motor response of the subconscious mind and is just another way of accessing this mind. Unless you are very careful, it will give you whatever you want to hear, and what good is that for divination?

Conscious prayer is another way of accessing the Subconscious Self. All prayer starts in the conscious mind and is directed to The High Self (our connection to Divinity) via Subconscious Mind. You cannot consciously access the High Self directly. You must get to it through the subconscious. Prayer is another form of conditioning or programming, but to be effective, it must be phrased properly.

The subconscious mind is very literal and understands only images and feelings. When we want to access the subconscious, we must use specific, precise words with meanings known to our subconscious self and provide a very clear picture of the desired result. The conscious mind actually translates our words into images and feelings, which are understood by the subconscious mind. You must see the outcome vividly in your mind, like it is already accomplished. If done right, we can truly get our prayers answered. It's called belief or faith!

6

The Eastern Disease Model

There are many models of how disease occurs. The oldest model (about 4000 years old), its origins buried in antiquity, is the Eastern Disease Model known to the ancient Chinese and Ayurvedic Hindus. It is as follows: **There is only one general cause for disease and that is improper functioning of the cells of the body**.

Each cell in our body has a **cell-mind** of it's own. These cells band together and meld their minds into a community mind, like for instance, the liver. Each organ has an **organ-mind** made up of a **group community mind** of the cells making up that organ. Each of the body's cells and each organic cell community is possessed of an instinctive knowledge of what is vital to its life work, and its own regenerative process. This community mind knows what it is to do in the body and how and when to regenerate. The liver, for instance, knows its job in the body. This community mind also knows how and when to regenerate.

The cells enable the body to carry on its work of continual regeneration. When cells regenerate, they simply clone themselves. They make new cells, exact duplicates of what they are at the time. If the cell is perfect, new perfect cells are generated. If the cell is imperfect, imperfect new cells are generated. Our liver is new every 8 months, our skin is new every 28 days, and our stomach lining is new every 7 days. Every 7 years or so, we are completely new.

In the case of the liver, for instance, the millions of cells composing the liver have a community mind that acts as the liver-mind, and is under the control of the subconscious mind unless interfered with by the Intellect (conscious mind). All body cell communities, through their minds, are amenable to mental control but require the Life Force (Chi) as the stimulator.

The cells making up the cell community minds need at least four things to be healthy: food, water, oxygen and the Life Force. If the cells don't have a sufficient quantity of any of these, they begin to regenerate as defective cells. If the deprivation continues, the cell community begins to dysfunction and physical disease takes root. Since cells regenerate by cloning themselves, they simply make exact copies of themselves as they exist at that moment. If they are imperfect, they make new imperfect cells. If the deprivation continues long enough, the cell community dies and the body can die. For instance, you cannot survive with a dead liver. We usually get enough food, water and air, even if it's not the best, but what does get cut off or reduced to the cells is the Life Force.

7

The Life Force

Prana, Chi, Ki, Ka, Mana. Each culture has a different term for the life force. *Prana*, a Sanskrit word is the Hindu term. *Chi* is the Chinese term. The Japanese call it *Ki*, the Egyptians call it the *Ka*, the Polynesians call it *Mana*, the Hebrews call it *Ruach* and the Germans call it *Orgone*. This energy is a force and not a chemical or gas. It is actually a bioelectric fluid like an electric current. I use the Chinese term Chi for this life force energy. The Chinese say that the *Chi* comes into the body from the sky through the head, from the earth through our feet, some of it comes from the food we eat and some comes from our parents and is stored in our kidneys. Ayurvedic healers say it comes in on our breath, and they call it Prana, the breath of life. However the Chi or Prana comes into the body, it flows into energy centers for distribution in our bodies. The Chinese say we have three energy centers and they call them *Dan-Tiens* and say they are located in the head, the chest and in the lower abdomen. The Ayurvedic healers say we have seven major energy centers and call them Chakras. I use the term Chakra in discussing the flow of energy through the body.

According to the *Ayurveda* (the ancient Hindu scripture on healing), Chi comes into the body on the breath, and into the energy centers, which are accumulators and transformers, called *Chakras* ("wheels"). Each of the body's seven Chakras is connected to one of the seven endocrine glands. The Chakras modify the Chi energy to be specific for the particular endocrine gland that uses it. The modified Chi flows through the body's energy pathways (meridians) to the cells via the endocrine glands and stimulates them to regenerate, do their job in the body, and gets rid of toxic wastes. **If the Chi cannot reach the cell community or is reduced, the cell community is deprived of its required life force and becomes degraded.** Blockages in the body's energy pathways (Chi Meridians) or in the Main Energy Centers (Chakras) cause this to happen.

Auras Are Electromagnetic Fields. How can we tell if the Chi is blocked? If we don't feel well or if our lives are messed up, it's a good indicator of blocked Chi and indicates that the cells are progressively cloning themselves in duplicates that are more and more degenerate. There is another way, which has to do with the laws of physics.

When an electric current flows through a conductor, an electromagnetic field forms around the conductor. The strength of this field is directly proportional to the amount of current flowing through the conductor. If there is resistance (blockage) to the current flow, the field is diminished. When the resistance is low, the current increases as a function of the resistance and the voltage. The strength of the electromagnetic field is directly proportional to the amount of current flowing in the circuit and inversely proportional to the amount of resistance in the circuit. This is **Ohm's Law** in electricity.

The Chi or Life Force can be compared to current flowing through the body (conductor). Blockages in the Chakras or the Energy Meridians are akin to resistance in the electrical conductor. The aura about a living body is the electromagnetic field and is a function of the flow of Chi through the body, just like the electromagnetic field of the electrical conductor. If the auric field is suppressed, this indicates a high resistance (blockages) to the flow of Chi through the body. The body's electromagnetic field can be photographed or detected with instruments.

If the body's auric energy field is strong, it indicates that there is little resistance to the flow of Chi current through the body. If the auric energy field is suppressed, the Chi current flow through the body is encountering high resistance (blockages). These blockages cut or reduce the flow of Chi current through the body and the cell communities are deprived of the Chi they need for health.

Chakras. The Chakras are the main energy centers of the body. These are vortices revolving at great speed, corresponding to a specific frequency consistent with each one's specific task, and manifested by the color of the vibration. Each Chakra vibrates (spins) at a different frequency consistent with the color traditionally associated with each Chakra. The colors are all the colors of the rainbow that combine to create white light.

There are seven main Chakras and they are centered on the body's seven endocrine glands. They are:

	Gland	Chakra Name	Vibration/Color
1	Testes/Ovaries	Base, Root	Red
2	Pancreas	Spleen	Orange
3	Adrenals	Plexus	Yellow
4	Thymus	Heart	Green
5	Thyroid	Throat	Blue
6	Pineal	"Third Eye"	Indigo
7	Pituitary	Crown	Violet

Chi comes into the Chakras on the intake breath. The Chakras act like transformers and accumulators (batteries) to change the character of the energy to that required by the different glands of the endocrine system. The Chakras modify the energy and feed it into the Chi Meridians (conductive energy channels) for distribution to the body's cell communities through the endocrine system.

The modified Chi energies all travel through the same energy pathways at the same time and are kept separated by frequency and phase. This is much like the way multiple telephone calls are transmitted through a single fiber optic cable simultaneously without interference. Each of the endocrine glands have receptors, which are really impedance matching networks that sense the proper frequency and phase that they need and allow the correct modified Chi to enter the gland's receptor gate. If the frequency and phase are not correct for that gland, the gate closes and the *Chi* moves on to its proper receptor. These Chi energies nurture and vitalize the cell communities and health ensues.

This is a beautiful and marvelous system attesting to the divinity of nature.

8

Negative Forcing Functions

Negative Forcing Functions (NFF) are caused by:

1. Bad things that happened to us in this life

2. Bad things that happened to us in past lives

3. Unresolved internal conflicts

4. Biological carry-overs from our genetic ancestors

5. Foreign energy attachments

Negative Forcing Functions (NFF) do three things:

1. They distort the body's energy field disrupting the flow of Chi through the energy pathways.

2. They install negative programs on the hard drive of our subconscious computer.

3. They continuously support the negative programs, imbedding them deeper and making them stronger.

The NFF's are really negative energy generators in our subconscious that continuously support and reinforce the negative programs installed on our subconscious hard drive. The distortions in the body's energy field by the NFF's cause blocks (resistances) to form in the Chi Meridians and Chakras, cutting the flow of Life Force Energy to the body's cell communities.

The integrated summation of all the programs on our subconscious hard drive determines our behavior, how we feel, and the way we respond to life. Unless the NFF's are released, the negative programs are continually reinforced and the energy blocks continually reform thereby disrupting health.

9

Energy Healing

My Grandmother could feel energy flow through the body and she told me that I could also. I tried it and sure enough, I could. I could put my hand between two areas of the body and feel the Chi flow. It feels like a clear tube with the energy gently pulsing along. I could pass my hands over a person's body and feel where the Chi energy was blocked. The blocks feel cooler than the surrounding area. At the same time, I get a visualization of a tube with a constriction in it, and the energy slowing down before the constriction and congesting at the blockage. When the energy is flowing unobstructed, it just feels clear. It is obvious to me. I found that I could clear the blockages temporarily by massaging the blocked area. This is what Shiatsu does.

After I realized that I could do it, I did energy clearing for about five years. People would come to me with all kinds of problems, both mental and physical. I would clear and balance their Chakras and clear their Chi meridians using Shiatsu (acupressure) and they would feel better. But, soon, back they came with the same problem, and I would clear them again and they would feel better. This went on repeatedly.

I realized I wasn't doing the person much good if they couldn't hold their healing for more than a short time. This also happens with other energy work, such as medicines, acupuncture, massage, chiropractic, and Tai Chi. They all clear the blocks temporarily.

10

Hypnosis

Hypnosis is the only modality that provides direct access to the subconscious mind. Since all our problems originate in the subconscious, you must go there to resolve the problems. I needed a way to get into the subconscious mind wherein are buried the causes of the distress (Negative Forcing Functions). Because of my own needs, I began to study and use hypnosis and soon started to see longer lasting results when I combined hypnosis with energy clearing. By accessing the client's subconscious and releasing the Negative Forcing Functions causing the problem and then positively reprogramming the subconscious so the Negative Forcing Functions would not be reestablished, proved to be the way to really help people heal permanently.

An example of this is: A child is told (by peers, parents, etc.) that he is worthless and believes what he is told. Children accept negative programming readily especially if it is from someone in authority, like parents. The Negative Forcing Function is his feeling of worthlessness. This installs a negative program of worthlessness in his subconscious, and the energy distortion causes Chakra and Chi Meridian blocks that restrict the flow of Chi, thereby starving the cells of the life force resulting in illness. The negative program of worthlessness affects his behavior and how he feels. As long as the NFF energy generator stays in the subconscious mind, it will continuously reinforce and support the negative program it installed on the subconscious computer.

Under hypnosis, the Negative Energy Generator of worthlessness can be found and released, and the negative programming causing the person to believe he is worthless can be replaced by programming which acknowledges the person's value. With the Negative Forcing Functions eliminated, the body's energy field normalizes by virtue of dissolving the energy blocks. With the energy distortion and Chi meridian blocks gone, the Chakras and Chi Meridians stay open permitting the Chi to vitalize the cells, and health is restored and maintained. Further, with the Forcing Function generator gone, the negative program in the subconscious hard drive is no longer reinforced and new positive programming has a good chance of permanently changing the person's life.

11

Effect of Foreign Energies

At first, I just used regression or parts therapy to uncover the Negative Forcing Functions (NFF) causing the blocks. This worked well but I often found I was doing therapy on attached entities and not on the client. By doing Spirit Releasement on the client first, I can be sure that I am dealing only with the client. Doing psychotherapy on attached entities doesn't help the client's problem. Actually, I found that just about any kind of therapy done on people with attached foreign energies is fairly useless because the results don't last. You just cannot reach the client's own subconscious self if foreign energies are present. You have to get them off before any other effective therapy can be done.

An attached energy of an earthbound spirit, for instance, brings with it the negative energy of its life and its death. This means that if a spirit in life was sick, or fat, smoked, or used drugs—this energy comes with it to the attached one. It doesn't mean that you will get the condition that the spirit had in life, but it does mean that the spirit's negative energy will come to you. If you have a predisposition towards the spirits problem, you can resonate with the spirit's energy and have a good chance of getting what the spirit had in life.

Even if you don't get the spirit's physical disease, you still get the bad energy of it and it can make you feel bad. The spirit's bad emotional and mental energy causes effects that are stronger because they exacerbate your own mental or emotional problems, like depression, anxiety and addictions. The spirit's bad energy reverberates with your own energy and can ignite a problem in you. You also get the energy of the deceased person's death, which usually has a lot of fear in it, amongst other things.

Even if the spirit is of someone in life who loved you, it still brings its own negative stuff with it. Just the attachment by itself drains your energy parasitically. **There is nothing good about an attachment, no matter who it is. The attached spirit must be made to leave and when it does—whatever energy it brought with it also leaves.**

Therefore, if the spirit brought the client's problem, when it leaves so does the problem energy. Consequently, the client is then free of that energy. That energy is what constantly reinforced the negative program of the spirit's life on the client's hard drive. So, you must also get rid of the negative program that the attachment installed on the person's subconscious hard drive. Since the negative program is no longer reinforced by the negative forcing function of the entity attachment, it is now possible to effectively reprogram the subconscious and get good results. This is done by positively reprogramming the subconscious hard drive with programs that cancel out the programs put there by the entity's negative forcing functions.

This reprogramming is very similar to noise cancellation procedures used in Anti Submarine Warfare. If you are trying to listen for an enemy submarine in the noisy ocean, you have to turn the gain up very high (amplify) to hear the submarine because the ocean's noise interferes with your ability to hear the submarine. If you record the natural noise of the ocean and play it back 180 degrees out of phase with the submarine's noise, the played back noise will cancel out the ocean noise and you can hear the submarine without the ocean noise.

This is what we do to cancel out the negative programs on the subconscious hard drive installed by the Negative Forcing Functions. By installing a good program, which counteracts the negative program that is no longer being supported with energy from the released forcing function, the new positive program opposes and supplants the old negative program. The old negative program will eventually die out because it is no longer supported, and the new positive program takes over and the person's behavior and response to life changes positively.

12

Post Clearing Therapies

Often, just releasing the entity attachment energy brings remarkable positive changes. Frequently, I must follow the Spirit Releasement with other clearing therapies to release any of the person's own Negative Forcing Functions from this life, past lives, internal conflicts and genetics.

This procedure works extremely well, but the process of repairing cellular damage caused by long imbedded negative energy and detoxification of the body from long-term medication is greatly accelerated by Cellular Regeneration Hypnotherapy and Acupuncture with Chinese Herbal Medicine. If the resolved problems existed for a very long time, the process of re-establishing normal healthy brain wave function can be hastened through Neural Feedback Training. The following post clearing therapies can be done after the client is cleared.

Detoxification

These can very effectively detoxify the body from the effects of all the medicines and toxins generated by the imperfect cellular regeneration going on with deprived Chi flow. But it must be done after the NFF's are cleared, or else it doesn't do much. In my own case, before I got cleared of my NFF's, I had 72 acupuncture treatments, and cooked and drank the terrible herbal tea for two years with little effect. After I became clear with Hypnotherapy and Spirit Releasement, it took about 20 acupuncture treatments and 6 months of terrible tea drinking to get better. When I first started to drink the tea, I became violently ill for the first 3 months until the detoxification had proceeded to the point where I became relatively free of the poisons and then it became much easier. It took that long to get the effects of all the drugs I had taken over the years out of my system.

Cellular Regeneration Therapy

Because the cells within my body had degenerated so much from the long term deprivation of Chi caused by my NFF produced blocks to the Chi flow, it was necessary to do cellular regeneration work on me. What I used was Cell Command Therapy. This therapy, developed by Dr. E. R. Martin of the PATH Foundation in Houston, Texas, is different from traditional hypnotherapy. The techniques cause regeneration and repair of body tissues and cells because of direct mental commands while the client is in a deep altered state of consciousness. Dr. Martin has trained other hypnotherapists in various parts of the country, including myself. The hypnotic techniques and procedures used are generally derived from material published by Dr. E. Arthur Winkler, Dr. Milton H. Erickson, and Dr. E.L. Rossi.

The effectiveness of Cell Command Therapy derives from its ability to communicate with the subconscious almost as if it were a servomechanism. The commands are given only when the subject is in a state of consciousness. Only then will these commands be accepted directly by the subconscious mind. The regeneration commands are given to cells after the body's energy is cleared, causing the cells to revert to their original pristine state, allowing cellular healing to occur in real-time.

Cell Command Therapy operates on the premise that each cell is capable of repairing and regenerating itself. The cellular command itself is directed to the cells of the systems involved, and is used in a hierarchical manner to restore any needed systems or organs. This cell healing and restoration ability appears to be intelligently directed by the mind or a mind in the cell itself. An example would be the restoring the cells of the endocrine system before doing any work on physical ailments that require a normally functioning immune system.

Error codes or blueprints, such as a free radical, are introduced into the cell coding by errant subconscious programming that blocks the flow of life force energy (*Chi* or *Prana*) to the cells. If the energy blocks are not removed in time, the deprived cells continue to clone themselves as errant cells, and physical dysfunction eventually results. The blocks to energy flow must be removed before attempting to use Cell Command Therapy.

Because the cell contains all of the necessary blueprints for repair and regeneration in the DNA and the internal magnetic, chemical and electrical coding of the cell, it only requires a method of communicating with that cell intelligence to cause it to begin and complete rejuvenation. The individual cells themselves always retain the original perfect coding or blueprint of themselves, just as they contain the blueprint for the entire organism. Cell Command Therapy causes the original blueprint or coding to be reenacted to cause restoration of the original perfect cellular state.

Results of Cell Command Therapy for clients with many diverse ailments have shown regeneration times that varied from 2 to 60 days for individual processes. The time required seems to be related to the individual's mental health state. In some cases, the restoration occurs on various levels or hierarchies simultaneously. In other cases, the higher levels need to be restored first before lower level restoration will complete. An example was an AIDS patient who needed his immune system to function correctly before the healing of the Kaposi's Sarcoma lesions could occur.

Cells are not limited by type or function, in their regeneration capabilities. It appears that this process can repair nerve, bone, and even brain cells. The regeneration of missing organs that do not contain the original blueprint is a process that has not yet been investigated thoroughly, although Dr. Martin is working on it.

In summation, this technique has shown dramatic results for many types of cell regeneration, and has assisted numerous people in completing their healing process and in restoring cells damaged by the ravages of aging. Any form of therapy can benefit from using Cell Command Therapy as an adjunct, for it seems to provide the shortest direct route to cell rejuvenation. The allopathic medical techniques that are accepted by the majority of our population could benefit greatly by Cell Command Therapy as a way to shorten the healing process.

Neural Feedback Training

Even though I now felt much better, I still had the erroneous EEG brain waves from the long established conditions I lived with, so I used Neural Feedback Training to correct the EEG brain patterns. Then I really began to feel well. As a result, my whole life changed.

The Neural EEG Feedback Training or Neuronal Regulation is like biofeedback because it requires patient and computer interaction. However, it is actually the brain itself that acquires this learning process of regulating different patterns of brainwaves without the patient being consciously aware of this learning process.

Biofeedback works by "feeding back" information about your physiological processes so that you develop an awareness of these functions. As this awareness heightens, you learn to consciously control your normally automatic body functions. To help achieve this consciousness, therapists hook up patients to instruments that monitor internal responses with sensitivity and precision thus converting them to visual or audible cues. The feedback relays information on muscle tension (EMG feedback), skin temperature (thermal feedback), brain waves (EEG feedback) and respiration. The monitoring instrument displays the results through sound or sight. The sound varies in pitch and visual meters vary in brightness as the response decreases or increases.

Using the cues provided by the device, patients adjust their thinking in order to regulate the pertinent body function. For instance, in electromyography or EMG feedback, sensors are attached to the skin to measure muscle tension. If the monitor indicates that your muscles are tense, you consciously try to relax them. The monitor then displays the updated results. A slowing down of the signal shows that you have relaxed your muscles. With practice, you learn what it feels like to be relaxed and how to altar your mental processes to achieve it. The instruments are just the means to the end, which is to reach a level where you can affect bodily processes on your own without the aid of devices.

Biofeedback works best when you are in a meditative state of deep relaxation. It is advisable to engage a qualified therapist to guide you through the exercise. A typical biofeedback program involves one-hour sessions once a week for ten weeks, but this can vary depending on the individual response and the disorder being treated. Once you fine-tune your technique, you practice it in your daily life to maintain your health.

Therefore, what I ended up with as a therapeutic process for my clients is as follows:

The Skillas Therapeutic Process

1. **Release all entity forcing functions through Spirit Releasement Therapy.**

2. **Use Parts Therapy, Regression Therapy, including Past Life Regression Therapy to resolve internal conflicts and to uncover and release Negative Forcing Functions buried in the past.**

3. **Resolve genetic/biological Negative Forcing Functions by correcting the subconscious' view of healthy normality.**

4. **Reprogram the subconscious so the old imbedded destructive programs are wiped out, and behavior and response to life changes positively.**

5. **Repair cell damage and detoxify the body using Cellular Regeneration Hypnotherapy and Acupuncture with Chinese Herbal Medicine.**

6. **Accelerate return to normal brain wave function with Neural Feedback Training.**

13

Significant Unique Therapies

Because Spirit Releasement Therapy (SRT) and Past Life Regression Therapy (PLT) are so important in my therapeutic process, I have chosen to discuss these therapies in depth.

Spirit Releasement Therapy

According to Dr. Bill Baldwin, a noted researcher and teacher of Past Life Regression and Spirit (entity) Releasement Therapies, the concept of Spirit Possession is very old and significant, and yet is mostly ignored in our modern society. He says that clinicians throughout the world find entity attachment prevalent among their people and in most cultures, the shaman, medicine man, or priest are the only ones who treat spirit possession.

All kinds of rituals are used to remove spirits—from chanting and using incense, to beating with sticks. Burning of incense is a widely used ritual in most Catholic, Greek and Russian Orthodox Churches to purify the surroundings. Christian Baptism is a kind of exorcism purification. Scandinavians and Russians sweat in the sauna and beat one another with branches for purification. Jesus cast out demons to heal and instructed his followers to do likewise. Protestant clergy do "deliverance" on those distressed with "demons." Spirit possession, which is a full or partial take over of a live human being by a discarnate entity or other foreign energy, is accepted in most cultures. Many authorities say that **ninety percent of the world believes in spirit possession.**

Many clinical situations suggest that the disembodied consciousnesses of dead humans and other foreign energies can affect living people by attaching to their subconscious minds causing negative physical and/or emotional problems. This situation is termed "spirit or entity attachment." When the clinician finds a person with a sore neck and clinical studies show there is nothing wrong with the neck, and you find an entity on the person who died from a broken neck, and you remove the entity and the neck pain disappears, it makes you think that something is going on here.

Traditional Western therapists generally reject the idea of past life therapy because it is based on reincarnation, and they also reject the idea of spirit attachment because it is scary. Accepted or not, entity attachment happens, it happens quite often and is a very ancient state of affairs that causes a lot of trouble in modern society, because its acceptance and treatment are ignored.

Spirit Releasement Therapy (SRT) often provides dramatic and immediate benefits, both mentally and physically. These benefits range from small positive changes to complete termination of otherwise relentless symptoms. The therapy is based on sound psychotherapeutic principles and clinical techniques and was developed by Dr. William Baldwin, Dr. Fred Leideker, Dr. Edith Fiore, Dr. Irene Hickman, and Carl Carpenter. **SRT covers the treatment of attached earthbound spirits, demons, soul-mind fragments of another living person's personality, extraterrestrials and thought forms.**

The Near Death Experience (NDE)

Since time began, people have always been scared and fascinated by death, because it is an unknown that affects everybody. All religions have defined scenarios of what happens after death. Books have been written about the "near-death experience," (NDE) in which a person "dies" and afterwards re-lives. After experiencing near death, many NDE people accurately describe actions occurring while their body was clinically dead, including medical actions taken during the revival process. Consciousness appears to separate from the body, but stays fully aware and is able to understand what is going on.

A common NDE experience is to see a tunnel with a brilliant light at the end of it, and often a holy person (for Christians, characteristically Jesus or a saint.) Sometimes NDE people also describe being greeted by dead friends or relatives. The light at the end of the tunnel magnetically draws the person's spirit but the holy being tells them that it is not yet their time and there is more for them to do on earth. The spirit then rejoins it's clinically dead body and the body lives again. These people say that the light is so attractive that they don't want to return to their body, but do so because the holy one insists. Lots of NDE people feel like they were going home and experiencing all those good feelings, and now were asked to delay their return. Those, I have spoken to seem to pine for the return to home, losing all fear of death, and instead look forward to death.

NDEs have occurred throughout history, in all parts of the world. It is even possible that experiences like these helped to create the world's ideas about heaven and hell, or at least about what may happen at or after death.

What is a Near-Death Experience (NDE)? Although most people who have come close to death say they remember nothing, a third or more may later report that "something happened." That "something" might be a near-death experience, an NDE.

No two NDEs are identical, but within a group of experiences a pattern becomes evident. The pattern (and any single experience) includes one or more of these things:

1. Feeling that the "self" has left the body and is hovering overhead. The person may later be able to describe who was where and what happened, sometimes in detail.

2. Moving through a dark space or tunnel.

3. Experiencing intensely powerful emotions, ranging from bliss to terror.

4. Encountering a light. It is usually described as golden or white, and as being magnetic and loving; occasionally it is perceived as a reflection of the fires of hell.

5. Receiving some variant of the message "It is not yet your time."

6. Meeting others: may be deceased loved ones, recognized from life or not; sacred beings; unidentified entities and/or "beings of light"; sometimes symbols from one's own or other religious traditions.

7. A life review, seeing and re-experiencing major and trivial events of one's life, sometimes from the perspective of the other people involved, and coming to some conclusion about the adequacy of that life and what changes are needed.

8. Having a sense of understanding everything, of knowing how the universe works.

9. Reaching a boundary—a cliff, fence, water, some kind of barrier—that may not be crossed if one is to return to life.

10. In some cases, entering a city or library.

11. Rarely, receiving previously unknown information about one's life-e.g., adoption or hidden parentage, deceased siblings.

12. Decision to return may be voluntary or involuntary. If voluntary, usually associated with unfinished responsibilities.

13. Returning to the body.

Most NDEs are pleasant, but others are deeply frightening.

The near-death experience (NDE) is among the most powerful experiences that a person can have, one of a family of experiences which may occur with or without being close to death. It may permanently altar a person's perceptions of what is real and important.

One most extraordinary aspect of NDEs is that the underlying pattern seems unaffected by a person's culture or belief system, religion, race, education, or any other known variable, although the way in which the NDE is described varies according to the person's background and vocabulary. There is no evidence that the type of experience is related to whether the person is conventionally religious or not, or has lived a "good" or "bad" life according to his/her society's standards. On the other hand, an NDE often strongly affects how life is lived *after* the experience.

An experience may include the feeling of being out of the physical body, moving through a darkness or tunnel, encountering the presences of deceased loved ones and other entities, and an indescribable light or menacing darkness. Many people say they have glimpsed the pattern and meaning of life and the universe, or have been given information beyond ordinary human capacities. For most people the experience is joyful beyond words, although others tell of unpleasant or terrifying experiences. When adequately understood, every type of NDE reveals issues of deep significance to the life of the individual and to humankind in general.

Is NDE Real?

Medical technology may rescue survivors, but science is not able to explain what happened in the process. Like all human experiences, the NDE no doubt has a biologically-based trigger; yet its impact is most often felt as a psychological or spiritual event. For people who believe that only physical events can be real, the NDE (or even the idea of such a thing) may be disturbing or seem ludicrous.

Yet the phenomenon cannot be dismissed just because we cannot explain it. **A 1982 Gallup Poll estimated that at least eight million adults in the US alone have had an NDE; the figure is now believed to be closer to thirteen million.**

Experiences have been reported through the centuries, from many cultures and religious traditions. Whatever the near-death experience is, it is neither recent nor local. *Something happens,* and it changes lives.

What Does NDE Mean?

Many people believe that the NDE *proves* there is life after death in a literal sense. To others, more cautious, the experience is not "proof," but it suggests that some aspect of human consciousness may be independent of the body and may survive physical death. To others, the NDE defines a value system based on care for others, knowledge, and service. Whether one sees the meaning of the NDE as religious or secular, there is much to learn.

Commonalities

Research has shown that NDEs in Western civilization occur with similar frequency and content to people of both genders and of all ages, races, levels of education, socioeconomic levels, spiritual/religious affiliations (or non-affiliation), sexual orientations (gay/lesbian, bisexual, or heterosexual), and precipitating circumstances (illness, accident, suicide, medical procedure, etc.). Research in non-Western cultures has not been as extensive but suggests that beneath great variation in specific NDE content, certain universal or very common themes may be present, such as a border or boundary between dimensions or domains of existence and one or more supernatural entities or beings.

Entity Attachments

Dr. Bill Baldwin, one of my teachers, says that there are five different kinds of entity attachments. I have encountered all of them in my practice. They are:

1. **Earthbound Spirits:** These are the disembodied consciousness of deceased humans who have died and not gone to the Light. My experience suggests that those who have died violently, such as being murdered, plane crashes, fallen off a cliff, automobile accidents, killed in a war, drowned, executed, etc. can become earthbound spirits. In addition, those who have been in much pain at the time of their death and were receiving massive amounts of drugs for the pain often become earthbound spirits. I also find spirits who just refuse to go to the Light

because they want to stay here to help a loved one. An earthbound spirit brings with it the energy of its death and the negative energy that was in its life. If the earthbound spirit before it died was beaten and had diabetes, it could bring the pain of the beating and a tendency towards diabetes to the attached person. Many earthbound spirits don't know they're dead. Quite often, I have to do regression therapy on an earthbound spirit that does not know it is dead and bring it through its own death. Fortunately, if the earthbound spirit can be made to leave, it will take with it whatever it brought. Earthbound spirits are usually relatively easy to get rid of.

2. **Demons:** Dark Force Energy (DFE) beings were created by the Source but chose a path of destruction and misery. Demons are easy to identify because they tell me that they are here to cause misery, pain, destruction and death. Demons are usually difficult to get rid of. They lie and are very arrogant, loud, profane and recalcitrant. You must protect your client and all involved from the demons. Demons will usually leave if you can get them to see their own light and become transformed.

3. **Soul-mind Fragments:** Disassociation or fragmentation is a survival coping mechanism of the mind that protects sanity. If something very traumatic happens to an individual, the mind in its survival mode disassociates into a sub personality frozen in time at the time of the occurrence with all the energy of the trauma stuffed within it and submerges that sub-personality into the subconscious mind. The conscious mind never knows that it's there. These are the "inner children," adolescents or adults and are often referred to as "ego states". Since children tend to disassociate easier than adolescents or adults because they do not have the coping mechanisms of older people, we find more inner children than any others. Sometimes these fragments can be lost and can attach to a person like any other entity. In this case, I must do soul retrieval to bring back the separated part and reintegrate it. Native healers such as Shamans use soul retrieval in their healing rituals.

4. **Extraterrestrials (ET's):** I don't mean little green men from Mars, but rather energies from somewhere else—other planets, galaxies or dimensions that are here in spirit form. In my practice, I usually find that demons hide behind ET's.

5. **Thought-forms:** Whenever anyone has an intense emotion, that energy does not immediately dissipate. Instead, it hangs around for a considerable period of time, like in a word balloon, and can attach to a person, disgorging its energy into the host. Thoughtforms usually do not have consciousness. They are also known as Vey Entities.

Differential Diagnosis and Treatment

The Spirit Releasement Therapist must determine if there is an entity attachment and the nature of it before treatment, because the Releasement Technique is different depending upon which kind of entity is found. Earthbound spirits are treated differently than demons, ET's or fragments of another person's soul-mind. In the case of self-fragmentation, inner children (ego states) must be found, the disassociation energy released and reintegrated rather than eliminated. Attached entities are parasites in the subconscious mind of the host and use the host's energy. One strong sign of entity attachment is persistent fatigue without physical cause.

Layers

Once any entity has attached to a host, a portal is created through which other entities can very easily enter and nest in layers within the host. I have only been able to release one layer at a time. I find that once a layer is cleared, that the aura becomes expansive and the person will feel good for a while. However, if there is another layer below the one just released, the same or other symptoms will redevelop. It is then necessary to release the next layer. Typically, I find two or three layers, but I have found as many as thirty.

Most Common Entities

In my practice, I find that Earthbound Spirits, Demons and Soul-Mind Fragments are the most frequently found attaching entities. With Earthbound Spirits, the disembodied consciousness of the deceased person attaches and joins with the subconscious mind of a living person, exerting influence on their thought processes, emotions, behavior and physical body. If the earthbound was depressed or had heart trouble or diabetes, it brings that energy to the host, and the host has a strong tendency to exhibit the same problems.

Soul-Mind Fragments tend to affect a person just like earthbound spirits do, bringing with them the fearful energy that created them. In addition, the silver cord that connects the Soul-Mind Fragment to the attached person acts like a full duplex data transmission link and there is a two-way communication of energies between them. Attaching Demons often bring with them earthbound spirits or Soul-Mind-Fragments of dead people who had serious problems in life so as to inflict that negative energy on the attached one they are trying to destroy.

I find that earthbound spirits are usually people who have experienced a sudden traumatic death, who have died while under strong sedating drugs taken for pain relief, or who just don't want to go to the Light because they want to stay with someone they loved. In the case of those who died traumatic deaths or were under sedation, these spirits often just don't see the Light and they wander looking for a place to settle. They are attracted by like energies. A sad spirit will be attracted to someone who is sad; a fearful spirit is attracted to someone who is fearful, etc. Anger, fear, jealousy, resentment, guilt, remorse or even strong ties of love can interfere with normal transition to the Light.

I also find many dead loving relatives on my clients. For instance, the grandmother who loves the grandchild and attaches to her to protect her, brings the energy of her death and the negative energy of her life to the poor child, who from then on has to suffer with those bad energies. Maybe Grandmother was a compulsive overeater, and the child grows up constantly wanting to overeat and having to always fight fat because of it. Maybe Grandfather died from congestive heart disease and brings that energy propensity to the child, who may develop heart problems because of the bad energy Grandfather brought with him when he attached to the child. Sometimes I find the spirit of a lover attached to the client. The dead lover had vowed never to leave her. When he died, he did not leave but stayed with the beloved.

Easy to Attach

Spirit attachment can occur simply because of physical proximity to the dying person at the time of their death. You can witness a fatal motorcycle accident and because your Guardian Chi (psychic defense system) is down from the fright, the dead motorcyclist can enter and attach to you, binging with him the energy of his death and the negative stuff of his life. I have encountered this situation in practice many times.

Dr. Baldwin says that attachments can be benevolent in nature, self-serving, malevolent in intention, or completely neutral and can be completely

random, even accidental. In my practice, many of the cases I encounter turn out to be completely random with no prior relationship in this or any other lifetime. With others, a family member is often the connection.

The Psychic Defense System

We have a Psychic Defense System just like we have a Physical Immune System, and the same things that lower our Physical Immune System lower our Psychic Defense system. Things like stress, sadness, rage, and fear lower both immune systems, and we are then vulnerable to invasion by entities. The Chinese call the Psychic Defense System the "Guardian Chi".

Attachments are quite common and caused by many things. Most people are open to spirit attachment on many occasions in their lives. Some investigators estimate that 70%–100% of the population is affected by entities at some time in life. Any mental or physical condition, strong emotion or need becomes a beacon that can attract an earthbound spirit with a similar emotion, condition or need. Anger, rage, fear, sadness, guilt, remorse or other negative feelings beckons entities with like feelings. In this realm, like attracts like.

A dead drug addict will carry his appetite for drugs in his spirit energy. If this energy attaches to you, you may also develop the same craving for drugs. Whatever were the needs of the dead one are now the needs of the attached one. **The attached spirit of a dead drug addict can be the source of craving for many living drug users. The same situation exists for other addictions like for food, cigarettes, alcohol and sex.** In practice, I often encounter these situations. When I remove the attachment, the addiction either leaves entirely or lessens greatly. What is left is usually due to some subconscious need of the client for the substance or the trailings of the physical effects of addiction.

Severe stress lowers the psychic defense system (Guardian Chi) and can allow access to an entity. Drugs like alcohol or hallucinogens that altar consciousness can also devastate the Guardian Chi and open the subconscious mind to invasion by entities. This can also happen when using strong analgesics and anesthesia necessary for surgery. A pain pill can sufficiently lower the Guardian Chi enough to allow a spirit to attach.

The openness, vulnerability and submission during sexual intercourse can make the participants open to the attached entities or soul mind fragments of their partner. Sexual abuse, like rape or incest can lower the Guardian Chi enough for the attachment of an entity drawn to the event, and it is often demonic.

Although many homosexuals are simply misplaced genders in the wrong body, entities of the opposite gender can influence the sexual preference and gender orientation of its host. I once had a homosexual client who was attached by 26 female earthbound spirits. I released them, and he lost his homosexual desires.

Physical invasions such as surgery or blood transfusions can cause entity attachment. When organs are transplanted, the spirits of the organ donors can tag along with the transplanted organ into the new body. Any severe disturbance can make a person vulnerable to an invasive spirit, because the Guardian Chi is "down" and not protecting.

Earthbound spirit attachment may occur because either the spirit or the living human chose it due to a strong emotional bond between them in this life or a past life. A brokenhearted person may welcome a loved one's spirit and then suffer from the negative energy that comes with it.

Demons, like other foreign energies, can attach to you when your psychic defense system is down, which occurs when you are under great stress like from sadness, fear, despair, rage, overwork fatigue, and the like. Demons want to destroy you…usually because you have a light that will benefit the planet. Their destruction methods range from exacerbating deeply embedded negative emotions already in your subconscious, to bringing into you earthbound spirits of deceased people who had terrible physical or mental/emotional problems in their lives or soul-mind fragments of distressed people living or dead. These attached energies bring to you all their negative stuff.

Often, I find that demons will bring in earthbound spirits to do their dirty work, because when they do, the energy of the spirit's death and the negativity from their lives are both brought to the attached client. Since most earthbound spirits die violently or in great pain, the massive fear energies of their deaths as well as other bad energies from their lives really wreak havoc with the client. All the depression, fear, and other misery energies are glued to the suffering client's subconscious as well as the physical propensity for the ailments of the deceased person. Earthbound spirits don't actually bring the diseases they had…but bring the disease's energies with them.

This is particularly bad if the earthbound spirit is genetically linked to the client. For instance, if there is a genetic cancer link, the cancer energy of the spirit is added to the client's inherited genetic predisposition for the disease. If someone in the family history had breast cancer, the cancer energy can often trigger or ignite the disease in the attached client. Since the attachment is a Negative Forcing Function, it continuously reinforces the disease energy in the client and installs and supports the negative program of breast cancer on the client's subconscious hard drive. Therefore, the probability of that person getting breast cancer is increased. This also happens with other disorders, mental and emotional as well as physical. I have seen this many times, not only with cancer, but with alcoholism, severe depression, obesity, heart disease, diabetes and a host of other conditions.

Attachment Sites

Entities can attach to any part of the body or the body's energy field. A physical weakness in any part of the body of the host can attract an earthbound spirit to attach to that area because of a corresponding physical weakness or injury in the entity before death. An entity that had heart trouble or died of a heart attack will often be found in the area of the heart, and the client will experience some kind of discomfort in that area until the entity is released.

Host Unaware

Most often, the attached host is unaware of the attaching spirits. The entity's desires, emotions, habits, behaviors and often physical symptoms will be experienced by the host as his own, and do not feel strange if they have existed for a long time, like from childhood. This is a prime reason why most people don't think they have anything attached to them. This is just as true for professional therapists as for people in general.

Free Will

A spirit can attach to a person without his consent, and this seems to violate free will. It also seems to refute the common conviction that each person is completely responsible for creating their own reality, and there are no victims. This apparent conflict stems from the fact that **ignorance or denial of spirit attachment is not protection against it**.

Your belief or disbelief in spirit attachment has no effect on whether or not spirits can attach to you. Most people do not actively deny permission to these intruding energies either because of ignorance or fear. We are all sovereign beings and have the right to deny invasion of ourselves by other beings. However, if we leave ourselves open to attachment by allowing our Guardian Chi to become weak, we are in effect, opening the door, giving permission and the spirits can come onto us.

Entity Attachment Through Channeling

Some "New Age" fans consider it smart to "channel" a higher power; a spirit teacher who speaks enlightened words through them. Channeling grants consent to an entity and makes the channelers vulnerable to entity attachment. Often, the spirits that come in won't leave when the channeling session is finished, and the channelers are stuck with them and everything they brought with them.

Attachment Symptoms

Symptoms of spirit attachment can be very subtle or decidedly apparent. An attached spirit may be present without producing any noticeable symptoms except fatigue. Fatigue is usually present because the entities are parasites and use your energy. Some common symptoms of entity attachment are, but not limited to:

- Physical or mental illness, (it may belong to the entity)
- Behavior inconsistent with normal conduct
- Physical sensations or symptoms without an organic cause
- Personal identity confusion (who am I?)
- A sense that a spirit or another person has taken control of one's mind and/or body.
- Personality changes after surgery, organ transplant, traumatic accident, severe emotional upset, or even changing residences

An entity attachment can change an individual's attitude, ways of thinking and can change tastes for food, sex, fashion, alcohol or other drugs. The biggest problem is that the attached earthbound spirit brings with it the energy of its death and the negative energy of its life (mental/emotional/physical sickness).

Soul-Mind Fragments of other people attached to you bring with them the negative disassociative energy that created the fragment in the first place. Thought-form energies like sadness, fear, or hate bring that energy to you and you will feel it. Whenever I find extraterrestrials, I usually find demons hiding behind them, so when I find ET's, I primarily have to deal with the demons.

Past Life Regression Therapy (PLT)

The foundation of Past Life Regression is reincarnation. Reincarnation is a concept believed by most people in the world. It was a belief within the Catholic Church until the Council of Nicea banned it. Most Christian religions do not believe in it and actively preach against it. Nevertheless, many Christians, in their deepest hearts, believe in reincarnation because it makes so much sense. I am Christian, and I firmly believe in reincarnation. When I was about three years old, I remember getting a revelation that I had lived before, I am living now and I will live again—ho hum! It was perfectly natural and made perfect sense to my three-year-old mind. It still does.

Reincarnation says that we live multiple lives to further our growth from ignorance to enlightenment. It is a way of expressing God, The Source Of Life. We live each life as a learning experience. When we die, our immortal soul, which is the part of us that never dies and is a part of God, transitions onto an astral plane of consciousness where we meet with spirit guides and teachers who help us determine what our next life should be as we develop.

If we did things in the previous life that were counterproductive to our enlightenment journey, then we have to do something in the next life to correct that shortcoming. This is karma. Once we live a sufficient number of lives to learn what we must learn, we then go back to God as a part of God and fuse into the everlasting source. Different people live different numbers of lives, but Dr. Arthur Winkler, who spent fifty years studying reincarnation says that we each live, on the average, about 2000 lives until we go back to God, from Whom we came.

Many illnesses, both physical and psychological, result from past life events. Much authoritative work is being done on Past Life Therapy (PLT), and many traditional psychotherapists are finding this therapy to be highly effective. They are finding that the present can really be healed through the past.

Traumatic events of past lives permanently impress our lives, and sometimes, manifest as today's illness. Hypnosis allows one to relive past lives and release the negative energy generators from the past permitting our bodies and minds to generate their own healing in this life. Even if you do not believe in Reincarnation, the therapy works just as effectively to produce healing.

Hypnosis and Reincarnation

The subconscious level of the mind, being a computer, has a memory bank or storehouse of memories. Every imprint, impression and experience we ever had is recorded and filed away in the subconscious computer memory bank. This is true regardless of whether the imprint or impression was experienced during the present incarnation or a past one.

In the hypnotic state, a person is capable of accessing those imprints or impressions out of the storehouse of the mind and recalling them in detail. When the hypnotherapist gives proper guidance and suggestions, the hypnotized person is capable of recalling any past life.

The Soul-Mind

Reincarnation is the process by which the soul-mind continues in another body. It is not the body that reincarnates; it is the Permanent Subconscious Memory and The High Self that reincarnate. This is the soul-mind and is the mechanism, which records the sum total of a being's experiences though all incarnations forming physical bodies and life-styles from their recordings. It is also called the Memory Bank, a permanent intellect or consciousness. It creates individuality, and like the immortal soul never ceases to exist.

What Reincarnation Is Not

Reincarnation is not a process that enables a body to come back to life again after it has died. When the soul-mind goes into a body, it stays with that body until the body dies. When the body dies, the soul-mind continues living in the "spirit plane." It remains there until it is ready to be reincarnated again in a new body.

Usually when the soul-mind reincarnates into a new body, the memories of all previous incarnations, as well as memories of the time in the spirit plane are **repressed** into the unconscious level of the mind, and cannot be recalled in normal everyday situations.

Reincarnation's Two Paths & Cellular Memory

We have two paths that we travel on during our journey from the Source (God) and back to the Source. The first path is our soul path, and the second is the genetic path. Actually, we can have many genetic paths depending upon into which genetic path we choose each lifetime. On our soul path, we carry with us all the stuff affecting our soul-mind: all the event memories, lessons and scars of each lifetime. This energy combines with the physical cell memory in the DNA of each of our particular genetic paths that we choose, modifying the cellular memory with our particular soul-mind energy, making it unique to the individual.

Past Life Regression Practice

In clinical practice, the competent hypnotherapist who understands Past Life Regression usually finds both past life trauma and spirit attachment. Spirit Releasement Therapy (SRT) and Past Life Therapy (PLT) are intimately related in clinical application. Often, whatever caused the spirit attachment is discovered in a past life and must be resolved with PLT.

The past life events of a client who is not cleared of entity attachments may be part of the soul memory of that client's attached entity. **Even the best psychotherapy is of little value if it is being performed on an attached entity and not on the client.** Past Life Therapy done on a client who has entity attachments is useless for the client. The client may experience some cessation of symptoms because the entity feels better, but the client's respite doesn't last.

We do not live in the past or the future. We have memory of the past and anticipation for the future, but the present moment is all there ever really is. Physical bodies are alive in this now moment but can be affected by past life trauma.

Dr. Edith Fiore, a noted psychologist and author, used hypnoanalysis and PLT with many of her clients to find the source of their presenting problems. Some of her clients told of events in past lifetimes as the cause of present-life emotional and physical problems. As I understand it, Dr. Fiore did not believe in reincarnation but she asked her clients to express whatever emerged in their exploration. **The beneficial therapeutic results so amazed her that she persisted in developing and using past-life regression in over 40,000 cases.**

Past Life Negative Forcing Functions (Energy Generators)

Physical and mental disease, disfigurements and accidents can happen because of karma or continuing consequences of traumatic past lives events. Healing in the now requires that we resolve incomplete stuff from past lives, which continues to affect this life. Negative emotional, physical and spiritual energy remains of past lives can contaminate the present life. Resolution and release of these negative energies is the purpose of Past Life Regression Therapy.

The subconscious mind receives and imbeds in permanent memory all evident sensory inputs from the environment. This mind records all these inputs and assesses them for any real or imagined survival danger. Subconscious assessments of any dangers are historically compared with similar previous conditions and a decision regarding present security and action to be taken for survival is made. **So, a present action can be a reaction to a similar set of conditions in a past life.**

These decisions and chosen responses take place below conscious awareness. The subconscious mind is always alert to any survival danger and therefore the **past is always present**. This means that the past is always affecting the present.

When the physical body recovers from damage, scaring can be observed. Scaring of the physical body usually happens after recovery from physical damage. This scaring indicates that some kind of damage occurred in the past. Even though the pain may be gone, the tissue is changed by the trauma, and function may be affected.

Past Life Negative Forcing Function traumas can scar the mind just like a physical scar. These mind scars, which are negative energy generators, can manifest as phobias, negative behaviors, and reactions of anger fear, sadness and guilt. Psychotherapy tries to get rid of these mind scar energy generators, but often is futile if focused only on the present lifetime if the scar source generator is in a past life.

Traumatic scar energy generators can be deeply buried in the subconscious memory banks and are long gone from the conscious mind, since it only has temporary memory. **These buried traumas are usually inaccessible in traditional talk therapy, which often is little more than an intellectual discussion of consciously remembered events.** If the source of the problem is in the subconscious, we have to go there to find it. Most people cannot consciously remember anything before the age of five.

Release

Past life trauma is a negative forcing function energy generator buried deep in the subconscious memory banks. That energy is still affecting us, even though we have no conscious memory of it. The energy of a traumatic event that distorted the body's energy field and is buried in the subconscious must be found and released. A basic therapeutic approach in psychotherapy is bringing the unconscious into the conscious and discharging the energy of it. Reliving is relieving. Recalling those traumatic events under hypnosis can release the buried negative forcing function's energy, and healing can then happen.

Reincarnation Perceptions

Many people are buoyed by the thought that they will live many lives. Living again and again can take away the fear of death that many of us have. If you have a miserable life now, the thought that you will live again can give hope to a better life next time. I myself am very comfortable with the concept that I will live again to learn and grow. As I mentioned in my discussion of my early life, when I was a very small child of three, the concept of living before and living again was very matter of fact to me. I didn't regard it with anything more than "that's just the way it all works" and didn't have any doubt about it.

Other people, however, hate the thought of living again. They feel that if this life is miserable, then they don't want to take the chance that they may have to endure another wretched life in the future. In Jess Stearn's book 'The Search for a Soul, Taylor Caldwell's Psychic Lives", Taylor Caldwell, the famous author in the epilogue says "*I confess that this is my dearest hope: that in the grave there is no remembrance and that once dead, (I am) free forever from horrible existence in this world or in any world hereafter*". She goes on to say "*I've written many books on reincarnation, and the very thought of it horrifies me. What person of intelligence could endure other rounds in this dreadful existence in this most dreadful world? What made them regard reincarnation as a promise and a hope? Surely, once is enough to suffer life*". (Doubleday & Co., 1973)

So, you see that some of us like the thought of reincarnation and others detest it. I guess it all depends on your point of view. I like it!

PART 3

Articles from my Practice

Maybe It's Not Your Problem!

Some people struggle with the same problems for years, maybe even for a lifetime. No matter what they do, they cannot seem to get rid of them. Physical or mental illness, persistent rotten luck, procrastination, continually failing at whatever you try to do, bad marriages over and over again, constant money problems, relationship difficulties, etc. Things just don't seem to work out; no matter how hard you try. Sometimes, you get some respite for a while. You take another course, read another inspirational book, see another new doctor, try a new therapy, move to a different city, change your spouse or go on yet another diet. Maybe things get better for a while, but it usually doesn't last. After a while, the same old stuff reappears, and you are back where you started or even worse. Why is this so, and what can we do about it?

Sometimes the problems stem from our environment. You were born poor or handicapped or sick; never got an education; your parents were bad or non-existent. However, even in these situations, we can always see examples of people who overcame the handicaps of a bad environment and became competent, happy people with great lives. If you really try, you can overcome all these impediments because within you is all the knowledge needed to solve your problems—God made us that way. In France, there is a church, which has an inscription on its door that says, "Our shoulders were measured at birth for the burdens we must bear". This means there is nothing within us that we cannot overcome.

So, why is it that good, intelligent, strong, sincere people cannot get out from under the terrible problems with which they struggle incessantly? **Maybe it is because the problems they are struggling with are not theirs—the problems belong to someone else!** Even though the problems affect their lives, the person is essentially a victim of circumstance—the problem is not really theirs—only the unfortunate effects are!

How can this be? Aren't we always told that we create our own reality, that there are no victims, that we are totally responsible for ourselves? Yes and No!

This is how it works. We are responsible for ourselves; that is a fact. We are completely responsible for protecting ourselves from the intrusion of negative energies and responsible for not attracting them to our energy fields. We have a psychic defense system just like we have a physical immune system. The physical system protects us from germs, viruses and other pathogens, which would invade our bodies and cause us to be sick. Our psychic defense system protects us from negative energies, which can attach to us just like a pathogen can. The Chinese call this psychic protection system the Guardian Chi. The same things that weaken our physical immune system to get weak also weaken our psychic system. Rage, sadness, fear, doubt, despair and other negative emotions weaken both systems.

If we have a weak physical immune system, we don't want to be going out to places where we can pick up germs and viruses because we will probably get sick. If we have a weak psychic immune system, we do not want to be putting out negative thoughts, which are energy, because the negativity in us will attract like negative energy. In the case of negative energy, like attracts like. That is how it works!

An earthbound spirit is the disembodied consciousness of someone who has died and not gone to the light. Spirits of deceased people do not always see that light we all hear about. For instance, if the dead person died under very traumatic circumstances, like murder, an airplane crash, a car wreck, in war, or just fell off a cliff, the chances are pretty good that they will not see the light and will wander. Others who may not see the light are those who die in great pain under the influence of heavy drug sedation. How do I know this? The earthbound spirits tell me during Spirit Releasement Therapy. This is not to say that all people who die violently or in great pain under heavy sedation become earthbound spirits, but the ones that I encounter are from these conditions.

If your psychic immune system is down and you are negative in your thinking, you are open and can attract like negative energies. An earthbound spirit who finds your energy attractive can attach to you. Likewise, a demonic entity drawn by your negative thinking may take the opportunity to attach to you to destroy you. You could also pick up the disassociated soul-mind fragment of someone alive as an attachment. Whatever you pick up as an attachment brings its own energy with it.

In the case of an earthbound spirit, the entity brings to you the energy of its death and the negative energy of its life. If it had heart trouble, an addiction, was depressed, a persistent failure, a compulsive overeater, had relationship problems or was consumed by rage and hate, it brings that energy to you. You can now have a strong tendency to have the same problems as the entity. Like so with a soul-mind fragment attachment…the horrific energy, causing the disassociation is in the fragment and it comes to you. If the entity is demonic, the demon will strive to make you miserable, do things not in your best interest, cause you mental and physical pain and anguish, and try to devastate you.

The only way out of these conditions is to remove the entities. There is no other way. While the entities are attached, they are forcing functions in the subconscious mind continuously embedding their negative programs into your subconscious self, and no therapy can be effective until the entities are removed. Sometimes the entities will leave by themselves, but you cannot remove them by yourself. Someone skilled in dealing with these energies must remove them. Once removed, the barrier to reaching the subconscious self is also removed and therapy will now be effective to change the person's life.

Why Will Power Doesn't Work

Many people believe they can solve most of their problems by diligently applying willpower. Sometimes, these problems are emotional, mental or physical, and sometimes they just seem to be as though life is against them. They cannot stop smoking, loose weight, get out of debt or resolve a physical or emotional problem they have struggled with for years.

They try willpower, vowing that things will change, recite affirmations *ad nauseam*, struggle incessantly against the problem, and still no permanent, significant change occurs. If we make our own destiny, why can't we resolve the issue through application of willpower? Isn't willpower our force for change against things we don't like about ourselves?

Let me tell you why will power doesn't work for long-term solutions, and what we have to do if we really want permanent change.

Willpower is a **short-term** power function of the conscious mind, NOT of the subconscious mind. Bad things happening to us result from bad programming of the subconscious, caused by Negative Forcing Functions in the subconscious. Forcing Functions are caused by negative things that happen to us either in this life, a past life, from an external energy attachment (Spirit Entities), genetics or from an internal conflict within ourselves. Unless the Forcing Function is found and released, it keeps on imbedding the negative program it created stronger and deeper. Since the subconscious is a bio-computer and must generate our behaviors from the programs within it, no permanent change in behavior or response to life will occur until the negative program is eliminated and a positive program replaces it. That's just how it works.

Willpower cannot change a bad program if there is a Forcing Function continually reinforcing the bad program. A temporary respite from the negative condition may occur, but the problem will reappear shortly, because you have not solved it, only alleviated it for a time. It is something like taking an anti-depressant if you are depressed. The anti-depressant can modify the brain chemistry so you do not feel the effects of the chemical imbalance causing the depression, but you have not resolved the problem permanently by finding the source of the chemical imbalance, which is the Negative Forcing function. As long as the Negative Forcing Function is there, the depression reappears as soon as you stop taking the anti-depressant.

Don't get me wrong: I am not against anti-depressants. They can provide relief while the search for the Negative Forcing Function goes on, but anti-depressants by themselves don't permanently eradicate the problem. I do not think that constantly using anti-depressants in lieu of eliminating the cause of the depression is the way to go. So, if you have a problem that willpower can't solve, find a good hypnotherapist, eliminate the problem's source, reprogram the subconscious and be done with the difficulty…but, be sure that any entities are first removed or the therapy won't work because you can't reach the subconscious self if entities are present.

Monsters of the Id

What are the monsters within us that keep us sick, that keep re-igniting the flames of misery? We think we have snuffed them out by wondrous therapies, only to have them reappear stronger than before. We do what the therapist says—we think we have cleared ourselves—we take the potions, guaranteed to heal us and maybe we feel better for a short while, only to have the malady recur and we feel bad again. What in us causes this to happen?

The culprits are monsters in the subconscious mind called Forcing Functions. These generators keep adding energy to the systems within us that are making us feel bad. Harmful things that happened to us in this life or a past life, unresolved internal conflicts, deleterious physical genetic encodings from our ancestors or attached entities cause forcing Functions. The effect of the Forcing Function is to keep re-stimulating the problem and to reinforce the negative program, which it created within us.

As long as Negative Forcing Functions remain in the subconscious, no therapy can be successful over the long term. As soon as therapy stops, the problem is restarted from the Forcing Function energy and the difficulty is re-created. The negative program created by the Forcing Function continues to operate and is continually reinforced by the energy. Since the programs in the subconscious determine the sufferer's behavior and response to life. He is miserable again.

The only way to achieve permanent healing is to eliminate the Forcing Function(s) from the subconscious self and the only way into the subconscious is through hypnosis. Therefore, a competent hypnotherapist will find and eliminate the Forcing Function(s) and reprogram the subconscious. Then the sufferer is healed permanently.

The reason most therapy fails is that the therapist cannot reach the subconscious self if there is an attached entity on the person. In order to find and eliminate the Forcing Function so that the subconscious bio-computer can be reprogrammed, the therapist must first release any entities there. Entity attachment is an impenetrable barrier to reaching the subconscious self.

Most therapists do not believe in entity attachments or are afraid to deal with them, so, they do not and their therapy is ineffective. For instance: if the Forcing

Function is from something that happened in a previous life, regression therapy is required to find and release the negative energy associated with the event. But, if there is an attached earthbound spirit on the person, the regression is done on the attached entity and not on the person. All the psychotherapy in the world on the attached spirit is not going to help the afflicted person.

So, if you have monsters in you that are preventing you from getting permanently well, seek out a Hypnotherapist who knows how to deal with Spirit Attachment and your life can really change for the better.

All or Nothing

Jonathan, 42, came to see me about four years ago asking me to help him. For many years, he had been suffering with severe pain all over his body, and his body was covered with lumps. He had been to many medical doctors over the years without much success in getting rid of the problem and had been taking pain medication, but he did not like to take medication all the time. I told him that I did not treat medical conditions because I was not a physician and did not practice medicine. He said he understood and just wanted to see if hypnotherapy could help him.

Jonathan had three layers of earthbound spirits on him. All the earthbound spirits had pain all over their bodies at death, and one of them had lumps all over its body at death. All had been severely beaten before they died. The one with lumps was beaten with a pole about 2 inches in diameter leaving lumpy ridges over his entire body. I got all the earthbound spirits to leave and then discovered a layer of Demonics below the earthbound spirits. In speaking to the Demonics, I found that they used the earthbound spirits to cause Jonathon's suffering, as attaching spirits bring with them the energy of their death and the negative energy of their life. I finally got rid of the Demonics, and the lumps and pain rapidly disappeared.

Now that the forcing functions (entities) were gone, it was necessary to reprogram his subconscious so that his behavior and response to life would change because the forcing function programs control these things. Reprogramming usually takes three sessions after the person is clear. Sometimes, getting rid of the entities does not totally clear the person and therapy on the self is required to clear the self before reprogramming can take place. In any case, it is an absolute must to clear all entities because the subconscious self cannot be reached if entities are present. Jonathon felt so good after clearing the entities that he did not come back for reprogramming because he did not want to spend any more money.

I did not hear from him again for two years and then he called me in dismay complaining that the lumps and pain were back. I explained to him that he had not let me complete the work on him so we would have to start over again. This

156

is because the old forcing function programs were not removed and replaced with new positive programs. Unless eliminated and replaced, the old programs will re-create a forcing function to reinforce it, and the original condition re-establishes itself. Jonathan's actions were penny-wise and pound-foolish.

Solve the Right Problem

People can struggle with a problem for years, perhaps all their lives, without getting to the solution. In hypnotherapy, I find this all the time. If you have a problem, it requires a particular solution. However, if the solution you use is for different problem, you will not get anywhere because you have not addressed the right solution for the right problem.

Dr. Richards, a 57-year-old physician came to see me through a mutual friend. He suffered from a persistent low-grade pain in the lower part of the abdomen for as long as he could remember. Being a medical doctor, he had ruled out all of the known reasons for this pain, having gone through many tests without finding anything physically wrong. I told him that I do not work on any specific physical or mental problem because I am not a physician or a licensed mental health professional, but he wanted me to try anyway. I explained to him my process for clearing energy, eliminating forcing functions in the subconscious and reprogramming the subconscious to change behavior and response to life. In particular, I discussed the effects of entity attachment on a person, and the necessity for getting rid of them before any effective therapy can be done.

He had a hard time accepting the entity part, but because he did not have any other solution to his problem, he wanted me to try. **Actually, it does not make any difference if the person believes in entities are not, the process works anyway. It is the same for past life regression therapy. People do not have to believe in reincarnation to have past life regression work.** It is like you do not have to believe in electricity to make toast in the morning. You just plug in the toaster and it toasts. However, for past life regression to work, you have to make sure that there are not any entities on the person, otherwise you are regressing the entity. All the psychotherapy in the world on the entity is not going to help the person. This is a common mistake of regressionists.

Dr. Richards had the earthbound spirit of a seven-year-old girl on him who had been raped and killed. She had been on him since his conception, since she said that she had been with him during seven previous lives and always came back on him when he was reborn. On questioning, she said that she had pain in her lower abdomen all the time from the internal tearing of her genitals that occurred in the rape. I got her to leave and go to the light, taking with her all that she had brought. Earthbound spirits always bring to their hosts the energy of their death and the negative energy that was in their life. In this case, she brought with her the pain in the lower abdomen.

When the doctor emerged from hypnosis, the pain was gone much to his amazement. He had never remembered being free of that pain without drugs. Now that he was clear, I reprogrammed his subconscious so the forcing function would not be recreated. That was eight years ago, and the pain has never returned. Draw your own conclusions.

Entities and Past Lives

Entity attachments are frequently the cause of an intractable problem in a person's life. Sometimes entities are just part of the problem and not the source of the problem and the therapist has to go beyond the entities to reach the root. However, even if the entities are not the problem source, they must be removed before you can get at the root forcing function of the problem, as entity attachment is a barrier to reaching the subconscious self.

Linda, 47, had been suffering from chronic fatigue all her life. She could not ever remember not being tired, even as a small child. She said she tried everything: medicine, supplements and psychotherapy without relieving the fatigue. She came to me as a last resort as most of my clients do. I told her, as I always tell my clients, that I do not work on any specific condition because I'm not a licensed healthcare provider but that I would try to help her using hypnotherapy.

I always check for entities first because if they are present, no other therapy can be effective until the entities are released. Often, removing the entities solves the problem because if the entity brought the problem, when it leaves, the problem leaves with it. I removed three layers of earthbound spirits and a demon from Linda, but the fatigue did not leave even though all of the earthbound spirits in life had chronic fatigue and the demon was using the earthbound spirits to wreak havoc in this woman's life. However, once she was free of the entities I could get to her subconscious self and explore further.

Using her chronic fatigue in an affect bridge induction, I was able to access a past life in which she was a male warrior and had been speared through the chest. All of "his" lifeblood (life energy) had poured out of him. Using hypnotic re-framing techniques, I pulled the spear out of him and repaired the wound stopping the flow of lifeblood energy. I then embedded a new program in the subconscious that related her fatigue in this life to the flow of lifeblood out of him in the past life and that the fatigue condition in this life did not exist because it never happened because of the past re-framing.

When I brought Linda out of hypnosis, she immediately felt more energized. Over the next few weeks, her chronic fatigue totally disappeared and she felt better than she ever felt in her entire life. That was six years ago and she still feels good.

In this case, the entities were attracted to Linda because of her fatigue and brought with them their negative energy contributing to her problem, but were not the *source* of her problem. The reason all her past therapies were unsuccessful was that the source problem was hidden behind the entity barrier, which had to be removed before any effective work could be done.

The Therapeutic Process

Back in 1981 when I first started doing energy healing work, I did not know much about the mind's effect on health. I did acupressure on blocked energy points and achieved some success in helping people feel better. However, the results did not last. Then, in 1985, I added Hypnotherapy to my healing work and achieved greater success in alleviating people's problems. Nevertheless, my success still was not very good. I did everything I had been taught to release the traumas in people's subconscious minds and still their problems persisted or the healing did not last very long. It was then that I discovered what effect entity attachment had on hypnotherapeutic healing. That was in 1990. Since then, I have great success helping people.

The objective in psychotherapy is to change the person's behavior and response to life (how they feel). Programs in the subconscious mind determine both of these. To reprogram the subconscious mind, it is necessary to first release all the negative forcing functions, which created and reinforce the negative programs. Once these are released, new positive programs can be imbedded into the subconscious and positive change results.

The problem is in reaching the negative forcing functions and accessing the subconscious bio-computer's hard drive where the programs are. You cannot release forcing functions or reprogram if you cannot reach the subconscious. Entity attachments form an impenetrable barrier to the subconscious, and until they are released, the subconscious cannot be accessed.

Vera, 42, came to see me about stress. During our discussions, she mentioned pains in her neck and head experienced since young adulthood. She tried conventional medicine and had taken many different pain relievers, but the pain always came back as she developed tolerance to the medicine or stopped taking it. I do not work on mental or physical illness per se, but she wanted me to try to help her, so I checked her out and got strong indications of an entity attachment.

I removed the entity, which was the earthbound spirit of a young man who had died by falling down stairs and broken his neck. He was very sad because his life ended so early. He said he attached to her when she was nineteen during a time of great sadness in her life. After releasing the entity and reprogramming her subconscious so that pain from the released entity was recognized as her pain, I brought her out of hypnosis. The pain left her and has never returned in two years. She remembered the sadness: it was when her father died. Our psychic defense system is impaired by emotions like sadness, which also attracted the sad entity…the entity brought the pain, and when it left, it took the pain with it.

Demonology 101

Demons are the second most prevalent entity I encounter in my practice. Earthbound spirits are the most prevalent. You can tell when you are dealing with a demon because they want to cause pain, misery destruction and death. They tell you so. God created demons just like everybody else, but demons went a different path (free will). Demons can come onto a person when the person's psychic defense system (Guardian Chi) is low. Demons are attracted by a person's light (innate energy) or by the negative energy the person is putting out.

If a person comes into this world with a great light to accomplish much good, this makes them a prime target of dark force energies that want to extinguish that light. If a person is very sad, angry, fearful or full of hate, that energy is a beacon to Demonics and they want to join that person as a kindred spirit. Once the demon is attached, it exacerbates the negative feeling, and then uses that strong negative feeling to produce more negativity in the world.

Carla, 37, came to see me because she had been in six major automobile accidents in four months. In each accident, she very nearly lost her life. Because of these experiences, she was afraid to drive and her job required that she travel by car. Since the accidents started, she experienced panic every time she got into the car. She was in a real quandary and quite frightened. She asked me for help, not knowing anybody else she could go to.

Under deep trance hypnosis, I spoke to a demon within her who told me that it was going to kill her and had tried to do so in the accidents. The demon said it wanted to extinguish her light as it was very strong and it had the assignment to get rid of her. It said it would continue until it accomplished its end. I finally got the demon to leave Carla and she has not had another accident since then. That was over 10 years ago. Since the Releasement, Carla says she is very comfortable driving and has no problem doing so.

Typically, Demons are afraid of the light and will not go near it, but many have told me that they eat a person's light as food to get the light's power without having the light directly on them. They do not like the light on them, believing it will destroy them. Releasing a demon involves getting them to see their own light within themselves, which transforms them from beings of darkness into beings of light. Then they can go to the light and, once there, they never return.

Heal & Improve Everything

Hypnotherapy, in addition to being a wondrous healing modality, has great utility in increasing performance in sports; job tasks, memory and artistic ability; and can improve relationships and other people dynamics. This occurs because: the person feels better, self confidence increases and stress is reduced, and: once negative forcing functions and programs are removed from the sub-conscious, it can then be positively re-programmed, positively changing the persons behavior and response to life. In addition, because the sub-conscious cannot differentiate between reality and imagination, it is possible to repeatedly rehearse a desired performance in the imagination, thus creating a program of excellence in the sub-conscious resulting in improvement.

Zachary, 51 first came to see me about 8 years ago because he was suffering from erratic heartbeats and it was scaring him. He did not like medical doctors for some reason and asked me to help him. I did some energy clearing on him using Shiatsu and the erratic heartbeats disappeared.

He re-contacted me about 3 years ago and told me his life was a mess. His relationships with women were terrible, he constantly felt very stressed, couldn't sleep, erratic heartbeats resumed, his golf game stunk and his law business was in trouble. He was lonely, unhappy and scared and wanted help again.

Several layers of entity attachments had to be removed before I could get to his sub-conscious self for regression therapy and reprogramming. Attached to him was an earthbound spirit of a man who died of a heart attack, the soul-mind fragment of one of his former wives and a demon. The earthbound spirit brought its heart attack death energy to Zachary. The soul-mind fragment of his former wife, who was still alive, was punishing him by bringing negativity into his female relationships and the demon wanted to destroy his life because Zachary had been a great light in a past life and the demon wanted to snuff out that light in this life.

After releasing the entities, I did Past Life Regression on Zachary and discovered several lives where he was a great healer and brought this knowledge to his conscious mind. I then reprogrammed his sub-conscious with positive programs of self-confidence, self-love and success and taught him how to rehearse his golf game under self-hypnosis.

Today: his relationships with women are beautiful; he is selling his law practice and becoming a Hypnotherapist in private practice; his golf game is dramatically improved; he looks and feels good with no erratic heartbeats; the insomnia is gone and he looks forward to life with enthusiasm and joy.

Leg Problems

Getting rid of entity attachments is often only the first step in helping the client. However, it is a vital step and makes the difference between success and failure. The original negative forcing function causing the problem (the core issue) may be buried deep in the subconscious self in an internal conflict, repressed memories from this life or a past life or from a genetic carryover. If entities are present, they may have been drawn to the person by the problem, which the person already had, and the effect of the entity is to exacerbate the existing problem. But, even if the core forcing function started in the person's self and was not originally brought by the entity, the entity must be removed first or you cannot get to the self and release the core forcing function.

Therefore, the first thing that should be done in any psychotherapy is to check for entities and remove them before proceeding. If an entity is present, psychotherapy on the Self is useless because entities are an impenetrable barrier to reaching the subconscious Self and nothing will change permanently.

Darla, 44 years old, suffered from swollen and aching legs since she was 8 years old. Medical doctors concluded there was nothing organically wrong. They especially checked her kidneys because kidney problems sometimes cause swelling. They prescribed water pills, but they dehydrated her so she discontinued them. She asked for my help.

I found a 63-year-old man on her who died in 1914 from kidney failure and heart trouble. He said that his legs swelled up and ached all the time before his death. He was on strong pain medication at death. He was attracted to Darla because she reminded him of himself. He joined Darla when she was 8 years old. I got him to leave and take with him all he had brought. When Darla came out of hypnosis, she said she felt lighter and her legs did not ache.

When Darla came back 4 weeks later, her legs did not ache, but the swelling had not disappeared. I then did regression therapy and found a previous life where she had her legs and feet bound up tight for torture and was been beaten to death. I released the energy of this event and brought her out of hypnosis. She felt very good and said her legs felt even lighter.

The original core forcing function was the past life event. It made Darla attractive to the entity, as like energies attract. The entity, attracted by the like energy, brought with its energy with it and compounded Darla's past life problem. Now that both forcing functions were removed, it was possible to reprogram Darla with positive programs of freedom from pain and swelling. Over time, the swelling in her legs subsided and she now lives comfortably with neither pain nor swelling.

Protection

Since foreign energy attachments can wreck havoc with a person's life, people quite often ask me how to protect themselves from these energies. Unfortunately, by the time a person asks the question, they are usually already attached and suffering the consequences. It is like closing the barn door after the horse has been stolen. There is a process that can protect you, but you must understand it to make it work for you.

We all have a psychic defense system that protects us against the invasion of foreign energies, just like we have a physical immune system that protects us from the invasion of pathogens that can harm our physical health. The Chinese call this psychic defense system, the Guardian Chi. The same kinds of things that lower our physical immune system like negative emotions of fear, sadness, rage and hate; and extreme fatigue, poor diet, etc. lower our psychic defense system. When our psychic defense system is down, we are vulnerable to the invasion of foreign energies attracted by our negative energy. Not only does the negative emotion lower our defense, but also it acts as a beacon to attract energies like itself. Like energies attract like energies.

Once these energies (entities) attach to us, they become negative forcing functions in the subconscious mind distorting our body's energy field and causing blocks to the flow of Chi through our bodies. These forcing functions also install and support negative programs in our subconscious hard drive that affects our behavior and response to life. The entities must be removed before any other clearing on the Self can be done. Forcing functions from trauma in this life, a past life, an internal conflict or a genetic problem can then be dealt with and cleared. Once clear, the subconscious is able to receive positive programs to replace negative ones so permanent change can result. Sometimes, entities will leave by themselves, but more often, someone who knows how to do it must remove them. Unfortunately, the attached person cannot remove the entities from himself.

To guard against attachments, keep yourself positive so that you do not lower your Guardian Chi or your physical immune system. Project positive energy rather than negative energy and you will attract positive energy (like angels) to yourself. Keep yourself physically strong and fit with exercise and good nutrition because this helps keep your energy positive and your psychic and physical immune systems viable.

I use an ancient Polynesian Shield and a Star Meditation for protection. These enhance my Guardian Chi and help me. You can get a copy at the Inner Space if you want one (attached). I also use and recommend prayer as an excellent way to stay positive. Knowing who and what you truly are guards against negativity in life.

Protection Techniques

The following techniques are for protection against negative energy. They should both be done at least once per day. The more you do them, the more secure is your protection. I believe it is best to do the **Polynesian Light Shield** first, followed by the **Star Meditation.**

Polynesian Light Shield:

Imagine an indigo blue light around you like a cocoon. While holding onto that light, imagine a pure white light surrounding the indigo blue light. While holding both the indigo and white lights, imagine both those lights surrounded by an ice blue light.

Star Meditation:

Close your eyes, focus inside to the very center of your being and find your spark of god's light there. Imagine that the spark of light begins to glow warmly and expand in every direction—upward and downward—all the way into the soles of your feet—up to the top of your head—from fingertip to fingertip—filling every cell of your body. Then, imagine the light expanding outward beyond the boundaries of your body, about an arm's length in every direction—a shimmering bubble of golden white light all around you. Then allow the light at your center to become very, very bright—like the sun, and have it expand out like a star. Feel totally protected.

Hypnotic Pain Control

Hypnotherapists use hypnosis in therapy because hypnosis allows direct access to the subconscious mind where all the negative forcing functions reside that causes our problems. Hypnosis itself is an altered state of consciousness, which has some collateral effects, which are useful in pain control. These effects are analgesia and anesthesia. Analgesia is elimination of pain and anesthesia is the elimination of all sensation.

The degree to which analgesia and anesthesia occurs is dependent upon the hypnotic trance depth that the subject can reach. There are many methods of judging trance depth, but the most commonly used are: Davis-Hubbard (30 levels); Le Cron-Bordeaux (50 levels); Stanford Scale (12 levels) and the Arons Depth scale (6 levels). The Arons Depth Scale is used by the NGH and is what I use in my practice. At one time only three levels were considered important, Light/Medium/Deep. This was found to be inadequate because greater degrees of differentiation were needed to determine levels needed to accomplish: dental work, surgery, childbirth and even Regression and Spirit Releasement Therapy.

Under the Arons Depth Scale, analgesia will begin to occur at Stage-4. This stage is also the beginning of the Amnesic stages. Subjects will actually forget their name, address, etc. The subject will not feel pain, but will feel touch. Stage-4 subjects can undergo dental work and most minor surgery without discomfort. Stage-5 is the beginning of somnambulism and complete anesthesia. The subject will feel neither pain nor touch. Positive hallucinations, where the subject sees things that are not there, will also occur at this stage. Stage-6 subjects experience profound somnambulism, anesthesia and negative hallucinations, where they will not see or hear things that actually are there. Beyond Stage-6 are the Hypnotic Coma and the newly discovered Ultra-Depth (Esdaile Level).

Surgery can be performed without discomfort on Stage-5 and up level subjects. Dr. Esdaile, a British surgeon, performed thousands of major surgeries on patients in India in the 1800's when he noted that patients under chemical anesthesia had a very high mortality rate. Under hypnotic anesthesia, the mortality rate was very greatly reduced.

Not everyone can reach the Stage-5 trance depth. In my practice, it is about 60%. Everyone has a trance depth that they can reach, and this depth is not usually reached during the first few hypnotic episodes. It can take up to 12 hypnotic episodes to reach maximum depth. These episodes can consist of self-hypnosis as well as external hypnosis. I know people who quite easily have root canals under self-hypnosis. I have read and heard about people who have had open-heart surgery under hypnosis. Surgeons are beginning to take note of hypnotic anesthesia because of patients who cannot tolerate chemical anesthesia.

Fortunately, much hypnotherapy can be done on subjects in the very light stages (Stages-1-3) and >95% of all people can easily obtain these depths.

Hypnotic Performance Improvement

There is an aspect of the subconscious mind that makes hypnosis of unparallel utility in increasing performance in all endeavors requiring practice to perfect. This aspect is the subconscious's inability to distinguish real from imaginary. This derives from the subconscious mind's need to protect us from any danger, real or imaginary, and the fact that it cannot discern the difference.

The subconscious operates on programs put into it. An imbedded program creates a habit, which is an automatic response to sensory inputs. Programs are consciously created, and with repetition are imbedded into the subconscious. Think of the subconscious as a computer. A habit is a program that has become imbedded into the subconscious computer's hard drive. The summation of programs on the hard drive determines our behavior and response to life. If the habit (imbedded program) makes the golf ball fly onto the green in one stroke, it is because the conscious mind got out of the way and let the imbedded program operate unencumbered.

When our mothers taught us to tie our shoelaces, we had to consciously do it very carefully at first—slowly moving our fingers in the proper motion to accomplish the correct knot. As we continued to tie our shoelaces repeatedly, the program (habit) became imbedded in our subconscious. In time, we did not have to think about tying our shoelaces, it just happened as we activate the imbedded habit and the subconscious tied the knot. Actually, if we consciously try to tie our shoelaces, once the habit is embedded, we will probably make a mistake because the conscious mind gets into the way of the perfect automatic subconscious program.

Take golf, for instance. We can consciously create a single stroke program in the subconscious by visualizing the ball coming off the clubface, flying through the air and going into the cup on the green. The conscious visualization actuates the subconscious to create the necessary coordinated body motion program to accomplish the conscious imagery. If we do this many times, the programmed action becomes imbedded into the subconscious mind. This then becomes a program on the subconscious hard drive.

When the golfer meets that same visualized situation on the golf course, the real life sensory inputs line up with the visualized sensory inputs and the subconscious executes the perfectly coordinated body motion to accomplish the feat, provided the conscious mind is out of the way. The conscious mind can be bypassed by putting oneself into self-hypnosis. The same technique can be applied to any sport or artistic endeavor where repetition is required for excellence. By consciously visualizing the desired result, the subconscious continuously rehearses the performance and hones the body's movements to perfection. The efficacy of this technique is demonstrated by the fact that most great artists and athletes use it.

Curses

Curses are a very ancient method for inflicting bad energy on people, places or things. Curses are a manifestation of Soul Mind Fragmentation (SMF) deliberately caused to affect a negative outcome. Normally, SMF is a survival mechanism the mind uses to protect our sanity when we are confronted with a situation too traumatic to bear. The mind creates a sub-personality (ego state) in which all the energy of the fragmentation is contained and submerges it into the subconscious mind frozen in the time of the fragmentation. The energy is always there but the conscious mind does not know it is there. This often is the underlying source behind persistent anxiety for which there is no apparent present cause.

The SMF can leave the body and attach to someone else, inflicting on that person the energy of the fragmentation. This not only damages the person onto whom the SMF is attached, but also damages the person who has lost a fragment of his own soul. Shamans heal by retrieving the SMF that is missing and reintegrating it into the afflicted person. It is called soul retrieval.

In a curse, a SMF is deliberately created by the curser through the powerful emotions of hate or revenge and deliberately projected onto the cursed person, place or thing. Because of the intent, the SMF usually picks up demon and the bad energy in the fragment is worsened thereby exacerbating the damage to the accursed. To heal this condition on the cursed one, the therapist must find the attached SMF, release the Demon and send the SMF back to the curser.

John called me about his 8 year old, son Nicky who had suddenly started acting crazy, screaming, cursing, fighting, spitting on his teachers and parents and trying to kill people with a knife. They had to take him out of school, restrain him and highly medicate him to control him. Traditional psychotherapy did not help. John thought Nicky was possessed. He was,—but not in the traditional sense.

Because of Nicky's age, I used his mother as a surrogate to do a remote depossession on him and found a demon attached to a SMF of Nicky's uncle on Nicky. It was a bad one and took 4 hours to release. Once released the child became normal and stayed so. It turned out that the uncle hated John and his family because John was wealthy and the uncle was poor. The uncle wanted to destroy them so he opted to destroy John's family by cursing John's son. After—John said that the mother, during the process, acted like the son as she was spitting, screaming and cursing. The mother is a very mild mannered and reserved lady.

Problem Places

Places and things can pick up negative energy (entities) just like people can. The effect can be devastating to large groups of people and last a very long time. Sometimes the energy attaches to a building or even to a whole area. Most people are familiar with haunted houses and battlefields. The attachment happens because of a curse or from an event that happened there. These attached places or things can be cleared using Remote Spirit Releasement Therapy.

About five years ago, Barbara 58 came to me because she and her husband had been trying unsuccessfully to sell their house in a development for four years. The developer went broke selling the homes to the original buyers at very deep discounts just to get rid of them. They desperately wanted to get out of the house because neither she nor her husband were comfortable there, nor had they been since moving there six years earlier.

Her husband was constantly sick going through the flu repeatedly and both of them were constantly very depressed. They weren't like this before moving to this house and decided after two uncomfortable years, that they would bite the bullet and move. The problem is they couldn't get anybody interested in the house, no matter what price, within reason, they offered the house at. Their neighbors also had the same problem. In an area of about 100 homes, 37 were up for sale and no one could get a fair offer.

I did a Remote Depossession on the house and area using a surrogate and found a very strong demon. The demon was attracted there by a massacre of around 300 peaceful Indians by whites a couple hundred years earlier. In my experience, demons are attracted by incidents like this because of the negative intent of the antagonists. The evil intent attracts a like energy and the demon came in and attached to the massacre area. The demon was also holding the souls of the murdered Indians captive in the area not allowing them to go to the Light.

This means that the death energy of those 300 Indians and all the negative energy in their lives were held in that place and exacerbated by the dark energy, which amplifies the death energy. The developer inadvertently, built the housing units over the site of the massacre and all that negative energy was still there. Once the demon was released to the Light, all the captive Indian souls also went and the area energy changed dramatically. Within 6 weeks, Barbara had a good offer on her house and many of her neighbors also.

Layers

Foreign energies can and do attach to us when our Psychic Defense System (Guardian Chi) is down. This defense system is lowered when we are very sad, fearful, enraged, fatigued, etc. Moreover, once an energy attaches, a portal or window into us is opened that makes it easy for other energies to attach. These energies establish nested layers within us that can build up and have to be cleared one layer at a time. If an energy (entity) that already has layers on it attaches to you, then you get that entity's layers also. I have dealt with as many as 30 layers. Some of my teachers have dealt with as many as thirty-five. Once entities get onto you, you get the negative energy of all the entities on all the layers. These additive negative energies can totally devastate a person.

If Earthbound Spirits (EBS) attach, they bring the energy of their death and the negative energies of their life to you. For instance, if an EBS had diabetes or heart trouble, was an alcoholic, was chronically depressed, or was a compulsive overeater, those strong tendencies are brought to you. If Demons are also attached, you get the destructive energy of the Dark Force Energies as well. If Soul Mind Fragments (SMF) of either living or dead people are attached, you also get the energy of the disassociations that caused the original fragmentation. All of these negative energies can destroy a life.

John, 47, was a Vietnam veteran who had been in and out of hospitals for over twenty-five years. He suffered from terrible chronic fatigue, stomach trouble, heart trouble, and recurrent bouts of extreme depression, insomnia, anxiety, and impotence. He took many drugs and had much psychotherapy but without any long-term relief. His life was agony and he had contemplated suicide many times. He was a shattered man.

I told John that I do not treat symptoms—that is the province of the medical profession. I only restore the body's energy using hypnotherapy. He asked me to try to help him.

John and his close friend were in a foxhole in battle. His friend got his head blown off and immediately went into John because of proximity to John and the fact that John was badly scared and his Guardian Chi was down. Not only did John pick up the EBS of his friend, but also a dead North Vietnamese soldier already attached to his friend and the soldier had a Demon attached to him. John got all of this.

I removed all these layers and John felt much better. He resumed his life free of the major symptoms and was able to return to work within a month. I heard from him once—a year later and he said his life was full and happy. That was over seven years ago.

Negative Forcing Functions

When a client comes to me with problems, be they mental, or physical, I always tell them that I do not work on illnesses or symptoms as that is for the medical profession. I do not practice medicine. I am a Hypnotherapist and I work on the body's energy using hypnosis. By correcting the body's energy flow, many of the symptoms, which the client may be experiencing, can disappear.

Bear in mind that illness symptoms are usually only the outward manifestations of an inner problem, which has screwed up the person's energy field. In the model for healing that I use, the symptoms may be temporarily eased, only to reappear when the treatment being applied is discontinued.

Negative Forcing Functions (NFF) are caused by bad things that happen to us either in this life, in past lives, from genetic carryovers from our biological ancestors, from unresolved internal conflicts or from attached external energies (entities). Negative Forcing Functions cause a distortion in the body's energy field, which inhibits (blocks) the flow of Chi (Prana or Life Force) through the body and installs a negative program in the subconscious mind's "hard drive". The subconscious mind is a bio-computer and it operates on the programs, which are installed in it. The NFF's continue to reinforce the negative programs it has installed and imbeds them deeper and deeper into the subconscious.

To achieve permanent respite from a NFF requires that it be found, the energy within it be released and a new program, which opposes the negative one, must be installed that overrides the negative program in the subconscious. If entities are attached to the person, they must first be removed; otherwise, you cannot reach the other subconscious NFF's as the entity is a barrier to accessing them.

Tara, 32, had severe panic attacks almost daily since childhood. Traditional medicine alleviated her condition with Xanax or other drugs. However, if she did not take the drug, the panic attacks reappeared quickly. Over the years, she developed tolerance to the drugs and so they did not work so well without increasing dosage and often had severe side effects. She tried psychotherapy several times to little avail, achieving some benefit but nothing permanent, so she decided to try Hypnotherapy with Spirit Releasement.

After removing a Demon that was attracted by her fear, I found that the panic attacks were caused by terrifying fears from childhood, which engendered an ego-state (inner child) frozen in time with the disassociation energy in it. This was buried in the subconscious and was the causal forcing function. Getting rid of the Demon, finding this fear forcing function, releasing its energy and then reprogramming the subconscious with a positive program, which opposed the reinforced fear program, caused the panic attacks to disappear and she began to live a comfortable life without drugs.

Earthbound Rescues

Most people and most therapists have no idea of the impact of Spirit Possession on health. Dr. Edith Fiorre, PhD, a clinical psychologist and author of several books, among them "The Unquiet Dead" has stated that Earthbound Spirits of the dead cause 80% of our illnesses. I believe this to be true and have devoted the past 10 years, along with other things hypnotic, studying, developing and perfecting a method of Spirit Releasement, which appears to work quite well. My Spirit Releasement work is an amalgamation of Dr. Fiorre's work and the works of Dr. W. Baldwin, Dr. Irene Hickman, Dr. Fred Leidecker and Dr. Carl Carpenter.

I usually find that an Earthbound Spirit (or spirits, since I usually find more than one) wants to be rescued from the uncomfortable situation they are in. I help them do that and usually have great success quickly and quietly. Most of the spirits that I rescue are physical, detectable energies, usually lost souls who do not understand their condition. Some do not realize they are dead, and now they have settled into an area that feels comfortable to them. Other common types of spirits (not discussed here) are Demons and Soul Mind Fragments.

Some of us attract spirits because we are emotionally weak and do not protect ourselves. Other spirits find a healer or, someone who can help them. In the first instance the victim will usually be emotionally stressed, experience anger and fear, and probably have migraines. These conditions all develop energy that can attract the Earthbound Spirit. Alcoholics, drug users and people who have been traumatized make excellent vehicles for spirits. Any trauma that weakens a person to the point of not wanting to be responsible for himself makes that person a good candidate for spirit interference. Earthbound Spirits bring with them the energy of their death and the negative energy of their life. Good physical, emotional and spiritual health is the best protection from possession.

Many people who attract spirits are healers. They do not realize that responsibility has been bestowed on them. It is a fact that at least 30% of the public are healers. In most old cultures, this was understood and healers were made aware of their responsibility while still young. I believe this current problem with spirits is because we, as a society, do not understand this phenomenon and in fact deny its existence, mostly because of fear.

184

Who knows if all I'm saying here is the whole truth. I can only say that many positive changes occur when I use this spirit releasement procedure on those affected. I can tell you that if Earthbound Spirits caused the problem, and I release them, the problem is quickly resolved.

Carlos' Problems

Carlos 68, a successful businessman, husband, father, and grandparent was utterly miserable. In fact, he had been miserable for the past 35 years. He suffered from incessant panic attacks and severe high blood pressure making his life a veritable hell. He was on potent tranquilizers for the panic attacks and four different blood pressure medications and felt out of control. In 5 years, he had been into hospital detox 4 times to get off the tranquilizers because he became addicted after developing tolerance to them having to take increasing amounts to get the effect. He also had been into the hospital emergency rooms 7 times over the same period with blood pressure at the stroke level, in spite of his medication. He was retired from his business, was panic-stricken and depressed and felt he had no options left but to die.

I found three layers of demons on him that had been drawn to him by his great fear. They exacerbated the terror he felt in the panic attacks. He got panic attacks driving in heavy traffic, speaking before groups, flying in airplanes and in the last few years by just leaving home. He became agoraphobic and didn't want to leave the safety of his house. Taking his medication sometimes caused strange feelings in his body and these feelings often triggered an attack. The attacks caused his blood pressure to rise precipitously and he got so scared of a stroke; the terror of it drove his blood pressure even higher. He was in a dreadfully dangerous cycle and couldn't get out of it.

Once I got the demons off him, there was some improvement, but not great. However, now that the entities were gone, I could look for other forcing functions in his subconscious that were causing his problems. I uncovered three major childhood Soul Mind Fragments (SMF) that were full of terror. SMF's are disassociated parts of the persons personality formed as a survival protective mechanism—they are also called ego states or inner children. He also had several terror induced adult fragments. We released some of the energy within these SMF's and the panic attacks subsided considerably, but his blood pressure was still high even with all his medication.

I then used an energy release technique called EMDR (Eye Movement Desensitization and Restructuring) on the childhood SMF's while Carlos was under hypnosis and his blood pressure responded dramatically. He was able, with his MD's concurrence, to cut his blood pressure medication by one-half and it remains under control. In addition, Carlos no longer uses tranquilizers because the panic attacks stopped completely. He is now living a panic free life and has embarked on a new career that pleases him.

Hypnotherapy: Rebirth of an Ancient Miracle

Hypnosis today is experiencing the greatest upsurge of widespread public acclaim that has been seen in the two centuries since Franz Mesmer had the French aristocracy agog with his healing miracles in the 1790's. Institutions now teach hypnotherapy. Bookstores are filled with a proliferation of hypnosis publications and its wonders. Medical doctors are recommending their patients to Hypnotherapists. Membership in the National Guild of Hypnotists, the world's premier Hypnotherapy Organization, has increased by 6000 per cent over the last six years.

Why is this happening? People are looking for alternative forms of healing and they have discovered the power of Hypnotherapy to change their lives for the better. It boils down to the fact that hypnosis is the only healing modality that allows direct access to the subconscious mind where all illness starts, and many authorities say that 85% of all illness is psychosomatic; some say 99%.

What is Hypnosis? There is no need to believe in hypnosis; any more than one need believe in electricity to toast your bread for breakfast or turn the light on. It just works. Hypnosis operates on its own. One simply uses it, the same way you plug in any electrical appliance when you require it. A Scottish physician, Dr. James Braid, coined the term hypnotism in 1841. Braid noticed that trances occurred when the subject was relaxed, eyes closed, in a state resembling sleep. So, he called this state "Hypnosis" from the Greek word *hypnos*, meaning sleep. Hypnosis is definitely not sleep. Whatever sleep is, hypnosis is not. Hypnosis is an altered state in which one approaches peak concentration ability. Hypnosis may look like sleep, but it is really nearer to total concentration that obstructs irrelevant sensory data. It is like the concentration experienced when engrossed in a very fascinating book. If you get very involved, you might not hear anything else.

Hypnosis is not sleep because the hypnotized person is awake and alert. Measured brain waves of a hypnotized person are those of one who is awake and not of someone asleep. Actually, in hypnosis you are more alert than in your normal

188

state of awareness. The subconscious mind and the conscious mind are completely inaccessible in sleep. In hypnosis, the subconscious is very accessible and highly suggestible. Rather than a form of sleep, hypnosis is actually an induced receptiveness of the subconscious mind in which awareness is focused and concentrated. Technically, hypnosis is simply bypassing the critical factor of the conscious mind and establishing selective thinking. The hypnotized person just stands back and lets whatever is there come through unencumbered by judgments, evaluation or analysis. It is just what is there in the imagination, as the imagination under hypnosis is the subconscious mind.

Hypnotherapy: Modality for the Millennium

People are hailing the newly rediscovered, yet ancient, healing modality of Hypnotherapy as the wonder of Alternative Medicine. But, why doesn't it always work? Is it because it really isn't that great? On the other hand, is it, maybe, because it's not always being done right.

Hypnotherapy heals because it can reach the subconscious mind, where according to medical authority, about 85% of disease originates psychosomatically. Some authorities say all disease is of the mind. Because of modern medicine's great cost and lack of insurance by so many, there is a great clamor for less costly healing approaches. In addition, hypnosis enhances people's lives by helping them to be more successful personally and professionally.

Hypnosis is a very old technique that permits the Critical Factor of the conscious mind to be by-passed. This produces a highly receptive subconscious state of mind into which beneficial suggestions can be offered. Hypnosis itself is no big deal. One can easily learn to hypnotize in a 3-day weekend course. What the hypnotist does with the client after he is in hypnosis is what makes the difference in whether the client is helped. It is here, that therapy is done and makes the hypnotist a Hypnotherapist.

Many hypnotists are trained to hypnotize, but are not trained to be Hypnotherapists. These hypnotists hypnotize a person and while in this receptive state, the hypnotist reads him a prescription to reprogram his subconscious mind. For instance, for smoking the hypnotist reads suggestions to stop smoking. The same technique is used for weight loss, addictions, etc. These are not very effective, achieving little more success than the placebo effect. This is why many such programs are so ineffective in the long haul.

Why is this so? For every difficulty a person has, there is a cause. This cause is always from things in this life, past lives, biological carryovers from ancestors, unresolved internal conflicts or from attached foreign energies. The cause must be uncovered and removed and only then, can the subconscious be reprogrammed so that the difficulty will not reestablish.

Techniques for uncovering the cause of the distress are many and the skilled Hypnotherapist has available an impressive array of uncovering methods with which to find the distress source(s). After finding it, the Hypnotherapist must then choose from an equally impressive list of techniques to eradicate the distress source energy. The well-trained Hypnotherapist will choose the most appropriate and effective uncovering and energy removal techniques depending on the particular needs of the client. Once the distress source is found and the energy released, the Hypnotherapist can now reprogram the subconscious and permanent healing can happen.

The National Guild of Hypnotists (NGH), which is the oldest, largest, and most prestigious certification organization in the world, trains competent Hypnotherapists. NGH has chapters all over the USA and is represented in 44 countries around the world. NGH certification requires a minimum of 100 hours of core curriculum instruction. This is very important because the States are moving towards registration or licensing governing the practice of Hypnotherapy and unapproved hypnotherapy training not meeting practice requirements will be useless in the future. The NGH and its affiliate The National Federation of Hypnotists (Local 104 OPEIU AFL-CIO) are in the forefront of this legislation around the world.

In the Atlanta area, The Inner Space offers classes leading to full certification by the NGH. The NGH Certified Hypnotherapy Training developed by Dr. Richard Hart of New York, is based on 40 years of research and proven field-tested behavioral programs. The Certification Curriculum provides a complete classical education in hypnotherapy enabling graduates to immediately become practicing Hypnotherapists.

On completion of the Certification Curriculum, graduates will be able to help clients with phobias, self-confidence and esteem issues, weight and smoking problems, sports performance, career counseling, sales performance and most other issues presented to Hypnotherapists in their practice.

This course is designed for:

- Those who want to work with people in a private professional practice of their own (full or part time)
- All mental health professionals including therapists, counselors, social workers and nurses desiring to enhance their skills and add Hypnosis as a short-term treatment modality
- Everyone interested in learning Self-Hypnosis for self improvement

- The modern Hypnotherapist interested in learning group leadership skills and programs which can be offered to private, corporate and government clients.

Addictions or Attachments? A Different Approach to Some Difficult Problems

"I've tried every diet in the world and I still can't lose weight,"—"This is the fourth time I've tried to stop smoking and even with the patch I'm back where I was."—"No matter how hard I try, I can't stop drinking even going to AA four times a week." These are familiar laments of those caught up in addictions, whether to food, tobacco, alcohol, drugs, sex or whatever. These poor souls are ensnared in one of mankind's most difficult to cure ailments, that of addiction, the overwhelming need to indulge in a substance or activity even though you know it is harmful or displeasing to you.

Each addiction is characterized by one familiar string that runs though all of them—Trying repeatedly to rid yourself of the craving for food, tobacco, alcohol and drugs, without success. Oh sure, sometimes will power can make you strong for a while, but will power is like adrenaline, it's only meant to be short lived and so most people revert to the addiction.—So, what is a person to do when they have this problem? Many people try hypnosis and other psychotherapeutic techniques, but the success rate for curing any kind of addiction is not that great, maybe 35%.

Many Hypnotherapists treat these problems with Direct Suggestion Hypnotherapy, wherein the therapist induces hypnosis and then gives the person suggestions that the subconscious mind is inclined to accept. Other Hypnotherapists use Regression Therapy to uncover the cause for the addiction in the person's present or past life and tries to remove the addiction energy at its source. Theoretically, if skillfully done, the person will lose the addiction. However, neither therapy works very often.

Why?—Maybe this is the answer!—It's a known fact that if a person is possessed by an entity, an earthbound spirit of someone who has died and not gone to the light, that the attaching spirit brings with it the energy of it's death trauma and whatever spiritual residue it carried in life. This means that if a person who is

193

addicted to eating dies, does not go to the light, and becomes a wandering soul, and if it attaches to a living person, that living person will be addicted to eating just as the dead person was. Now the problem with these attachments is that no matter what the living person does to stop overeating—using will power, going on endless special diets, etc. and no matter what therapy the person receives, unless that therapy gets rid of the attaching entity, no solution to the person's problem will be found.

Most psychotherapists do not believe in spirit possession and therefore do not treat it. The poor addicted person with an entity, who only finds therapists that treat the self, never gets rid of their problem. Therefore, the unfortunate one stays fat, smoking, drunk or drugged. For example, following death by drug overdose, a newly deceased spirit keeps a strong desire for the drug, and this desire cannot be satisfied in the nonphysical state.

The spirit must experience the drug through a living person who uses the substance. This can only be done through a parasitic attachment to the person. The attached spirit of a dead drug addict dominates many addicts.

The condition of spirit possession, that is, full or partial takeover of a living human by a discarnate being or energy has been recognized or at least theorized in every era and every culture. In ninety percent of societies worldwide, there are records of possession-like phenomena. Extensive contemporary clinical evidence suggests that discarnate beings, the spirits of deceased humans can influence living people by attaching to them, and imposing detrimental physical and emotional conditions and symptoms. This is called "spirit or entity attachment." Earthbound spirits, the surviving consciousness of deceased humans, are the most prevalent attaching entities. The disembodied consciousness attaches itself and merges with the subconscious mind of a living person, exerting influence on thought processes, emotions, behavior and the physical body. The entity becomes a parasite in the mind of the host.

Spirits can be bound to the earth plane by emotions and feelings connected with a sudden traumatic death. Anger, fear, jealousy, resentment, guilt, remorse, even strong ties of love can interfere with normal transition. It is very easy to pick up an attaching spirit when our psychic defenses are down which is the case when we are depressed, sick, fearful, etc. Researchers say that 85-100 % of all people experience some kind of entity attachment during their lives. Occasionally the entity just leaves by itself. Mostly, however, they must be removed. People cannot clear entities from themselves; it requires a skilled therapist to do so.

For those of you who have tried everything to rid yourself of an unwanted problem or behavior, maybe it is time for you to consider Spirit Releasement Therapy. It just might change your life.

Energy (Chi)—Feeling Good—&
Hypnotherapy

The great Henry David Thoreau said "Most men live lives of quiet desperation" and he was right. So many people go through life feeling lousy, never feeling good and just put up with it. Amongst the elderly, so many are miserable experiencing their "golden years" in pain and despair. In Kazanzakis' *Zorba The Greek* the old women when asked how she felt replied, "When you are old, you never feel well". Does this miserable state of existence have to be? Well, if we only understood what makes us feel good and bad, then maybe we could do something to correct the situation.

We feel good when our Life Force energy is free to run through us and nourish all the cells in our body. All the cell communities in our bodies require four things to be healthy—nutrition, oxygen, water and the Life Force—called Chi by the Chinese—Prana by the Hindus—Orgone by the Germans—Manna by the Polynesians—Ka by the Egyptians—Ki by the Japanese. All cultures recognize the existence of this force and its effect on health, happiness and longevity. Usually, we get enough food, water and oxygen for health, but keeping the Chi flowing unimpeded through our bodies to nourish all the cells is something else.

There are invisible energy channels within our bodies through which the Life Force (Chi) flows. The Chinese call them Chi Meridians. There are also seven energy centers in our bodies, which convert the Chi into the specific kind of energy required by the different parts of our body. These converters or transformers are what the Hindus call the Chakras. Each Chakra is centered on one of the seven glands in our endocrine system. The Hindus say that the Prana (Chi) comes into our bodies on the breath—the Chinese say it comes from the sky, the earth, our food and some of it from our parents. However, it comes in, it must flow uninterrupted to our cells to keep us feeling good.

If the transformed Chi energy flows from our Chakras into our Chi Meridians and thence to the different cell communities in our bodies in sufficient volume to allow the cells to regenerate and clone themselves as perfect cells, we are healthy and feel good. If the flow of Chi is reduced or cut off to the cell communities, we get sick and feel bad. That is how it works!

What causes the flow of Chi to be impeded are blocks or resistances to the flow, which are formed by a distortion of our body's energy field when life's experiences cause errant programming (negative forcing functions) to develop in our subconscious mind. When this happens, the flow of Chi is diminished or stopped and those cell communities depending on the Chi no longer clone as perfect cells and begin to clone as defective cells. When this happens, we begin to feel less than perfect. If the blockage continues for an extended time, the cell communities dependent on the blocked Chi begin to dysfunction and disease happens.

Since the problem is in the subconscious, you must go into it to find the problem and release it so that it will no longer cause the energy field distortion resulting in blocks to the flow of Chi. The only healing modality that can reach the subconscious mind is Hypnotherapy. Using Hypnotherapy, the negative forcing function can be uncovered and released. This corrects the body's energy field and the blocks disappear—allowing the Chi to flow unimpeded again to the cells and health is restored.

The Chinese knew this, thousands of years ago—but they did not know how to get into the subconscious mind. However, they did know how to develop physical techniques, which could open up the Chi Meridians when they were blocked and they did so with Acupuncture and Tai Chi exercises and herbs. Acupuncture uses needles stuck into the Chi Meridians at key points where the blocks usually occur and this temporarily opens the blocks. Tai Chi is an exercise, which also opens the energy channels. Tai Chi, because of its movements, also produces grace and beauty and strengthens the joints and ligaments with no adverse side effects. Other cultures use Allopathic Medicine, Chiropractic, Yoga, Massage, Exercise, etc. to temporarily remove the energy blocks.

So, what does all this say about alleviating human misery? Just this—if you have problems, some of your Chi channels are probably closed. You can correct this by getting rid of the negative forcing functions in the subconscious mind with Hypnotherapy and permanently restore the uninterrupted flow of Chi in the body—or you can have Acupuncture or do Tai Chi or one of the other clearing techniques to temporarily clear the blocks to energy flow. As long as you keep the energy channels free, you will feel good and stay healthy. The nice thing about hypnotherapy is that once you clear the negative forcing functions, they are gone permanently and healing lasts. With the other healing modalities, when you stop doing them, the problems return.

Energy, Entities, Hypnosis &
Healing

'I have spent all that money, and all that time going to doctors and I still feel lousy. Is there no way out for me or am I condemned to walk the earth in misery until I die?' This is often heard from many people as they struggle under the cloud of persistent illness. In spite of medical science, there are still people who live out their lives in desperation. Consider this: The Eastern model of disease is based on blocked cellular energy flow. Negative forcing functions in the subconscious cause the energy blocks. Hypnotherapy can release these forcing functions, which releases the blocks and energy can then flow unimpeded, permitting permanent healing. A prime difficulty in releasing the blocks is spirit attachment. If there is an entity present, unless it's released, most therapy is ineffective. Release the entity and hypnotherapy can create permanent healing. Maybe, just maybe, this is the way out for you.

Eastern Disease Model: There is only one general cause for disease and that is improper functioning of the cells. Each organ has something that might be called an organic mind made up of a group mind of a number of cells, each of which, moreover, has a cell-mind of its own. The cells enable the body to carry on its work of continual regeneration. Every part of our bodies is repaired constantly by fresh material. Our entire body is new every seven years. Our liver is new every six months. Our skin is new every 28 days.

Each cell possesses an instinctive knowledge of what is vital to its lights work and its own life. It takes physical nourishment, water, oxygen and Life Force Energy (Chi) to reproduce itself. The cells have a memory and in other ways manifest mind action. The cells are built up into organs, tissue, muscles and form cell communities in which their minds are seen to combine in addition to having independent mental action. The liver, for instance, has millions cells composing it and has a community mind that acts as the liver mind and is controlled by the subconscious mind unless interfered with by the Intellect. All organs, through their minds, are amenable to mental control and direction, but must have the

Life Force Energy as the motivating principle. But, if the cells don't get the Life Force Energy they need, they begin to reproduce as defective cells and ultimately the cell community to which they belong dysfunctions and disease begins.

Energy Clearing: I did energy clearing for about five years. People would come to me with all kinds of problems. I cleared their energy and they would feel better. In a couple of weeks, back they came with the same problem. I would clear them again and they would feel better. This went on repeatedly.

Hypnosis & Entities: Then is when I became interested in hypnosis to get to the subconscious, wherein all illness causes are buried. Hypnotherapy can release negative forcing functions and reprogram the subconscious problems do not reestablish themselves. This is the way to permanent healing. At first, I used regression therapy alone to find the negative forcing functions. This worked well, but sometimes I found I was doing therapy on an attached entity and not the client. By first releasing the entities on the client, I can be sure I'm dealing only with the client. Psychotherapy on the entity doesn't help the client's problem.

Just releasing the entity negative energy generators often brings remarkable positive change, but frequently I must also release the client's other negative forcing functions with Regression or Parts Therapy to resolve issues from this life, past lives, internal conflicts or genetic problems to achieve permanent healing. This procedure works extremely well, but the process of repairing cellular damage caused by long imbedded negative energy, and detoxification of the body from medication is greatly accelerated by Cellular Regeneration Hypnotherapy and Acupuncture with Chinese Herbal Medicine for detoxification. If the resolved problems existed for a very long time, the process of re-establishing normal healthy brain wave function can be hastened through Neural Feedback Training. Therefore, what I ended up with as a therapeutic process is:

The Skillas Therapeutic Process

1. Spirit Releasement to release all entity forcing functions.

2. Regression and Parts Therapy, including Past Life Regression, to uncover and release Negative Forcing Functions buried in the past and, to resolve internal conflicts.

3. Resolve genetic/biological Negative Forcing Functions by correcting the subconscious' view of healthy normality.

4. Reprogram the subconscious so the old imbedded destructive programs are wiped out, and behavior and response to life changes positively.

5. Repair cell damage and detoxify the body using Cellular Regeneration Hypnotherapy and Acupuncture with Chinese Herbal Medicine.

6. Accelerate return to normal brain wave function with Neural Feedback Training.

I find that the Huna Light Shield along with the Star Meditation are effective protections from entity attachment and teach this to my clients to prevent any further attachments, once they are clear. I have seen these therapies work for many people who didn't have anyplace else to go as that's usually when I get to work on them. Ultimately, the Truth shall set you free, and it is freedom from the misery of illness that therapy is all about.

More on Hypnotic Pain Control

We have within our brains some 100 billion cells, there are literally trillions of connections, and our memories are stored there. These connected memories are kind of a signature of what our life is. We can remember what it is to be without headache. If you're told that something will cure the headache and you believe it, you'll cure yourself of the headache because of remembered wellness.

Hypnosis is becoming a powerful tool for healthcare professionals. A Pain Control Hypnotherapist is extensively trained to teach the client how to use the mind—body connection to ameliorate unwanted fear, tension and anxiety concomitant with emotional or physical pain. The Pain Control Hypnotherapist always gets a referral from a medical doctor before shutting off pain, because the pain is a signal that something physical is wrong.

Conventional Western Allopathic Medicine emphasizes outside intervention to treat disease. Hypnotherapy emphasizes internal healing philosophies to treat disease. The most important concept in Hypnotherapy is the understanding that the healing does not come from the therapist and go to the client. The client already possesses the healing—they received it as a gift at birth. This gift is the Chi (Life Force Energy), which flows through your body and keeps you alive. Healing is a natural part of your physical body and is intuitively connected to your mind and Spirit. The therapist is only the teacher who shows the client how to awaken the path of consciousness that allows the healing to happen on demand.

Healing of the human body occurs on three different levels: physical, mental, and spiritual. The physical is the body, the mental is the mind and the spiritual is the soul. From the time you were conceived, your body began to detect disease and started the healing process as the embryo developed and continues to detect and heal throughout the lifetime of your physical being. The Chi life force energy is the healing force.

Consider the Physical Immune System: DNA structures in each cell are transmitted into RNA structures that cover the replacement of every individual cell. Because of the almost infinite number of cell replacement and generation messages that need to be produced, mistakes can happen. Sometimes the instructions become garbled and the cell receives misinformation causing it to replicate in a manner that interferes with the natural functions of surrounding cells or organs. You might call these misinformed cells a type of cancer, as they do not follow laws of physiology prescribed by the original DNA molecules. If this happens, the body naturally senses the offending cells and eliminates them via the immune system. The immune system also diagnoses and repairs the body when foreign organisms that cause disease invade it. The immune system is a natural process of the body healing itself and is a direct function of the life force flowing through the body.

The human brain has 10 to 15 million neurons in which to process and store information. Each neuron has the capacity to store a tremendous number of bits of information and memories. The brain also has one or more synapses or switches on each single neuron. The sum of limitless possibilities, associations, or potential interactions for memories, feelings, ideas, and attitudes staggers the imagination.

These interactions in the brain operate on a system of words, thoughts, feelings, and mental images. Positive thought processes promote healing of the body and negative thought processes inhibit healing and health. Every thought in your mind produces a physiological reaction in your body, even if the thoughts occur on a level beneath normal conscious awareness.

Because the Pain Control Hypnotherapist understands the psychology of pain, he is able to alter the way the afflicted person perceives the pain and achieves relief. Some of the techniques used are: Creating Numbness—Visualizations—Regression—Progression—Altering the Sensation, and Changing the Location of the Pain to somewhere it is not and then getting rid of it. The Hypnotherapist does not actually get rid of the pain, but alters the way it is perceived. For instance, if the subconscious mind accepts that pain is only pressure, then the body's physiological response must be a response to pressure rather than to pain.

The Hypnotherapist, because he deals with the subconscious mind wherein all of this is controlled, can uncover the forcing function(s) causing the body's distress and eliminate them, thereby restoring natural healthy function. What this means is that the Hypnotherapist has the ability to remove the blocks to the flow of Chi (Life Force Energy) within the body—and when the Chi is flowing unimpeded, the cells are nourished and regenerated and the body heals itself.

Spirit Possession and Reality

So many people are screwed up. Their lives are either living hells or they are gray worthless boring monotonous existences devoid of love, joy and future. They just go along—living from day to day—just getting older, a little more desperate and wondering about what might have been. I see people like these every day in my practice—there are lots of them.

A principle cause for this "miserable existence" is the attraction of entities to ourselves by the way we think. We have a psychic immune system, just like we have a physical immune system. Our physical immune system protects us from the invasion of pathogens that cause physical disease. Our psychic immune system protects us from external negative energy. The same things that depress the physical immune system depress the physic immune system. The Chinese call this psychic defense system the 'Guardian Chi".

There is a law of the mind that states—"thoughts are things and when mixed with emotion, they will create after their own kind." Or, simply, thoughts plus emotions (feelings) = creation. To be enlightened is to know that thought is creative. Thought creates everything...good or bad.

According to Patanjali, "Mind is a process, a process of thinking." We have been told that life is everlasting; but we are conditioned to believe that death is the end to our existence. Death is really evolution, a transition to another level of existence. We conquer the fear of death by knowing Truth.

Thoughts and spirits can be considered the same. They are both simply vibrations. The spirit lives within and is manifested through the physical body. The physical body is a vehicle and is temporal; the spirit is eternal. The physical body is a mirror of the mind—a reflection of our beliefs and thoughts. If thoughts of love flow through the body, we are well. If the flow of love is blocked by the lower vibrations of fear, guilt, anger, resentment, and sadness—all are illusions—we develop a sickness of the body and Mind.

Upon death when your physical and etheric body is shed, the "real you" is still fully alive in its "astral body". The "astral you" will raise and move to the frequency to which it mainly lived on the physical plane. A spirit is still a being of consciousness, albeit not complete, as we know life on earth. A spirit can become earthbound and may only rise no higher than the lowest astral plane. It can be earthbound by its own attachments to family, friends, lovers, lust, addictions and negative emotional ties, by sudden traumatic death, or in dieing when severely drugged.

It can be a loving father, son, mother, daughter, friend, lover, etc. The emotional ties between a spirit and a living person can hold it earthbound. A person obsessed on earth can still be obsessed in the astral. However, while in spirit this obsession can never be satisfied and the spirit will seek out a person through which to satisfy it's obsession. If it attaches to you, you gain the energy of its death and the negative energy of its life. If it was obsessed, sick, addicted, fat, mean, depressed, etc.—it brings that energy to you.

For a long time, we, as collective humanity, living in the physical plane of Earth, have forgotten who we are. We know we are a body that carries a brain, but do not know we are also mind, soul, and spirit. Most of us do not know this because we have forgotten—especially in our age of technology and things. We are very much into the physical and have lost sight of the spiritual. We are out of balance and have forgotten who we are. We are focused on the conscious mind. We stay there most of the time, limited to less than two percent of what is our reality. More than 98 percent of our reality is unknown to the majority of people.

Thousands and perhaps even hundreds of thousands of years ago, it was known that man had three minds—three separate and distinct minds that also manifested as one mind. Down through the ages the three minds became known as the "Trinity," a Christian concept. These three separate and distinct minds are the Conscious, Subconscious and Superconscious. Each has its purpose, and yet they manifest as one mind when in perfect balance and harmony. Out of balance, we feel incomplete, devoid, and empty. Most of humanity is out of balance!

The mind comprises soul and spirit, as well as our lower system of thought—our ego—while our body reflects our mind. When our life is discordant, negative forcing functions are created in the subconscious and they distort our body's energy field and cause blocks to the flow of Life Force Energy (Chi). The deprivation of Chi to the cellular communities of the body results in illness of the body and mind. The forcing functions can be caused either by something that happened to us in this life, a past life, unresolved internal conflict, genetics or by attached entities.

So, what is spirit possession or demon possession? It is to be possessed by or in possession of negative thoughts and feelings that are magnetically attracted to us, according to how we think. A possessing spirit is the thought imbued with feeling. When someone dies, we can become possessed of that person's spirit because we attract according to how we think and feel. A thought is a living, vibrating thing that cannot be destroyed, but it can be changed. Change your thoughts and you change your reality.

Our thoughts are of two natures. They are either of love or of fear, which can equate as good or bad, positive or negative, God or devil. Love is synonymous with God and fear with illusion. Love leads to joy and everlasting life, while fear leads to sickness, poverty and misery, culminating in death. The subconscious mind will kill or cure you according to how you think. That is why you cannot afford the luxury of a negative thought. It will bring you everything you do not want.

A demon is intense negative energy. This energy draws to us when we think negatively. Hate draws hate, anger draws anger, guilt draws guilt, fear draws fear, etc. These truly are killer forces and will work towards extinguishing your life in a variety of different ways: suicide, drug overdose, alcoholism, sexual abuse, and a myriad of other ways. A demon demonstrates various levels of intelligence and tries to destroy the possessed person.

We must realize that when we think in an incorrect manner, or when our mind is out of control because of lack of discipline or because we are just ignorant of how our thoughts create our reality, or when we choose to live in a state of denial—**we must pay a price—and that price is a miserable existence or no existence at all.**

Hypnotherapy is an excellent way to get your life back on track and balance. There is a lot to know and understand. Be prepared to love and feed your spiritual self for the rest of your life. We learn for our own souls growth. Expand your mind and awareness; move on to the High Road, for it beckons to you now. Remember, a journey of 1000 miles begins with a single step. Take that step NOW.

Past Life Regression Therapy (PLT)

Many people call me and want to be regressed back to previous lives to find out who they were in other lifetimes, just as a matter of recreational interest. I also get calls from people who are having great difficulty in this life with mental and/or physical problems that say they want to be regressed back to previous lives to resolve their present illness. Other people want me to reprogram their subconscious because someone regressed them back to previous lives but their problems are still with them and they think that reprogramming will complete their healing process. So, what is this Past Life Regression and what is happening?

Regression Therapy is a very powerful uncovering technique used in Hypnotherapy to find the initial and subsequent sensitizing events responsible for the present problems in a person's life. The past life problem is a negative forcing function in the subconscious of the afflicted one. In Regression Therapy, the therapist hypnotizes the client and then uses an affect bridge induction in which the client feels the difficulty he is experiencing and regresses back in time to the source of the feeling. Since the subconscious mind has permanent memory and stores everything that has ever happened to the client since he was first created in memory banks, the affect bridge induction takes him back to the part of the subconscious where that feeling was first created.

All the difficulties that any person experiences in this life are caused by things that happened either in this life, in past lives, unresolved internal conflicts, biological carryovers from our ancestors or from attached external energies. There is no other place where these difficulties can come from. In Direct Regression Therapy, a person can be directed to go back to a specific time or place in this life. For instance, if the person consciously recalls that a traumatic event happened at some particular time of this life, it might be wise to go back to that event and release the energy connected with it for healing. In Indirect Regression, the therapist simply asks the subconscious to go back to the source of the present life difficulty. In my practice, when I do this, the client goes back to a past life 75 percent of the time.

However, there is a problem with all Regression Therapy. If there is an attached external energy on the person, you cannot reach the Subconscious Self. If, for instance, there is an attached earthbound spirit of a person who has died and not gone to the light, the Regression takes place on the attached earthbound spirit and not on the client. All the psychotherapy in the world on an attached entity is not going to help the client. In order to do effective Regression Therapy on the client, whether for this life or a past life, he must be free of any attached external energy. Otherwise, the Regression is in vain and no benefit results.

I have found that the presence of an attached entity on the client is the principal reason why so much psychotherapy fails. It is imperative that any attached entities be removed before any therapy is begun. Actually, removal of the entity, if there is one, in many cases solves the client's presenting problem. In my practice, when the entity is released, the problem disappears, 70 percent of the time. If the entity brought the problem, when it is released, the entity takes the problem with it.

So many therapists will put a client into hypnosis and try to reprogram their Subconscious Self by embedding beneficial suggestions into the subconscious without knowing if the Self is accessible. If the client is not clear, the beneficial suggestions fall on a deaf subconscious ear and nothing changes. This is like throwing good grass seed onto a concrete driveway. It will not grow. In order to make it possible for that grass seed to take root and grow vigorously, it is necessary to first remove the concrete and prepare the soil. This is analogous to clearing the client's Subconscious Self before trying to embed beneficial suggestions into the subconscious and expect them to result in change.

Sometimes, if there is an entity on the person, and you remove it—the problem persists. This means that the entity did not bring the problem that the person is complaining about. However, the therapist can, at least, now find the source of the problem, because he has access to the Subconscious Self once the entity is removed. Here is where Regression Therapy is so valuable.

Because the Self is now accessible, Regression Therapy can be very healing. Moreover, if the source of the problem is, indeed, in a past life, it is now possible to access that past life and release the energy associated with the sensitizing events and the person can be cleared. Once cleared, reprogramming of the subconscious with beneficial suggestions that will produce positive change is possible and the person's life will be changed.

Therefore, whether for recreational or therapeutic purposes, you cannot do effective regression, including past life regression if there is any kind of foreign energy attached to the person. The effective therapist will always ascertain if the client is free of attachments before continuing therapy. Unfortunately, not many therapists are aware of spirit attachments or know how to deal with them—so, much therapy is unproductive since 90%—98% of people have attachments at some time in their lives.

Depression: What Can You Do?

It takes the joy out of life. It makes you feel rotten on a beautiful day. It colors with a gray pall everything you do. You say to yourself, "Is this it? Is this all there is?" Some men have it so bad, that when they shave in the morning, they have to consciously keep from cutting their throats. Women might say, "What happened to all of my dreams of love and sweetness and sharing, of the good times?" It's insidious. For some, it comes when they least expect it. For others, it's always there, but hidden until we are alone and have to think. Therefore, we avoid being alone or, at least alone with our thoughts, for we cannot bear them. "What happened to my dreams of glory and love? Is this all there is?"

"All I can say is that I'm not happy. My wife or husband doesn't look good to me anymore. What happened to them? She's fat—he doesn't care. Is it really she or he, or is it in you? Maybe if I build a wall around myself, I won't feel the pain, the anguish. Let him go his way—I'll go my way. It doesn't matter" But it does!! This is your life, this is your existence, and it has to matter. It's all you have for now. Thoreau said, "most men live lives of quiet desperation". But is this anyway to live?

Many therapists say that depression is anger that's been turned inside of you. Anger that's been stuffed. Anger that things didn't turn out the way you had dreamed, or anger from a rotten childhood of abuse and neglect and no love, or just anger that you are as you are rather than how you wanted you to be. Just anger!

Many wise men say that much disease, particularly cancer, comes from anger turned inside. Is this why cancer is so prevalent in our society today? If depression is, anger turned inside and cancer comes from anger turned inside, then maybe those who are depressed are in danger of cancer. It makes sense! Maybe this is Nature's way of ridding us of the unhappiness of depression by causing death.

Allopathic medicine chooses to treat depression with anti-depressants and this is good to a certain point. It relieves the symptoms of depression because these powerful agents have the ability to modify the brain chemistry that has been driven awry by the anger/depression negative forcing function that is causing the depression. I think that anger is a natural, primitive reaction to something that

209

has happened to you which is not to your liking. I believe that if you express that anger and release the energy associated with it that it simply was and now is gone. However, if you stuff that anger do not express it, it will show up in depression and from depression, comes all kinds of problems.

I am a Hypnotherapist and not a licensed professional like a medical doctor or clinical psychologist who can legally treat depression and so I do not. I treat the body's energy field and the mind, using Hypnotherapy. Why Hypnotherapy? Because Hypnosis is the only modality, that allows access to the subconscious mind and that is where the problems (The Negative Forcing Functions) are. The problems are not in the conscious mind—you can talk to the conscious mind until you are blue in the face and the problems will persist. You must enter the sacred realm of the subconscious to find the problem, and release it. Once released, the subconscious computer can be reprogrammed so that the new program opposes the old programs caused by the Negative Forcing Functions.

Once the new program is imbedded into the subconscious mind, change results…for the subconscious is a bio-computer and it must operate on the programs, which are in it,…it has no choice. However, you cannot reprogram the subconscious bio-computer if there are still Negative Forcing Functions within it. Trying to reprogram a subconscious that is not clear is like throwing good grass seed onto the concrete driveway—it will not grow. You must first clear it by removing the concrete and preparing the soil for the seed. Once you do that, the seeds will grow. It is the same with the subconscious.

These Forcing Functions come from bad things that have happened to us in this life, from previous lives, unresolved internal conflicts, genetics or from attached external energies. There is no other place they can come from. If there are external energies on the person, then they must first be removed before any work can be done on the self for this life, or a past life because access to the self is blocked until the external energies are removed. Often, the external energy has brought the Negative Forcing Function and when it is removed, the problem disappears—for if the energy brought the problem—when it leaves, it takes the problem with it. If the external energy did not bring the problem, at least now, with the external energy released, access to the self is possible and uncovering and releasing the Self Negative Forcing Functions can now be accomplished.

Uncovering the cause of the anger and depression and releasing it is the only sure way to resolve the problems of despair and unhappiness. Anti-depressants only help, they do not solve the underlying problem cause, for it is in our subconscious mind. An old comic strip called Pogo, created by a genius named Walt

Kelly once said, "We have met the enemy—and he is us". We have to find the enemy and get rid of him to be happy.

Daniel's Sadness

Daniel, 31 yrs old, came to see me because of intense persistent sadness that was so severe that he found it very difficult to keep from committing suicide. He had been under the care of a psychiatrist for several years and was on anti depressants. Although the sadness was ameliorated somewhat, it was still severe enough that he could not work. He was married, without children and his wife was supporting them.

I do not treat depression or any other physical or mental condition because I am not a licensed professional and am prohibited by law from doing so, but I agreed to try to help him by correcting his energy. Negative Forcing Functions (NFF) in the subconscious mind cause blocks to form in a persons Chi Meridians restricting the flow of Chi energy through the body. When this energy flow is restricted, we can feel dysfunctional physically, mentally, emotionally and spiritually. The NFF's are caused by bad things that happen to us in this life, past lives, unresolved internal conflicts, biological carryovers from our ancestors or from external entity attachments. To get at and release the internal NFF's, all entity attachments must first be removed because they form a barrier to reaching the rest of the Subconscious Self.

On questioning, Daniel revealed that his previous girlfriend, Marsha, with whom he had a long relationship before marrying his wife, was still on his mind a great deal. When he sees her, he feels good, but on leaving her, his sadness becomes almost unbearable and he has thoughts of suicide. Actually, whenever he is close to her energy field he feels good and when leaving it feels badly.

I removed two layers of demons from Daniel, which were drawn to him by his great sadness, and he felt somewhat better, but the sadness persisted and the suicide thoughts remained strong. Going further, I found a past life when Daniel was a physician who committed suicide because he could not save his wife, Arlene whom he loved dearly. He felt that he had neglected Arlene for his patients and the guilt caused his suicide. That energy carried over to this life. Arlene in that life was Marsha in this life. Releasing that past life's energy of guilt and reframing the whole situation freed Daniel from that past life state and he lost his sadness and desire to kill himself.

Without getting the demons off Daniel, past life regression therapy would have been useless, because I would have been regressing the attached entities and not Daniel. By opening up clear access to Daniel's subconscious by releasing the demons, I was able to do substantial and effective therapy and solve his problem.

Lorrie's Dilemma

Lorrie, 40, was successful, beautiful, intelligent, single and a cancer survivor. The cancer struck her in her early twenties and chemotherapy put it into remission. She had a great job, made lots of money and to look at her, you would never believe she lived in terror. She lived in fear that the cancer would reoccur and she had incessant daily panic attacks, which made her life wretched. In addition, she wanted to get married and have children, but found herself attracted to men who were not the marrying kind or who were already married. She asked me to help her.

She had been having panic attacks since her early teens, so they were not from the cancer fear. She came from a family of highly intelligent but emotionally ill people, who could not show love and spent their time carping at one another so she was very unhappy and hated her family.

She exhibited a badly suppressed aura indicating strong blockages to Chi energy flow through her body. This is caused by negative forcing functions in the subconscious mind. I figured that her problems with men might be due to her early family life, but I couldn't do regression therapy on her to release that negative energy, because I suspected she had entities on her and it is impossible to do effective regression work until all entities are released. Entities block access to the person's own past Self so any regression on a person with entities is useless. Hypno-Kinesiology also indicated entity presence as did ideo-motor response diagnostics.

She had eight layers of demons on her, all drawn by the misery of her early life. They said they were partly responsible for her cancer and panic attacks. She also had a Soul Mind Fragment (SMF) of her mother on her, who had panic attacks and died of cancer. Once I released the eight demon layers and her mother's SMF, the panic attacks totally ceased. Now, I could get to her Subconscious Self, liberate her from the early family trauma, and positively reframe the past using regression therapy.

In regression, many traumatic events from her early family life were freed from her subconscious. Slowly, building on each release and positively reframing each event, we constructed a different past that freed her from the agony of her early

214

life. Using Parts Therapy, I was able to resolve the internal conflict, which caused her attraction to men who wouldn't give her a family. This conflict protected her from ever having a family, which she related as misery because of her own miserable family history. Last, I heard, she was dating an eligible man and her prospects look good. Her fear of reoccurring cancer is also much reduced and the panic attacks never came back.

Affirmations: Why They Don't Work!

Many people try using affirmations to change their lives. Louise Hays has affirmations for all kinds of conditions. Maxwell Maltz in Psycho-Cybernetics speaks about the power of affirmations to radically alter your life. Other authors keep hammering that all you have to do to change is to keep repeating positive phrases and your life becomes better. All these people are sincere, their affirmations are well written, and we do them and they don't work. Why?

I wondered about this in my own life when I tried using affirmations assiduously and nothing happened. Was it only me, or do others have the same problem? From the people I've talked with, most of us do. Why? I didn't find the answer until I was well into my Hypnotherapy training and practice. Unless you are clear of the forcing functions in your subconscious mind that are causing the difficulties you are trying to correct, affirmation fall on a deaf subconscious ear.

Behavior and responses to life are changed by positive reprogramming (affirmations). Positive reprogramming of the subconscious to change a person is nothing more than repeating affirmations. No matter how many times an affirmation is repeated, even under hypnosis when the subconscious is very receptive, it is of little or no avail in the long term if the person is not clear. In addition, to make matters worse, you cannot even reach the Self to clear it if an entity is attached to the person.

Virtually all illnesses, mental and physical, originate in the subconscious. Negative subconscious programming from forcing functions (traumas) cause the body's life force energy (Chi) to block up, depriving the body's cells of this energy. This blockage, over time, results in dysfunction. By moving the conscious mind aside with hypnosis, the subconscious mind can be communicated with directly and the forcing functions identified and released. The negative programs can then be replaced with positive programs, thereby permanently removing the energy blocks and restoring health.

The energy blocks result from problem issues in this life, a past life, an internal conflict, or a genetic carry-over or from the attachment of foreign energies, as in

Spirit Possession. If a spirit is attached to a person, no therapy will be successful until that energy is removed. An earthbound spirit brings with it the energy of its life and death. The energy of any illness or addiction the spirit had is brought to the attached one. When the spirit leaves, whatever came with it also leaves. This may explain why so many people cannot resolve long standing illnesses and problems like excessive weight, smoking, alcohol, drugs, stress, etc. no matter how hard they try or how many wonderful affirmations they say. The problem may belong to the attached energy and not to the person.

Once all entities are removed, the Self may be reached and dealt with using Regression Therapy, including Past Life Regression, Parts Therapy, or Gestalt Therapy. Once all traumas are removed, the subconscious can be effectively reprogrammed and the released difficulties will no longer reoccur. Now affirmations (reprogramming) will work because the subconscious is clear and you can reach it.

Gerry Kein of Deland, FL, one of my excellent teachers puts it this way "The subconscious mind is awesomely powerful. It can make you into anything you would like to be. Rich and famous, thin, happy or sad. **It is the real us.** The subconscious mind is like a computer and it operates just like one. When you buy a computer, it's worthless until it's programmed. A computer can only operate on the programming placed in it. If you change the programming, it no longer operates on the old program. It must operate on the new program. This is how our subconscious mind works. It's a computer. It functions just like an electronic one, only it's much more powerful. We program our computer through our present and past life experiences. When we were created, our computers were unprogrammed. Everyday, through every life, we add programming to our internal computer. The primary rule of our computer is this. It must make us into the type of person that it perceives us to be based on all the programming it's received."

Remember that affirmations are just reprogramming of the software in your internal computer. If you can't get to the software because of an attached entity or unresolved traumas in the subconscious self, you can't do any reprogramming. Once you are clear, you can reprogram and IT MUST HAPPEN. You are changing programming, and your inner mind must respond to its new program so marvelous changes can occur in your life.

Hypnotherapy and Pain

A person in intractable pain who can't take pain medication is in a lot of trouble. What about the person who just doesn't like to take pain medication or the prospective mother who would like to eliminate or at least cut down on medication for herself or her baby's sake. The subject of Hypnotic Pain Control was featured at the 15th Annual International Conference of the National Board of Hypnotherapy and Hypnotic Anesthesiology which took place in Phoenix AZ, May 12—16, 1999. About 350 health-care professionals interested in complementary medicine attended the conference. Medical doctors, psychiatrists, clinical psychologists, registered nurses, and Hypnotherapists attended.

Hypnotherapy is a frequently recommended treatment for chronic pain. The National Institute of Health has strong evidence to show that hypnosis is very beneficial in the management of cancer pain, TM J. disorders, tension headaches, and irritable bowel syndrome, amongst many other painful conditions. Relaxation techniques are shown to be very useful for reducing chronic pain. Chronic pain affects over 34 million Americans. Most are significantly disabled by, and some are permanently disabled. Over $40 billion is spent annually on treatments and over 25% of all sick days are from pain. Pain patients may experience an increase in stress, metabolic rate, blood clotting, and water retention. They can have delayed healing, hormonal imbalances, impaired immune systems, mobility difficulties, and loss of appetite, sleep disturbances, low self-esteem, and depression.

I was one of the featured speakers at this conference and spoke on the subject of Energy, Entities, and Hypnotherapy. Most of the papers discussed reducing pain by relieving the anxiety, tension, and fear associated with pain for childbirth, dentistry, surgical anesthesia and pain management. There were several papers, which spoke of techniques that are more esoteric for relieving pain, and I will describe them below:

Energy, Entities, and Hypnotherapy—Charles Wm. Skillas, PhD. This talk focused on the Eastern Energy Model of Disease that says all physical and mental dysfunction are caused by life force deprivation to the cell communities of the body. The life force is prevented from reaching the cells by blocks, which form in the body's energy channels. Negative Forcing Functions in the subconscious mind causes these blocks. The forcing functions occur because of traumatic episodes in this life, a past life or from an external energy attachment. Using hypnotherapy, the forcing function can be found and released—the blocks disappear, life force energy flow is restored, pain subsides and health ensues. If an external energy is attached, it must first be removed before any productive long-lasting work can be done on the self.

Soul Reintegration—Walter Stock, Ph.D. For untold centuries, shamans have utilized altered states of consciousness to achieve knowledge and healing for themselves and others. As shamans view the universe, each time we undergo a trauma, a portion of the soul detaches and becomes lost and frozen in time. The traditional shaman retrieves and integrates the soul fragments. The shaman undertakes a journey on the client's behalf, traveling through non-ordinary reality to the Upper or Lower Worlds in search of the missing parts. This is often done while the shaman remains in physical contact with the client while listening to the beat of a drum. The shaman would then blow the retrieved soul part back into the client, most often through the crown or heart Chakra. This produced alleviation of pain and healing.

Body/Mind Healing—James R. Raimy, Ph.D. We must realize that we are all mortal beings and will die sometime, regardless of the efforts of any practitioner or medicine. However, it is comforting to know that if we work with our mind and body, we can effect change, which will promote rapid healing and alleviation of pain because our body was not meant to remain sick or injured. Also, the physician doesn't heal anyone; the physician merely stabilizes the body or mind in a crisis, allowing the body or mind to heal itself. The body is born with the blueprint for restoring and repairing itself. Each cell of our body contains the DNA imprint, coding and intelligence needed to function properly, and also contains the instructions for whatever repairs need to be made. Hypnosis is the pathway to healing because it allows the Hypnotherapist to directly access the subconscious mind and command the cells to restore and regenerate to their original blueprint and proper coding and perfect cellular functioning reoccurs causing alleviation of pain and healing. Cell Command Therapy, developed by E. Martin, Ph.D. of Houston TX, is based on this premise and Dr. Skillas practices this therapy.

Soul-Mind Fragmentation
Its Effect on Human Behavior

Whenever we experience a shattering trauma, the human mind uses a survival coping mechanism called disassociation to maintain sanity. This mechanism, however, has a downside—that of producing fragmentation of the soul-mind.

The soul-mind is the mechanism, which records the sum total of our experiences through all incarnations, forming our physical bodies and lifestyles from these recordings. It's also called the memory bank and is a permanent intellect or consciousness, which composes a person's character or individuality and never dies. It may be synonymous with the subconscious mind, a sort of ethereal bio computer incapable of discernment or decision-making, but recording the concepts, suggestions, ideas, and emotional evaluations of the conscious mind.

When fragmentation occurs, a sub-personality is formed containing the energy of the disassociation. It is then submerged into the subconscious where the energy continues to affect the person but is unknown to the conscious mind. An extreme example of this fragmentation is Multiple Personality Disorder, which is usually a product of severe childhood sexual abuse.

The sub-personality is the so-called inner child, adolescent or adult, depending on the ages at which fragmentation happens. Children fragment more often than adults because they don't have the adult's coping skills. These fragmented parts have all the feelings, emotions and memories of the trauma even if it happened many years ago, as if they were frozen in time. For example, if an inner child is formed at age 6, that child will still have the same fear energy causing it's creation and will be at the same age (6).

The soul fragment can go to another living human being, such as a family member or friend, a loved one as part of mutual soul sharing, through physical and sexual abuse, or the desire of one person wishing to take another's pain. Casting spells and curses during Black Magic or witchcraft can cause the practitioners soul to fragment. The fragment then attaches to the victim. Usually when this happens demon entities are attached to those soul parts giving power to the curse or spell. In a curse, you will a piece of your soul to go to a person you are angry at, and the curse becomes operational.

If a soul-mind fragment goes onto another, that person will experience the trauma energy that caused the fragmentation. Likewise, the person who lost the fragment receives the attached person's negative energy through the mystical silver cord connecting them. The silver cord always connects the soul-mind fragment to its origin and effectively serves as a full-duplex data transmission link.

Clients who have departed soul-mind fragments report seeing the silver cord leading out from their etheric body under hypnosis, even when they have no conscious knowledge of the cord. Likewise, a person may be attached by another's soul-mind fragment and experience that person's disassociative trauma energy. The person who owns the fragment now receives the negative energy of the one to whom his fragment has attached.

Treating soul-mind fragmentation requires the therapist to discern that there is a sub-personality and then integrate it back into the person's personality. If the fragment has left the person and gone to another, the fragment must be retrieved and re-integrated as shamans do. Soul retrieval is a shamanic approach to healing. In the native tradition of shamanism, illness indicated that a part of the soul had vacated the body. Shamans journeyed into the underworld to retrieve the soul-part and return it to the sick person, restoring health.

If the fragment is from another, then the therapist must treat the fragment as an entity attachment and return it to its original owner. In treating people for the symptoms of Spirit attachment, it is not unusual to find a mind fragment of both living and dead people as an attached entity.

The trauma causing the fragmentation must be processed before the fragment rejoins the main body of the soul. The small fragmented portion of the soul is usually so badly damaged that it cannot be returned to the main body of the soul unprocessed, because it contains all the memories and feelings of the traumatic event. The small fragment of the soul was sacrificially isolated to protect the main body of the soul.

It is very important that every soul part be returned to the main body of the soul for the emotional, mental and physical health of the client. Recalling, reliving and releasing the trauma and resolving the conflict using hypnotherapy processes the trauma.

Freeing the Captives: The Emerging Therapy of Treating Spirit Attachment
By Louise Ireland-Frey, MD

Review for the Aquarius Magazine
By Charles Wm. Skillas, PhD

I do not know of any other book on Sprit Depossession written by a medical doctor, and that is why I looked forward to reviewing this book when asked by the Aquarius Magazine. The ancient concept of Spirit Possession is largely ignored in our modern scientifically oriented society and particularly by the allopathic medical profession.

Dr. Ireland—Frey, MD holds a degree in medicine from Tulane University and became a Hypnotherapist at age 67 in 1978 after being healed by Hypnotherapy. It was while using Hypnotherapy on a patient that she was confronted with the problem of spirit possession and began to take this kind of therapy seriously. She saw the therapy's power and began to develop her own techniques of using it. This book illustrates how she goes about the process and the results she obtains.

She regards the invading entities as suffering captives needing to be freed from the prison they created for themselves within the host. By doing so, she rescues the entities and relieves the host of what the entities brought with them. She describes what conditions make such invasions possible and what can be done to prevent obsession or possession and how to get rid of the attachments. She discusses the type of entities she encounters and her methods of Releasement featuring Remote Releasement. Her book gives details on how to handle haunts and ghosts, poltergeists, wanderers and Demonics. She also advises about how to obtain assistance from Bright Discarnate Beings for protection and council during the Depossession Process. Much of the book is devoted to case studies in which she summarizes the exorcisms.

I know a number of the Spirit Releasement Therapists she quotes in her book, having been taught by some of them. Notably, Dr. William Baldwin, PhD; Dr. Edith Fiore, PhD; and Dr. Irene Hickman, DO. Curiously, my other two teachers, Dr. Fred Leideker and Dr. Carl Carpenter, whom I regard as in the forefront of this therapy, are not mentioned either in the text or in the bibliography. The bibliography does, however, include noted people like: Ruth Montgomery (*Strangers Among Us*), Dr. Carl Wickland (*Thirty Years Among The Dead*), Roger Woolger (*Other Lives, Other Selves*) and Betty Eadie (*Embraced By The Light*), to mention a few.

The book is easy to read, but with all of the exorcism examples she gives, it is sometimes difficult to keep the entities separated in your mind. For those who have no background in Spirit Releasement Therapy, this book provides a wealth of information on the general subject. Even experienced practitioners will find a number of novel and interesting approaches. However, as an experienced practitioner, I have a problem in three areas of her technique. These are: Most Releasements are done remotely; She does no re-programming of the Subconscious after the release; and she depends greatly on the ideo motor finger response.

Remote Releasement: Even though Remote Releasement of entities is effective, I have not found it to be as powerful as having the afflicted host present for the release. I only use Remote Releasement when the afflicted host is far away and cannot be present, or when the host is a child. Because children are so easily fragmented, I use a surrogate for Remote Releasement to prevent the child from having to go through the experience, as it can get very scary if you are dealing with a strong Demonic.

Re-Programming of the Subconscious Mind: Because the attached entity is a Forcing Function in the Subconscious Mind and by being such, creates a program in the Subconscious Mind affecting the host's behavior, it is necessary to reprogram the Subconscious Mind once all the Forcing Functions are cleared. If the old programs, which created the aberrant behavior, are not countered, the old programs still operate and the behavior does not change even though the energy is different now that the entity is gone.

Ideo-Motor Finger Response: Dr. Ireland-Frey seems to totally depend upon the subconscious control of the fingers to ascertain if there are entities in the person—how many and what kind. I use the ideo-motor finger response after I have gotten the entities released, but find that if there are Demonics present that the finger response can be wrong.

The reason is that Demonics usually lie and since they can manipulate subconscious control of the fingers, you cannot trust them to say that there are no entities on the person when there may be. If the finger response says, "Yes there are entities", you can pretty much believe it. However, if it says, "No, there are none" you cannot be sure. I depend more upon the suppression of the aura and Hypno-Kinesiology muscle testing to indicate entity presence. Actually, though, I am never sure that an entity is present until I actually hear it speak to me through the host under deep trance hypnosis.

Terrorism: Evil Masquerading As Faith

Our world was shattered when Islamic suicide bombers flew hijacked planes into the Twin Towers, Pentagon and a Pennsylvania field on Sept. 11. Reaction for most was shock, fear and then terrible anger. I know that's how I felt and I still feel it somewhat, especially anger. It has helped that we have driven the Taliban out of power in Afghanistan and we wait for Osama bin Laden's capture. However, the problem of terrorism will not end with his death, or the death of all al-Qaeda terrorists. For the problem is as old as the planet. It is called evil.

Evil is not confined to Islam any more than it is to Christianity, Buddhism, Judaism, Hinduism, Shintoism or any other religion. During WW2, we called the Japanese Shintoists evil and the German Christians evil. We couldn't understand how German Christians could commit the atrocities they did and how Japanese Shinto Kamikaze pilots could fly their planes into Allied ships. All religions, including Islam, teach love and peace and yet men are able to distort the teachings to accomplish evil things. What is happening? Why do men do, in the name of religion, what religion forbids? The answer is again, evil.

Evil is personified as Satan or demons in much of the world. Evil wants to destroy, to cause pain, anguish, suffering and put out the Light of love that is in the heart of every person, for we are all born of love no matter what the circumstances. Each person has within them the Spark of God's love that created them and this is the most powerful force there is. And, because this force within is so potent, it can make men do anything. Men who are already possessed by demons are dedicated to the Light's destruction, and they know that this force within us, if harnessed to their purpose, can make people do anything. So, they distort the love energy to hate, instill fanaticism and use it to control men to do evil in the name of religion.

It is easy to do this. If you can get men to hate, their psychic defense system goes down and they become extremely vulnerable to attachment by demonic energy. Once attached to people, it can and will destroy them because it hides their internal Light. By disguising hate as defending their religion, evil men can get other men to hate and then demonic energies can attach and it's all downhill from there.

How do I know this? Every day, under deep trance hypnosis, I talk to demonic energies within suffering people and the demons tell me their purpose, which is destruction. If I can get them to leave, the person is saved, if not, they are destroyed. Thank God, I am mostly successful.

Weight Loss

It seems like most people want to lose weight. It has become the passion of our time that you can't be either too slim nor too rich, regardless of the fact that some people genetically are heavier and not everyone can or wants to be rich. This article is not about money—it is about weight loss.

If you are a stevedore on the docks and haul heavy weights around all day or an athlete doing strong physical effort, you require more food than someone who sits at a desk. Some people also have medical problems like low metabolism, thyroid dysfunctions, etc. that cause weight problems, but most people are heavier than they should be because they eat more than their body requires for it's energy needs. Why do they do this?

People eat and drink more than they physically require because of subconscious needs. These needs come from subconscious negative forcing functions caused by bad things that have happened to them in this life, a past life, from unresolved internal conflicts, from biological carryovers from their ancestors or from attached foreign energies.

The only way to find the underlying cause of these needs is to go where they are and that is into the subconscious mind and the only way into the subconscious is through hypnosis. The reason why so many hypnosis weight loss programs fail is that it is virtually impossible to access the person's own subconscious if there are foreign energies present. Foreign energy attachments are a barrier to reaching the subconscious. They must first be removed and then you can get at the other forcing functions to release their energy, which is reinforcing the negative programs in their subconscious hard drive causing them to eat or drink excessively.

Sometimes an attached energy (entity) is of someone who ate or drank too much because of his or her own needs. In this case, their need energy is imposed on you and you begin to eat to assuage the entity's need. Sometimes the entity is attracted to you because you are sad or fearful and the entity is sad or fearful (like attracts like). You may have your own need for excessive food or drink because you are lonely or sad and eating/drinking are palliatives. In this case, you must get rid of the attachment first or you cannot get to your own subconscious negative forcing functions causing your need.

Once you clear access to the subconscious by removing entities, it is then possible to find and release the energy of your own forcing functions causing your need to overeat or drink. Once this energy is released, your subconscious hard drive can be effectively reprogrammed changing your consumption behavior positively and permanently.

Anxiety & Stress

Anxiety is normal when you are confronted with an uncertain situation. The uncertainty causes stress and stress is a normal part of daily life. Stress is actually the fuel our minds need to function. Many people come to me complaining of being constantly anxious without any obvious cause. In many cases, they are taking anti anxiety medications and some of them suffer from side effects. Medical Doctors and Psychiatrists prescribe these medications to help anxiety sufferers get through stressful situations, but many end up taking the drugs on a long-term basis because the anxiety is always there. Using hypnotherapy, I help people find and eliminate their anxiety sources so there is no need to continue taking medication forever.

"Bad things" that have happened to us in this life, in a past life, unresolved internal conflicts, biological carryovers from our ancestors, and attached foreign energies cause long-term anxiety without apparent cause. These "bad things" form energy sources called Negative Forcing Functions (NFF) and they reside in the subconscious mind. Under hypnosis, it is possible to enter the "sacred realm" of the subconscious, find the energy sources causing the anxiety, and release them.

NFF's actually do two things to us. They distort the body's energy field so that the flow of life force (Chi, Prana) is blocked and they also install and continuously reinforce negative programs in our subconscious computer's hard drive. The integration of all these hard drive programs determine how we feel and how we behave. You cannot simply reprogram the subconscious and expect respite without first releasing the internal negative energy source supporting the negative programs manifesting your anxiety.

An example: Fragmentation is a disassociate survival coping mechanism of the mind that protects sanity. Children tend to fragment easily under stressful situations like fear. The fragment, sometimes called an "ego state" is frozen in time at the fragmentation age and submerged into the subconscious. The conscious mind is not aware of the fragment, but the energy affects the person throughout his life. He still responds to the fear and feels anxious even though there is no apparent cause for fear in his life now. The "inner child" fragment is still afraid and the fear energy of the child is still affecting the grown man. Under hypnosis the fragment can be found and its energy released so it no longer can affect feeling and behavior and, with new programming, the anxiety response is gone.

Similar appropriate release techniques can be employed to eliminate other negative energy sources and release anxiety. The only caveat is that if there is an attached entity, it must first be released or else you cannot effectively find the internal negative energy source. In many cases, the entity itself is the anxiety source and its removal releases the anxiety.

To Be Alone...It's Okay!

Some men and many women come to me complaining of being depressed and lonely as their lives are empty, because they have no "significant other" to share it with. They believe their happiness depends on someone else sharing their lives and if only this "wonderful" someone was with them, they would be "fulfilled and happy".

Of course, this is not true. Our happiness never depends on others. This dependency feeling reflects our security needs. Within the need for security is the fear of poverty, of old age, of ill health, of criticism, and the fear of death. So, loneliness depression is really related to security. In hypnosis, we can strengthen the ego by reprogramming the subconscious, but it doesn't work well unless the person is clear of all Negative Forcing Functions (Subconscious Negative Energy Sources) because the old dependency programs are constantly energized by the Sources and new independence programs are overridden.

I recently had a case involving a very depressed young woman of 40 who wanted to die because she couldn't find a man to share her life. I released the Negative Sources in her including entities, present and past life issues, and internal conflicts and then tried ego strength reprogramming, with some success. She greatly improved on the issues stemming from her released Negative Sources, but she was still unhappy being alone.

Because she was now clear, I was able to get her High Self to provide visions of previous lifetimes that affected her loneliness issue. In one past life, she lived happily in Mediterranean Crete. Her father married her off to a Northern Lord, requiring her to move to a cold country where the people were unfriendly and her husband mostly ignored her. She was unhappy. After he died, she moved back to beautiful Crete and was happy for the rest of her life living among friendly people, developing many friends and engaging in intellectual stimulation and work. In a 2nd past life, she was the daughter of a tyrant who treated both she and her mother with contempt and cruelty. She finally married to get away from her father, only to find her husband was like him. He finally died and she moved to a pleasant climate with friendly people and developed relationships and work, which made her happy.

These wise visions provided by her High Self clicked within causing her to understand that just being married didn't bring happiness. Actually, here it caused unhappiness. Her happiness came by taking charge of her life, living where she liked and engaging in satisfying relationships and work. This deep perception changed her life and she is now happy with just herself.

How It All Works, In a Nutshell

Many people have asked me to succinctly tell them how hypnotherapy with spirit releasement works to heal them. I get this request from both clients who are contemplating seeing me and from those who have already benefited from the therapy. Here it is.

Most of us do not realize that our mental, emotional and physical health depends on the flow of life force energy (Chi) through our bodies and if it is blocked, we have problems. The more severe and long-lived the blocks, the worse the problems become. The blocks are caused by "bad things" that happened to us in this life, past lives, unresolved internal conflicts, genetic carryovers from our ancestors and from foreign energy attachments. These "bad things" produce negative energies in our subconscious mind called Negative Forcing Functions.

These Negative Forcing Functions do two things: they block the flow of Chi through your body and they install negative programs onto your subconscious computer's "hard drive" and then **constantly reinforce them.** The programs on your "hard drive" determine how you behave and feel. To change how you behave and feel requires that the programs be changed. This can only be done effectively by first eliminating the negative energy that is reinforcing your bad programs and then positively reprogramming your subconscious hard drive. Then change happens and it is permanent.

The only way to find and release the negative energies and reprogram your subconscious hard drive is with hypnosis because it is the only way to directly access the subconscious mind. If there are any foreign energies on you (entity attachments), they must first be removed before any other work is done because entity attachments block access to the internal subconscious. Sometimes, just releasing the entities brings remarkable change, because if the entities brought problems, when they leave, they take their problems with them. Usually, however, the entities were attracted by your problems and just add to them. Your problems are what caused your "Guardian Chi" which is your protective psychic defense to be down and that's how the entities were drawn to you and were able to get onto you.

So, if you feel bad, mentally emotionally or physically, try to get to the source of your problems and get rid of them rather than just continually "band aid", and struggle with life. Most western medicine is allopathic in that symptoms are treated with medicines so that we don't feel the symptoms anymore. This is of great help, but eliminating the source of the symptoms is better I think. Remember that the symptoms—pain, fatigue, anxiety, depression, addiction, and feelings of worthlessness, hopelessness—are just the symptoms, not the cause.

Want to Live Well? Then Get Yourself Fixed!

If you feel rotten in mind or body, you need to get fixed. Your will to physically live or die exists at the root of your Subconscious Mind. Life or death is directly tied to your Subconscious Mind's fundamental need to create. If this need is frustrated, the Subconscious will kill the body. The will to live pushes the Subconscious to heal the physical body when it is injured or sick, but it does this only because it wants to continue to express its creative ability. If this expression is thwarted, then the will to live becomes the will to die. If this happens, the Subconscious may aggressively destroy the body through accident-proneness or by refusing to support the body against invading pathogens by turning off or attacking the immune system.

Subconscious Mind safeguards our physical life. It generates hunger pangs if food is required and exhibits preferences for the foods we need. In its protective role, it alerts us to survival threats—or it can engender an environment favorable to illness and injury. Unless we have a strong desire to live, it will not try hard to keep us well. Unless we are positive about life, Subconscious Mind will not provide the energy to attain our goals. Subconscious Mind directly mirrors our will to live. If you hate life or are continuously unhappy, subconscious mind will see to it that you don't have to live very long. If you have no positive dreams for your life, that is tantamount to rejecting life and you will die. Subconscious Mind won't keep you around if you really don't want to be here.

Subconscious Mind controls our physical body, but we can influence it. Consciously, we can command it to provide the energy we need to accomplish goals or to heal us if we are clear. Both of these commands require that we be passionate about life. The Subconscious is crazy about passion. With passion, you can get it to do almost anything. Without passion, no matter how much you might want something—forget it. You won't get it. To be passionate about life, you must feel good. To feel good, you must be clear.

Only our Subconscious Mind can heal us. There is no medicine, person or thing outside of us that does this. Through Subconscious Mind using Hypnotherapy, we can heal by clearing Subconscious Negative Forcing Functions and reprogramming positively. Entity attachments (one of the Negative Forcing Functions) must first be released and then the rest of the Subconscious can be cleared and reprogrammed for life instead of death. Then you feel good instead of rotten and live long and happily.

Demons: They Want to Destroy You

In my practice, I find many demons when doing Spirit releasement Therapy (SRT) on troubled clients. Demons are Dark Force Energies (DFE's) that seek your destruction because they want to eliminate your light. They are attracted more to people with positive energy and that's why they want to get rid of you. I have literally dealt with thousands of demons and they all invariably have the same objective—to destroy you.

Demons can attach to you when your psychic defense system is down which occurs when you are under great stress like from sadness, fear, despair, rage, overwork fatigue, etc. Their destruction methods range from exacerbating deeply embedded negative emotions you already have in your subconscious, to bringing into you earthbound spirits of deceased people who had terrible physical or mental/emotional problems in their lives.

Often, I find that demons will bring in earthbound spirits to do their dirty work, because when they do, the energy of the spirit's death and the negative stuff from their lives are both brought to the attached client. Since most earthbound spirits die violently or in great pain, the massive fear energies of their deaths as well as other bad stuff from their lives really wreck havoc with the client. All the depression, fear, and other misery energies are glued to the suffering client's subconscious as well as the physical propensity for the ailments that the deceased person had. Earthbound spirits don't actually bring the diseases they had…but bring the disease's energies with them.

This is particularly bad if the earthbound spirit is genetically linked to the client. For instance, if there is a genetic cancer link, the cancer energy of the spirit is added to the client's inherited predisposition for the disease. If someone in the family history had breast cancer, the cancer energy can often trigger the disease in the attached client. Since the attachment is a Negative Forcing Function, it continuously reinforces the disease energy in the client and installs and supports the negative program of breast cancer on the client's subconscious hard drive and the probability of that person getting breast cancer is worsened. This also happens with other disorders, mental and emotional as well as physical. I have seen this many times, not only with cancer, but with alcoholism, severe depression, obesity, heart disease, diabetes and a host of other conditions.

The client's own life may have caused its problems, but if you have to fight an uphill battle against extra odds, your chances of losing are greater. So, if you have problems, make sure you have the best chance of winning by ridding yourself of extraneous negative energies and give yourself a break.

Energy Therapies and Negative Forcing Functions

Energy therapies can relieve emotional distress for a time and I have used them over the years. The problem with these therapies is that they simply relieve the symptoms...like taking Prozac to relieve depression, when the underlying sadness source is buried in the subconscious. This source is always from one or more of the Subconscious Negative Forcing Function Energy Generators caused by bad things that have happened to you in this life, past lives, unresolved internal conflicts, biological carry-overs from ancestors or attached entities.

Thought Field Therapy (TFT) and The Emotional Freedom Technique (EFT) are examples of excellent energy therapies. Roger Callahan, PhD discovered and developed TFT and Gary Craig modified it to EFT. It's quick...especially for anxiety and phobias because it works directly with the energy causing these. It can relieve phobias in minutes rather than in months. The relief rate is reputed at 85-90%. No faith or confidence is required for success.

A phobia is a persistent irrational fear and there are many phobias. Some are very powerful, like Agoraphobia (fear of open spaces), and can dominate a person's life. People with severe Agoraphobia live lives of desperation and are often afraid even to venture to the corner store.

We have a complex electro-chemical system that creates an electromagnetic field called the aura around our body when energy flows through it. Negative Forcing Functions distort and unbalance the body's energy field blocking energy flow. Thought Field Therapy opens these blocks by balancing various body acupuncture points and actuating both hemispheres of the brain. This is done by having the client look to the left and right, rotate the bead alternately in two different directions, hum a tune and count out loud in a systematic pattern coupled with tapping acupuncture points, while holding the phobic feeling in the mind. The therapist must first correct any psychological energy reversal situation.

The client must also rebalance at home because the energy can flip out of balance. With each rebalance the energy field becomes more stable. You have eliminated the symptoms...but the causes are still there constantly reinforcing negative programs in the subconscious. You still have to find and eliminate the initial causes of the problems or new symptoms will develop. You really have not solved the problem, but only displaced it, like pushing on Jell-O...it pops up some other place.

The initial causes are the "bad things" that produced the Negative Forcing Functions in the subconscious. These negative energy generators must be found and released so they no longer screw up the body's energy field and stop supporting their negative programs in the subconscious. Then you reprogram and get permanent healing.

Prisons of the Mind!

How tragic it is that those who so much need what Hypnotherapy can give are so locked into their prisons of thought that they suffer needlessly without hope and then ultimately die thinking that life is so miserable, so unfair. The cages we build around ourselves to protect us from what might appear to challenge our beliefs are so formidable that there is no way out of them or into them. The public media that most people are exposed to speak little of what Hypnotherapy can do and when it does, it is mostly derision. Those who have no metaphysical bent, locked up into the materialistic scientific fabric of our society or so insulated by their religious beliefs, never take the opportunity to explore the wonders of the real world that God created. The world of the mind and how a cleared mind and new beliefs can change lives.

I write about the great healing power of Hypnotherapy which, when coupled with Spirit Releasement Therapy (SRT), changes peoples lives from misery and despair into lives of hope and accomplishment. But who gets to read it? The answer is: mostly only those who already know about it. The "preaching to the choir" syndrome. The other 90% out there who need this work never hear about it or if they do, are afraid to explore it for fear of ridicule or even religious condemnation. And, so they only do what is "acceptable" to save themselves and when it doesn't work they continue being wretched until they die.

I continually see people who have suffered a lifetime of misery and help them by releasing them from their mind's imprisonment. People, who have been in traditional therapy for twenty years without much relief, consistently get better in twenty hours of hypnotherapy with spirit releasement. Why is this so? It is because any spirit attachment forms an almost impenetrable barrier to reaching the subconscious self and that's where the problem sources are. Moreover, an earthbound spirit brings its death energy and negative life energy to exacerbate or ignite problems in the one attached. In addition, if there is demonic energy attached, the demons flagrantly seek to destroy the person and often use other foreign energies to help accomplish this purpose.

In the August 15, 2002 issue of Time Magazine on page 40, there is a sub-article on Bipolar Disorder that illustrates my point. A case is mentioned of a 17-

year-old girl who was fine and then, as she puts it "Everything was perfect…and then I went insane". Her grandfather was Bipolar, diagnosed the year she was born. She was diagnosed the year he died. She says, "You might say that we passed the baton". She takes drugs for the condition, which helps her, but suffers terrible side effects.

Because of the mindset of the western medical community, no thought was given to the possibility that perhaps her Grandfather *very directly* had something to do with her problem. I would have looked at her problem much differently. Because of the genetic link between she and her grandfather, she may have a genetic predisposition to the bipolar condition. Her energy is resonant with the condition.

When her grandfather died, he may have attached to her, not having gone to the Light, as he should have. People with such conditions often do not see the light or for other reasons just don't go to The Light and attach to others, particularly family members. Family attachments are especially common. Her grandfather's bipolar sickness energy could easily exacerbate her genetic predisposition to the disease and cause her illness. Get him off her and she could be fine again. I constantly find this kind of thing in my practice. It is the rule, not the exception.

Because she is locked into the prison of this condition using drugs in order to live, and has no knowledge of what I just said, she is doomed to put up with the condition for the rest of her life. Western medicine is allopathic in that drugs are used to treat illness symptoms. This is of great help, but eliminating the source of the symptoms is better. How heartbreaking it is that she and so many others like her don't have the opportunity to check it out, maybe find permanent release for herself, and rescue her grandfather at the same time.

For if her Grandfather is attached to her…he has not gone to the light and is left a wandering lost soul ordained to be forever off his path to enlightenment and ultimate reunion with God. When she eventually dies, unless she sees and goes to the Light, she will also wander like him and perhaps end up attaching to others thereby bringing her energy to them, like her Grandfather brought it to her. I hope that along her lost soul path and her Grandfather's, someone will recognize the real problem and release both of them to the Light rescuing them and those they might infect.

Even without the genetic link, the energy of their sickness can still wreck havoc with anybody to whom they fasten to because attached spirits bring their bad energy to the afflicted unfortunate. Wouldn't it be worth while to step out of the mind's prison long enough to at least try Spirit Releasement Therapy (SRT), just in case negative spirit energy is the problem source? I use SRT all the time and miracles happen!

War and Terrorism: How They Affect Us

Many Americans and much of the rest of the world are afraid. Since Sept. 11, 2001, we have all been riding the monster of fear, and feeling that we are not safe anymore. With that fear has come economic chaos: people loosing their jobs; our 401k's becoming 201k's and general uneasiness as we no longer feel comfortable any longer. This produces great stress in us.

We are at war with terrorism. We went into Afghanistan and got rid of the Taliban and some of Al Qaeda, but terror cells are still active throughout the world. President Bush wants us to go to war with Iraq to remove Saddam Hussein before he builds weapons of mass destruction to use against Americans and American interests like Israel. Never mind that we should have, and could have finished Hussein during the Gulf War in a few more hours of fighting. That was then and this is now. Now we have to contend with what Hussein threatens and with terrorism at home and abroad. A lot on our plate!

No longer can we simply board an airplane to do our business or go visit our families or take a vacation. The whole travel thing is a nightmare. The long lines at the airport, the parking problems, the security indignities and the biggest item…the fear. We don't feel safe—our security, our survival is threatened. What will happen when we go to war with Iraq? What additional bad things will happen to the economy and how will war with Iraq further affect traveling, our safety, our economics and our future? We are dancing with fear and fear is leading.

War and terrorism are outside of us, but they affect us greatly because they threaten us, causing apprehension, which disrupts our energy fields. Remember the uneasiness you felt at the scary movie or how you felt walking down the alley at night in a bad neighborhood or when the unleashed pit bull started after you? The energy change results from our primitive fight or flight syndrome getting us ready to either run or fight the saber tooth tiger in the tree. All kinds of changes happen to us…the adrenaline flows, pulse rate increases, digestion stops, blood clotting enhances, etc. This is how nature protects us as it reacts to our energy field change.

Because most of us have little or no control over terrorism or war with Iraq, we feel powerless about the situation. All we know is that we are afraid or angry or both and our physical and emotional systems are responding. Our security, our survival is threatened and these are basic human needs. This threat produces fear and all that goes with it.

The survival threat fear is a negative force generator in our subconscious mind that cuts the flow of life force energy (Chi) through our bodies and installs fear programs on our subconscious hard drive. Because the subconscious mind is an analog parallel processing computer, it has a hard drive and the integrated summation of the programs there determines our behavior, and how we feel. Therefore, these outside energies of war and terrorism acutely affect our behavior and feelings by the fear they generate within us.

Depending on their personalities and emotional makeup, people will be affected differently by these external forces of war and terrorism. If a person has a strong full Chi flow through their body because they are clear, they are less affected by these foreign energies than the person whose Chi flow is blocked. When the Chi is blocked, the reduced energy flow causes the person's energy field to suppress their protective Guardian Chi and outside energies can affect them more easily and deeply.

The external energies of war and terrorism are rooted in fear and insecurity, and act just like other foreign energy attachments. These outside forces can greatly exacerbate existing negative energy generators lying relatively dormant in us. If our Chi flow is blocked by deeply embedded fear or insecurity energies from bad things that happened to us in this life or past lives or we are attached by other fear energies—the addition of the war and terrorism energies can ignite and magnify our pre-existing internal negative energy generators thereby increasing our stress.

The best protection that we can collectively have against the negative energetic effects of war and terrorism is to keep ourselves clear. When we are clear our Guardian Chi protection shield is strong and we can better resist the imposition and magnification of the external fear energies of war and terrorism. If we are not clear, these exterior forces can destabilize and wreck havoc with us.

Hypnotherapy can change our lives from desperation and stress to anticipation of ultimate good because it can clear the subconscious of all negative energy generators, including fear based ones, and reprogram the subconscious with hope and courage. This makes us more sanguine instead of scared, stressed and depressed. You can't as an individual, do much about war with Iraq or terrorism, but you can change the way you react to these things. So, get yourself clear and feel less stressed in these troubled times.

Holiday Blues

For most people the Thanksgiving and Christmas holidays are times of love and joy, but for many, these holidays are times of great depression and anxiety. What should be a time of enjoyment can be a yearly devastating emotional experience instead. Many suicides are recorded during this holiday period. Why is this so and what can be done to help these unfortunates?

The feelings we experience at these times stem from childhood events in this life or from past lives. Lucky people had loving families and good times, but unlucky people had bad experiences during the holidays. The lucky ones will remember the feelings of joy and love, but the unlucky ones will remember the feelings of sadness, anger or envy. Because of the emphasis given to these holidays by our society, the triggers are all around reminding of the past. Amongst the triggers are shopping, music, TV shows, movies, etc. These triggers re-ignite the old feelings, both good and bad and cause a re-experience of the past feelings.

The old feelings are from energy generators in our subconscious minds that are tied to, and support the programs they initially installed on our subconscious hard drive. They can be either joyful or depressive. These programs determine our behavior, how we feel and how we respond to life. We want to keep the joyful ones, but get rid of the depressive ones. To effectively clear ourselves so we can feel and behave better, we must rid ourselves of the energy generators supporting the depressive programs in our subconscious hard drive. This can be done with hypnotherapy.

With hypnotherapy, the subconscious depressive energy-generators can be found and their energies released (cleared), and new positive programs can be installed on the hard drive so we feel good instead of awful. If foreign energies are attached to you, they may carry the holiday sad energy problem and bring that sadness to you. If you have your own problem, the attached energy exacerbates it, making it worse. If the sadness is not from your past, you can still feel the depressive influence from the foreign energy attached to you. These foreign energies can be from either the attachment of earthbound spirits of deceased people, or soul-mind fragments of disassociated people living or dead who were depressed.

The solution to the holiday blues problem is to release the foundation of the problem, whether it's from your own past, or from someone else's past whose energy is attached to you. Whatever the source, once you get rid of it and reprogram for joy instead of depression, permanent change takes place and you feel much better about yourself and about life.

Comprehensive Hypnotherapy Training

People study hypnotherapy for many reasons. Some want to become practitioners to help people and make a living; others want to learn about how the mind works to help them in their professions and others simply want to enhance their own health and capabilities. I got into hypnotherapy to save my own life after unsuccessfully trying for years to get help from traditional western medicine, psychiatry and psychology. Hypnotherapy saved me and I turned from my established profession in technology to learn and help others with this wonderful, awesome healing modality.

Many schools and individuals teach and certify hypnotherapists. All the teaching is good because it opens up awareness to how the mind works and helps people to varying degrees. You can learn to be a hypnotist in a weekend as the techniques are relatively simple. Knowing what to do once you are in the subconscious makes a hypnotist, a hypnotherapist. Hypnosis is a tool that allows direct access to the subconscious wherein are the programs that determine your behavior, how you feel and how you respond to life. Change the programs and you change the person's life…and this is what hypnotherapists try to do. So, why is it that not all hypnotherapy is successful, particularly for the long term?

The answer is that standard hypnotherapy only helps if the problems are relatively simple bad habits and most problems people have are more than just those. Habits are programs imbedded by repetition and most are rather harmless. Significant bad programs installed and imbedded by negative forcing functions cause serious life problems. These distort the body's energy field cutting the flow of Chi (Life Force Energy); install negative programs on the subconscious hard drive and then continuously support those programs. Forcing functions are actually negative energy generators created by damaging things that happened to you in this life, past lives, severe unresolved internal conflicts, detrimental genetics from your ancestors or the attachment of foreign energies.

Hypnotherapy only heals permanently if the negative energy generators supporting the bad programs on your subconscious hard drive are found and released and new positive programs installed that are capable of overriding the old bad programs. Then you get permanent change. To accomplish this requires much more training than is usually provided.

The National Guild of Hypnotists (NGH) will only certify hypnotherapists taught by NGH instructors (CI's). This is because the NGH course teaches hypnotherapists the fundamentals of reprogramming and the needed basics to understand and move onto advanced courses where the techniques of finding and releasing all the negative forcing functions are taught. The NGH Hypnotherapy Certification Course opens the door to the complete healing process.

Agoraphobia, Fibromyalgia, Depression and Addictions: A Wretched Life

Agoraphobia is the fear of open spaces and Fibromyalgia is a pain disorder in your muscles and joints. It may also cause poor sleep, headaches, and stiffness or muscle aches. Stress or lack of sleep can make the symptoms of Fibromyalgia worse. More women than men have Fibromyalgia, but the disorder is common—it is seen in about 5% of the population. However, it isn't life threatening and it doesn't cause permanent damage but it makes life miserable. Psychotherapists treat Agoraphobia and Depression and medical doctors usually treat Fibromyalgia with pain medication.

Doris, a 43-year-old single female spent the last four years imprisoned in her house, afraid to go out and wracked with intractable pain for nine years that was diagnosed as Fibromyalgia. She was being treated with benzodiazepines for sleep, anti-depressants for depression and heavy pain medications; including cortisone injections and oxygen treatments from a chiropractor. She was addicted to the sleep, pain medications, and also to get relief, drank upwards of 5 liters of wine every day to help her sleep and relieve the pain. She added the wine because she had developed tolerance to the medications and was at the upper limit on drug dosage. Drugs such as these usually don't work for people in the long term and the wine seemed to help her to bear her misery. Her life was shattered and she was an emotional wreck when I met her. Because I am not a licensed medical doctor or psychotherapist, I cannot treat these conditions, but I agreed to try to generally help her using hypnotherapy at her urgent request.

Although she was a beautiful and wealthy woman, Doris had very low self-esteem and never had a healthy relationship with men. The two men in her life were non-supportive and treated her badly. The first man beat her and the second with whom she had a child, now a teenager, was indolent and sought to keep her dependent on him so she would financially support him. He wanted her sick so he could take care of her and not have to work. She had a very beautiful and wealthy domineering mother who from childhood belittled her. She had 10 unneeded cosmetic surgeries at her mother's insistence by the time she was 35 years old. Her mother was ashamed at her illness and had once sent her to a mental hospital for 5 weeks to "straighten out", an experience that left her "shaken" and worse than before. Doris loved her father but he died of cancer when she was very young.

Using regression therapy, I discovered that when Doris was 6 years old, her mother started making out with men in the house and would make Doris put on a nightgown and kiss the men mother was "entertaining". Doris had great fear that her mother would abandon her and would try to sleep with her mother so the men could not. At 7 years old, she was attacked by a swarm of wasps stinging her all over her body and in another lifetime, she fell down the stairs severely injuring her. These regression incidents proved to be the source of her Fibromyalgia pain. The fear that enveloped her created soul-mind fragmentation (ego states) within her that were still highly energized. The fear lowered her psychic defense system and demons came upon her to destroy her using the fragmentation, fear and the energy of the wasp episode as their tools of destruction. Doris is a fine woman of great light and demons seek to destroy people like her.

Without going into the therapy details, this is what I generally did for her. I released the demons, and was then able to resolve negative issues from the past by means of this life and past life regression therapies. Using Parts therapy and Gestalt therapy, we were able to work out her self-hate, mother forgiveness issues and soul-mind fragmentation. Once these were taken care of, I reprogrammed her subconscious for ego strength and self-value. I also provided her with her own internal safe place with self-induced triggers to access it, and made her aware of her own Guardian Angel's protection. (Her Inner Protector)

The entire course of therapy took 21 hours. About one month after completing therapy, Doris resumed her life free of the negative forcing functions that were destroying her. She now drinks one or two glasses of wine in a day, just for the enjoyment of it. She no longer takes sleep medication and the pain of the Fibromyalgia is practically gone and will soon be totally gone. Her medications are drastically reduced and she is successfully weaning herself of them entirely. The depression, having been caused by the devastation of her illness, has lifted now that she has pain relief and optimism. She is driving her car, which sat idle for 4 years and interacting with her daughter in a positive way helping her with schoolwork and taking her shopping. She visited her mother, felt at peace with her, and has told her leach boyfriend to get out of her house, which surprised and distressed him causing him to become much more truly helpful to Doris. This relationship may have a chance to become positive if he receives help.

Truly, releasing the negative forcing functions within her subconscious mind and positively reprogramming it, has enabled her to find herself and her life has changed from one of misery and unhappiness to one of hope and anticipation of the future.

Reincarnation's Two Paths

Because I deal with past life negative forcing functions, amongst others, in my work to free suffering people from their afflictions of mind and body, I am often asked how reincarnation works. Past life scars can affect us in this life cutting the flow of Chi through our bodies, just like the other negative forcing functions of: Internal Conflicts, Repressed Memories of This Life, Genetic Effects from our biological ancestors and Attached Foreign Energies.

During our journey from whence we left Source (God) until we finally return to Source, our soul-mind joins with many separate and distinct genetic paths in order to experience growth towards ultimate enlightenment. Our soul-mind is always ours and is the true us, but our physical body during any particular incarnation is only a temporary home for us. It carries the genetic history of the biological line from which it springs along with the strengths and weakness of that particular genetic strain.

After death we meet with our guides and teachers who assist us in determining what life we will next live on our journey to enlightenment. Each life is a learning experience and what we don't learn in one life will have to be learned in another. This is Karmic balancing. For example, if you lack compassion in a life that you should have learned it in, then you will have to learn it in another life—often the hard way.

My research tells me that once the decision is made to reincarnate into a particular body, the soul-mind energy enters the body during the fifth breath at birth. Before that, the fetus is just a biological animal. Once the soul-mind enters the newborn, the divinity of the High Self, which is a part of the soul-mind, makes the person a Child of God and Divine as the High Self is.

The soul-mind energy binds with the energy of the DNA within the biological self and the particular body then becomes and remains until death, intimately connected to the soul-mind dwelling in it. The cells of the body, because of the DNA level binding of energy, adopt and retain throughout the body's physical life, the permanent memory contained in the soul-mind energy. This then becomes the cellular memory of the physical body.

To clear past life scarring from the physical body, past life regression therapy (PLT) must be done to find and release the energy of past life trauma which has been encoded into the cellular memory of the body causing distress to the person. It is important to make sure, before doing PLT, that any attached earthbound spirits or soul-mind fragments of other people are released first, because if they are not, you are finding and releasing the past life energy of the attached entities and not of the client. Therapy must be done on the client's own past lives to relieve him of the scarring effects of past life trauma. All the psychotherapy in the world on the attached entities is not going to help the client. Since many people have foreign energies attached to them and most therapists don't deal with entity attachment, most past life regressions are fairly useless in permanently helping the client.

The Problem with War

Psychologically, war is a confusing phenomenon in how it affects us. Some people become very patriotic, while others rail against it as inhuman. Others draw themselves into a mental cocoon and try to ignore it…pretending it isn't happening. Still, others feel the cold grip of fear surrounding them. What is common to all, however is that stress is increased because of the uncertainty of what will happen. The future is unknown and it may be dark.

Even those who are very hawkish and want to level the enemy with overwhelming firepower and know that we have the ability to do it are under more stress. Certainly, those who are afraid are under stress. Fear is the biggest stressor there is and excess stress can cause bad things to happen to our minds and bodies.

Stress is simply a response to life. If you live, you have stress…so it is a normal part of life. However, if it gets too high or is too long lasting, things can break. Depending on our personalities and how closed we are to the flow of life force through our bodies because of negative forcing functions in our subconscious; our breaking stress levels are different.

Even if stress levels go very high, but do not exceed our breaking strength, while we are still in the elastic response mode, nothing bad will happen to us. We actually may be able to step back, view with a kind of elegant detachment what is happening, and perhaps gain perspective on our own lives and its difficulties. In essence, we are sharper in discernment and can grow in positive insight and strength.

However, if our breaking strength stress levels are exceeded by the addition of the war stress, it can produce deleterious consequences for us. The extra stress can send us reeling into mental and emotional illness and even into physical illness if the situation persists for too long. You will get warnings of impending breaking stress levels by how you feel. Sweating for no reason, headaches, undue fatigue, irritability, sleep disruption, anxiety and depression amongst other symptoms can signal the approach of the break. These warning signs call for corrective action before things get worse.

Some sufferers will respond by taking medicine, praying, visiting psychiatrists, psychologists and counselors. Others will do nothing and try to brave it out without breaking. Others will just break. Some may even enlist the aid of conventional hypnotherapists, who cannot legally treat the symptoms, but can help them to relax thereby somewhat relieving their stress. An enlightened few will find a hypnotherapist who can get to the root of their high stress and release the negative forcing functions of the source problems within them. With this release, the breaking stress threshold is greatly increased and the sufferer can handle the war stress without undue difficulty.

War & The Ostrich Syndrome

Many of my clients and some famous people, like Cher are completely ignoring the war with Iraq because they disagree with it or can't emotionally handle the trauma of war. Is this good for their emotional health?

Being at war is stressful because of the uncertainty it engenders within us regarding our own security. Apprehension about reprisals against the American people by extremists, negative effects on the economy, concerns for people losing loved ones in the war and a host of other disquieting elements can add to our overall stress level. If this level is already high because of negative forcing functions already imbedded in our subconscious minds, the added stress of the war can tilt us into illness, both emotional and physical.

Some people choose to cope with this added stress by simply pretending that the war doesn't exist and wall themselves off from the reality of what's going on by consciously burying their heads in the sand as the ostrich does when it doesn't want to see what's going on in it's reality. As the war goes on, this approach becomes increasingly more difficult to maintain because of the inundation of media news and the interests of other people who are glued to their TV's watching what is happening.

Whether we like it or not, life goes on with or without our participation. If you choose to not involve yourself, you may, at least on the surface, keep your stress down…maybe. But, does disregarding reality really protect you from stress? I think not!

In building our wall of self-protection, at some level of consciousness we still know what is going on. We cannot truly divorce ourselves from reality no matter how deeply we bury our heads in the sand. The uneasiness is always still there, the fear is still there and so the stress is still there, albeit concealed temporarily by our avoidance behavior. We cannot truly escape the stress and it is, most assuredly, affecting us.

It is far better to accept reality and the stress of life openly and deal with it. If your stress level is already too high, then find a good hypnotherapist who can help you uncover and release the stressor sources buried in your subconscious and accept ongoing reality as it unfolds. We learn and grow by accepting actuality and not hiding from it. This makes us stronger as we overcome adversity in life and release our deeply imbedded stress sources within. After all, we are adults and not children. We don't have to live in a never-never land of deluding fantasy for protection. Instead, grasp life for what it is, solve your problems and become stronger and wiser. This process is called maturing.

Have a Little Patience!

It is very disconcerting that some people, who have long-standing debilitating physical and/or emotional problems, sometime for 20+ years, will come to me and expect me to resolve their problems completely in one session. I guess there are healers like Jesus and Buddha who can do this regularly, but I cannot. Sometimes, I (and the client) luck out and the problem disappears completely with one session, but this is the exception, not the rule. I think it has to do with the fact that most problems are caused by a multiplicity of negative forcing functions and not just one—and even if it is just one, there is the predicament of cellular memory, particularly in conditions involving pain or physical distortions over a long time period.

Illness—mental, emotional, physical, and even spiritual are caused by the interruption of Chi flow through the body which deprives the cell communities of this Life force Energy that is necessary for healthy functioning of the cellular community, including it's regeneration. When the Chi is reduced or cut off to the cellular community, the cells begin to regenerate as defective cells and illness results. This model of illness is based on the oldest Model of disease that exists, the Eastern disease Model, which is over 4000 years old.

Bad things that happen to us in this life, past lives, unresolved emotional conflicts, genetic carryovers from our ancestors, and foreign energy attachments cause negative forcing functions. These act as energy generators in our subconscious, which distort the body's energy field reducing the flow of Chi, install negative programs in our subconscious and continually reinforce them. These programs determine how we behave, how we feel and how we respond to life. It is very unusual to have only one negative forcing function in an ill client. I have found as many as 35 layers of them, but a good number of my clients have only three to eight layers.

To feel differently, the negative energy generators have to be found and released of their energy, which shuts off support of their installed negative programs in the subconscious. One the bad energy source is shut off, the subconscious can be reprogrammed and the person begins to feel better. However, the cells of the body are used to the negative conditioning and it takes time to reprogram them to proper functioning. I usually use Dr. Ed. Martin's (PATHE Foundation, Houston, TX) Cell Command Therapy to accomplish this, but occasionally if the person has been on long term heavy medication and has had the condition for a very long time, I refer the client for Acupuncture and Chinese Herbal Medicine for detoxification and pain analgesia, and sometimes Neuronal EEG Feedback Therapy to correct brainwave function. These are very powerful therapies, but they don't work by themselves—the client must first be cleared and reprogrammed properly and then this protocol works wonderfully.

It is impossible to do all of this in one or two sessions. The progenitors of disease do not come instantly, and the generated symptoms do not usually leave instantly when the negative energy generators are removed. In my own illness, before I discovered SRT, I didn't know that removing entities was necessary before the other therapies would work on me. I had regression therapy and Parts therapy and Gestalt therapy, and energy therapy and breath therapy, and Chinese therapy and countless other alternative therapies in addition to western allopathic medicine, psychiatry and psychology without permanent improvement. For instance, I had 72 acupuncture and Chinese Herbal Medicine treatments over a 2-year period and saw psychiatrists for 20 years without success.

Finally, with much trepidation because I was afraid of it, I agreed to SRT because there was nowhere else for me to go. Once cleared of entities, the other therapies began to work for me to release the non-entity related problems and I was on the road to health. After I finally got clear with Spirit Releasement Therapy (SRT) and additional hypnotherapies to remove my other imbedded negative forcing functions, I began to rapidly improve, but still had some pain and EEG brain wave distortions from a lifetime of negative conditioning. These were corrected with the Chinese and EEG Neuronal therapies and, thank God, the almost total degradation of my life ceased, and I was able to begin enjoying and using my life, rather than just enduring it.

It took years and much expenditure of money to finally get where I needed to go. Even after cleared with SRT, there is much work to do. It doesn't happen overnight, but you must stay with it or continue to suffer. You have to be patient. Maybe that's why the medical profession calls their clients patients.

Women's Men Problems

Many of my female clients have big trouble with men. I also get many men who have trouble with women, but the preponderance is with the women. This may be due to the increased sensitivity of women to emotional turmoil or maybe men just don't admit their problems as readily as women do. Many of these problems come from early childhood in this life, but they can also come from past lives or any of the other negative forcing function programs embedded in the subconscious which affect our behavior, how we feel and how we respond to life. A common problem theme for women is their relationship with their fathers.

Dorothy, 39, intelligent, well educated and model beautiful came to me a couple of years ago complaining that she was very unhappy with the men she attracted and that her relationships always ended without any commitment or long term security for her. She had a history of headaches and persistent depression that interfered with her job and enjoyment of life, but her biggest complaint was her man problem. She would like to be married and have children, but it never worked out. She wanted help with the headaches and depression and in drawing the right kind of men into her life.

It took four sessions to get rid of entity attachments, which were drawn to her by her depression. She had two demons, an earthbound spirit and a soul-mind fragment of someone else on her. These entities were able to attach to her because her Guardian Chi psychic immune system was down because of the sadness she felt. Her light attracted the demons to her as she was very spiritual and they brought in the earthbound spirit and soul-mind fragment, which caused the headaches and exacerbated the depression sadness.

Once the attachments were gone, using Parts Therapy, we were able to ascertain that she greatly loved her father and was very close to him but he left because of divorce when she was 4 years old causing her great fear and loss. Her child mind concluded that if she were to ever get close to another man like she was to her father, and he left her, she would re-experience the same 4-year-old grief agony so she unconsciously protected herself against this happening by never allowing any true intimacy into her relationships to prevent being hurt again. It turned out that her man problem was not in the men, but rather in her, and it

262

was she, not the men that were causing her problems with men. Within two weeks, her headaches and depression were gone and with her new insight, she was able to re-examine her current relationship from a different perspective.

Recently, I received a call from her telling me that not only was she still free from the headaches and depression, but that she was looking forward to getting married. She said she was experiencing an inner peace that had eluded her all of her life and was truly happy.

Remote Healing

A great deal of my work is with people who either do not know that they are being worked on or who cannot or will not come to see me. Often a parent will ask me to work on their children who are into drugs, alcohol or exhibiting behavior that is deleterious to their future. Like if they keep on behaving as they are, they will either end up in jail or in a morgue. The kids would not come to see me voluntarily and if forced by the parents, would actively resist my work so it would not be of much use. Remote work can help these situations dramatically.

Wives will ask me to work on husbands who will not or cannot stop drinking, smoking, exhibiting infidelity, physically or mentally abusing them and generally acting like a lout. Again, if the husband is coerced into seeing me, he would actively resist the work and the sessions would be of little or no benefit. Remote work can be of great value here.

Many clients who hear of my work from my lectures, my writing or via my website on the internet come to see me from all over the United State and from all over the world. I have had clients from every state and from over 40 countries come to Atlanta and stay for whatever time is required to do the work. Many clients have returned three or four times to complete their work. The problem is that a lot of clients not from the Atlanta area who need my work just cannot afford to come see me for the time it takes to resolve their problems. For all of these people remote work is a viable alternative for them to consider.

Remote work requires a cleared surrogate who is conditioned to easily go into hypnosis and has been trained to accept the images and feelings coming from the subconscious connection to the remote client's subconscious mind, and who allows those images and feelings to be expressed freely without consciously filtering them. In addition to the hypnosis surrogate, a trained cleared person provides protection to the process by holding all involved in the Light. And of course, I am directing the entire procedure and conducting the therapy.

The therapy consists of finding and removing the energy of negative forcing functions buried in the subconscious self that have negatively programmed the subconscious computer and supports the negative programs in the computer. These negative forcing functions are from: "bad" things that have happened to the person in this life, in past lives, unresolved internal conflicts known or unknown to the client, biological genetic carry-overs from the ancestors, and from attached foreign energies (spirit attachment). Remote work does not resolve internal conflicts or biological genetic carryover problems, but is quite effective in dealing with this life and past life issues and entity attachments. Remote work also does not permit reprogramming of the clients subconscious computer. This must be done in person. However, clearing repressed memories from this life and past lives and the removal of foreign energies is very beneficial, and can restore a person to health and happiness, where if it was not done, the person might be destroyed.

I am able to clear some negative forcing functions (energy generators) from the afflicted person and restore the flow of life force energy (Chi, Prana, etc) through the person's body affected by the particular energy blocks. If the person had entity attachments, their effects are negated. For the other remote responsive negative forcing functions, the clearing of the "negative energy generators" from the client's subconscious mind is of great benefit to the client by removing the blocks to Chi flow, which restores physical health and positively influences behavior.

In the case of children under age twelve with very serious problems, I almost always use remote work to help them because if the child is infected by a demonic energy, the clearing process could be very scary to the child and the child might self fragment in which case I would then have to deal with that problem in addition to the original problem that brought the child in. I sometimes use a parent as the surrogate if the parent is willing and is clear. Most often, however, the parent is not clear and it would take a lot of time and money to clear them, so it is easier and less expensive to use my trained professional surrogate.

In summation then I would say that it is better to deal with the client directly for hypnotherapy work to resolve the problems that are interfering with a happy and healthful life. However, if it is not possible for whatever reason, to have the client see me face to face, then remote work is very beneficial bearing in mind that some things just cannot be done remotely. Fortunately, most of the more serious problems I encounter with people are from this life or past lives or attached spirits, and remote clearing does a wonderful job in helping these cases. Remote work is certainly infinitely better than doing nothing. It can make the difference between happiness and destruction.

More on Remote Work

Remote work is very interesting because substantial life altering changes can be made to a person who hasn't any idea that someone is working for their benefit. It is like prayer for someone in trouble who doesn't know that they are being prayed for. Prayer can produce dramatic changes without the person being consciously aware that they are being prayed for. As a matter of fact, I call my remote work, prayer because it is so similar to it.

Prayer accesses the person's High Self, as does remote clearing work. The High Self is the part of us that connects us to God. Permission of the person's High Self is always obtained before proceeding with remote clearing work. Unlike prayer, which can be done without permission of the High Self, remote work requires this permission. Regular prayer goes to the High Self of the person being prayed for in hope that the High self will make the desired outcome happen. Since the High Self works through the afflicted one's subconscious mind, the resultant solution to the afflicted person's problem can be of a nature that the individual would not desire.

This can happen because the subconscious mind is not rational and so the solution to the person's problem might be totally out of synch with what the person might have consciously desired. For instance, the afflicted person being prayed for may have diabetes and the prayer would be for the person to be released from the diabetes. Since the person offering the prayer is unaware that the diabetes may be caused by a past life trauma or an attached entity or an unresolved internal conflict, the release of the diabetes may trigger an even more potent and life threatening condition like cancer to use up the unreleased energy of the negative forcing function causing the diabetes which had not been dealt with. The subconscious cannot be allowed to determine the solution to the problem because of its irrationality.

With remote work, the High Self cooperates with the conscious mind of the hypnotherapist in resolving the negative forcing function and discernment of a rational approach to the release of the negative energy can be made. This way, a much more sane solution is directed to the subconscious mind that carries out the action to resolve the afflicted one's problem without worsening the situation. It is actually taking responsibility for the solution of one's problems rather than just letting an irrational subconscious interchange take place, which may actually worsen the person's overall condition even though the apparent problem is resolved. I call remote work like this "Intelligent Guided Prayer". It is the "easy way" as opposed to "the hard way" which is often the subconscious mind's irrational solution.

Remote Clearing

I do remote clearing work on many clients prior to their first visit to see me in person because it makes therapy go quicker and sometimes even better than if the client starts out seeing me in person. Remote work does not resolve internal conflicts or biological genetic carryover problems, but is quite effective in dealing with this life and past life issues and entity attachments. Remote work does not allow reprogramming of the clients subconscious computer, which must be done in person. However, the release of the negative forcing functions of repressed toxic memories and entity attachment can really help the client even if you cannot get to reprogramming.

Some people are resistant to hypnotherapy because of their logical and analytical minds. Accountants and engineers are prime examples of this problem. Others are too concerned about what the therapy costs and cannot relax and let whatever is in the subconscious flow into conscious awareness. The client lives far away and cannot make appointments in person; the client has a resistance to the therapy for religious reasons. These are two examples of problems for which remote work can dramatically help. Even though the client may resist consciously, we always get permission from the High Self of the person before proceeding with the remote clearing. We will never do any work against the person's higher will. Usually, the High Self will agree to the work because of the greater good done for the person.

Parents of children who are on drugs and who will not engage in conventional therapy often find remote work beneficial in getting the child into a frame of mind to have direct in-person therapy. This is especially helpful if the child is zonked out on drugs. I have had many parents who have brought their children in to me for help and I cannot work with the child because they are high on drugs. I always tell the parents to make sure that the child is drug free for a couple of days before bringing them in to me, but then they show up and the child's eyes are fully dilated with the drugs and I cannot work on them. Even if we never get to the point of direct therapy, the remote clearing helps the child.

Spouses, whose marriage partners are unwilling to have therapy for such problems as physical and verbal abuse, drug or alcohol addiction, laziness, etc, have an alternative to use for these situations with remote clearing. Even though the spouse never comes in for reprogramming, just clearing the negative forcing functions can dramatically improve the miserable situation. If we can only get them partially cleared, there are still benefits in attitude, behavior and health. Quite often, however, when many of the negative forcing functions are removed remotely, the affected person improves so much in attitude that they are quite willing to come in for reprogramming and other in-person direct therapy.

APPENDIX

The Rules

Over the years I have picked up sayings that have impressed and helped me. I offer these for your consideration:

Christian Science Stuff

1. My true identity is immortal and always intact.

2. There is no life, no God, in matter. Mortal mind and body are inverted likenesses, misrepresentations of the real man and Mind.

3. Detect fear as the illusion. Prove the fear to be illusion by absolutely facing it. Then the fear vanishes. Face the fear—demand its disappearance.

4. Feeling free is feeling healthy.

5. It was the understanding of the perfection of man's real, spiritual being as created by God that enabled Jesus to heal those who were sick blind and lame.

6. Sickness, no matter what name it goes under, is a supposition, an illusion, a dream.

7. Sickness has only the strength we believe it to have. It has no real, no divine origin.

8. I am in perfect harmony with God's universe and I am healed.

9. The God who is love itself does not send evil. The God who is mind does not send blight. There is nothing loving in creating a man full of dishar-

mony. There is nothing intelligent in creating a man who doesn't have dominion.

10. The laws of God exist forever and never change. They guarantee everyone the freedom to be whole and healthy.

11. Accidents, mistakes, or illness do not belong to the real man, God's image, and they can be ruled out of our lives. Nobody stands between God and man. In truth, God and man are one, and God communicates directly with man. No darkness of fear, no darkness of doubt, no darkness of sickness or death—our families and we are safe.

12. It is your right to be consistently happy and productive. When we reach out to God to save us, we realize that He is already here. Depressing moods are not from God, nor are they representative of our true being. We can dispute them on that basis. We are always free.

13. Man must rise above the level of believing himself only a helpless victim of material circumstances to the point of having dominion over his life. Express gratitude for the good already evident in your life. Gratitude, I soon discovered, is a powerful destroyer of self-pity. I became more aware of my native reservoir of strength, intelligence, peace and real substance. I began to trust God and let go—planning how my life should work out.

14. Your precious, unique identity is much more than a material personality. It is the eternal, individual expression of all the infinite, spiritual qualities emanating from your soul. You are the expression, in your own unique way, of the intelligence and wisdom of Mind, the energy and vitality of spirit, the compassion and kindness of divine love, and the radiant qualities of your Soul. If you don't feel special and needed, your real need is to discover more about who you really are. And, to bring out in your life, in your thoughts and deeds, what you are discovering.

15. Man is one with life. Man doesn't need to walk an impossible tight rope to avoid illness or disease. In reality he lives securely in the un-invadable realm of good, governed by divine law. In addition, Spirit maintains harmony throughout all creation. Fear and sin are two primary detractors from mental and physical well being. Stemming from material belief, they tend vividly to reinforce negative belief, effectively hiding from our perception the spiritual and real nature of things.

16. Man, God's image, is not a sinner! The sin that needs punishment or correction is the belief that there is a power opposed to God that can make us act contrary to our true nature as a perfect, spiritual, loved child of God. No matter how serious a sin, once it has been genuinely given up—replaced with the truth—it ceases to exist and cannot penalize us.

17. A loving God does not subject his creation to negative conditions. He is no more the author of sickness as He is of sin.

18. If, as we perceive a negative activity, we realize it is a falsity—we're not influenced by the activity itself. So, we mentally reverse it and it ceases to affect us.

19. Physical law with its inevitable consequences of sickness, wrongdoing, and death loses its supposed control over us to the degree we understand that matter is not real. Mental denial of matter and material law opens the way for the harmonious law of spirit to be proved the only force in our lives. Man never waivers in his obedience to this law, nor is he ever, in reality subordinate to physical law.

20. God created man in His image. The logical conclusion of this is that man's true identity is spiritual, not physical.

21. The metaphysical fact that healing takes place in consciousness emphasizes the necessity for us to guard against negative suggestions that tend to initiate or worsen an undesirable condition. As we affirm spiritual truths and deny the falsities of material sense, we are healed.

22. God is mind: all that God, is, or hath made, is good. Moreover, He made all. Hence, evil is not made, and is not real. Any action of evil is a hypnotic illusion. No matter how great in evil circumstance, it remains just that—hypnotic illusion. We can and must refuse to accept it. The real man that God made cannot be harmed for this man is immortal, invulnerable.

23. If depression is not indulged in, it will not prevail.

24. Sickness and sin are both illusions—they can only hurt me as long as I believe in them.

Life Principles & Hypnotherapy

1. There is none so blind as he who will not see.

2. Laugh and the world laughs with you, cry and you cry alone.

3. A man who is warm sees and feels things differently than a man who is cold.

4. Don't sweat the small stuff—and it's all small stuff—*Richard Carlson PhD*

5. Thought is creative. By thinking, we can manifest things in our lives. Intent is what channels energy to our purpose. But, intent and thinking without passion doesn't do much. Passion makes the difference.

6. Love is life's energy.

7. Love accepts everything; it is patient, tolerant, kind and not judgmental.

8. Other people will treat you the way you treat yourself.

9. If you want to complain, offer a solution.

10. Listening is the most important part of communication.

11. To stay miserable, always be right.

12. What you say and think is what you get.

13. Would you think about expands—your results are your teacher.

14. Others will always mirror yourself.

15. Your reality results from your thoughts and beliefs.

16. No one is the victim of anyone else.

17. You are a victim only of your thoughts.

18. There are millions of levels of reality, and everyone is right about *their* reality.

19. Every problem is a gift.

20. The way to heal is to forgive.

21. Nature doesn't really have laws, it has habits—and habits can be changed. There are no limits.

22. Our reality reflects our mind and we can change our mind.

23. Parents are our first gurus (teachers).

24. Anything unresolved with your parents will come up in your relationships for the purpose of release and healing.

25. 95% of our behavior is from role models; 5% is from what we are told to do.

26. We tend to copy the kind of relationship your parents had with each other. We try to work it out for our parents.

27. Fear of something is like training for something you don't want. It'll manifest because emotions amplify the power of manifestation.

28. Some people get sick to control their reality: they need sickness to be loved.

29. Love does not have to be earned.

30. In my life I wrote the movie, hired the actors and produced it, so I can change it. Life is my movie.

31. I am never a victim.

32. We are here to participate in the evolution of consciousness into matter.

33. The ego believes you are wrong and bad, and it has to gather evidence to prove this. The ego would rather be right than happy.

34. All healing starts with us.

35. Whatever you feel is not wrong.

36. Your internal law—I am perfect and innocent just the way I am.

37. Peace is the absence of internal conflict.

38. I am my own guru.

39. I do know it all; my guru is the God within me.

40. Physical immortality: act as though it is true for a year and see what happens! Unravel family traditions of death; get rid of your death urge.

41. Eliminate rigidity in your life. Be flexible in your body and in your thinking. No struggle!

42. You must and can lose your fear of death.

43. Self-esteem: your relationship with yourself is the most important relationship. Treat yourself with love, respect and caring. Loving yourself and being in this highest space is a gift to everyone else.

44. Become the kind of person you want to attract.

45. Practice loving yourself. Stop criticizing yourself; mistakes are opportunities to learn.

46. Acknowledge your success! Whatever you focus on expands. If you love, appreciate and accept your body, you'll become more beautiful.

47. Do the career you want to do: God will have fun being you!

48. People love to pay you for doing what you love to do.

49. Focus on what you want. This empowers it. Don't focus on what's bad; don't empower what you don't want.

50. Many people will give you what you want. Go for it!

51. Jealousy is a result of a belief system that says loss is possible, and that not loving yourself and not appreciating yourself doesn't make anything wrong.

52. Illusions disappear when we stop believing in them.

53. To have good sex, ask for what you want. Always stay in the present. Get anger out, it anesthetizes your body. You express God most fully when you have sex.

54. You are always innocent.

55. Consciously create the kind of relationships you want. You can create with the power of your mind. Be clear on what you want. Ask for what you want with self-esteem, and be willing to receive it. The Source doesn't let up once you ask.

56. You always get what you ask for, or what is in the way of it.

57. Refuse to accept "I don't know" from your own mind—it knows all. You will know when you get the right answer by how it feels. TRUST THE UNIVERSE.

58. There are no limits.

59. Surrender to life—flow with it. You can live kicking and screaming, or with an easy flow. You have to go through life, so do it *elegantly.*

60. The physical is to serve the Spirit. The body is only a vehicle, and you must treat it as a separate thing. Get rid of all the rule books written by people who have love-hate relationships with the body. You must be firmly in your body to grow.

61. Do what you feel! Begin to operate without the need to do it.

62. The subconscious mind knows the cause and solution to all our problems.

63. The subconscious mind never forgets anything. It has permanent memory.

64. Guilt requires punishment of us.

65. Never, ever punish yourself.

66. Guilt causes fear—remove guilt and fear and enhance your life.

67. Guilt is the original sin.

68. The original sin is the statement that we are not God.

69. Guilt energetically pulls us into punishment.

70. We think that if we punish ourselves enough, we avoid greater punishment.

71. We are all innocent; we don't have to punish ourselves.

72. Being responsible and feeling guilty are not the same.

73. Forgiveness of one's self is the most important. The past is nothing but learning experiences. You went through it; now forget it. The way to heal is to forgive.

74. The past is like the wake of the ship. Just let it go. It does not steer the ship, it just tells you where you have been, not where you are going. The future is created out of your decisions in the present moment.

75. Forgiveness frees the forgiver.

76. Forgive yourself.

77. Forgive the other person.

78. Give up all claims to punishment.

79. Don't make your forgiveness dependent on the other person.

80. We tend to suppress guilt and project it as anger.

81. Forgiveness is unconditional love.

82. Forgiveness is the eraser of guilt and fear.

83. If there is no forgiveness, there is no change. If you don't forgive, they don't suffer, only you do.

84. There are three places to live: the past, the present, the future. You have the choice.

85. The ultimate fear is the fear of rejection.

86. The subconscious protects us against threats, real or imagined and it cannot tell the difference

87. For every amount of love you give, you get back tenfold.

88. Karma is erased by knowledge.

89. You are the only one that can heal you.

90. Establish rapport with your client, without it, you cannot do anything.

91. Hypnosis is a tool to produce receptivity.

92. Abreaction is a blessing: venting gets rid of negative energy.

93. The Hypnotist must create a state of receptivity

94. People don't know that they are hypnotized.

95. When clients come out of hypnosis, they usually say two things: "I was not hypnotized," and "I was only making up a story." But, it is the right story for healing.

96. In hypnosis we interfere with our clients ability to analyze, to critically reason.

97. The idea behind hypnosis is getting past the critical analytical mind and focusing on helpful suggestions

98. The therapist must take clients out of their comfort zone to get change.

99. Manage your boundaries. Always know where you are with your clients. Don't get sexual.

100. Clients actually want you to take control; they want a fix.

101. Resistance is conflict about losing control.

102. You must work with the clients belief system, not with yours.

103. Never define hypnosis for client. Instead, define what hypnosis is like.

104. Don't do hypnosis when challenged, like at parties with friends.

105. The belief system is where the power is.

106. Never give advice. Instead, open up options for them to choose from.

107. It's all right to be wrong; it really doesn't matter.

108. When we worry, we take ourselves out of the moment and into the future.

109.Build their egos (self-esteem); then they take care of themselves.

110.There are two kinds of people:

    1) To Have People, those who want it right now,

    2) To Be People, those who are willing to wait.

111.Monotony, rhythm, repetition: that's how we hypnotize.

112.To be assertive is to be persuasive without being abusive.

113.Suggestions, under hypnosis, are programs, and they dictate how we behave. Suggestions are thoughts.

114.In self-hypnosis suggestions are given to yourself in the hypnotic state. Auto-suggestion is suggestion given to yourself in the waking state.

115.The client should always develop his own suggestions.

116.Suggestions are about making a commitment, which can be measured.

117.Suggestions to create hypnosis are the only primary suggestions. All other suggestions are secondary suggestions.

118.Highly suggestible people are usually deep hypnosis subjects, but deep hypnosis subjects are not necessarily highly suggestible.

119.Behavior cannot sustain itself unless reinforced either positively or negatively. Otherwise, it disappears.

120.All you have to do as a therapist is find out what is reinforcing a client's negative behavior, and get rid of it.

121.If you listen carefully, the client will tell you exactly what is wrong, and how to fix it.

122.The unconscious mind always needs tension. Tension is fuel.

123.People speak in feelings and in thoughts.

124.People are afraid to lead with "I feel." People are scared of feelings.

125.Three psychological things are going on all the time: how you think, how you feel, how you act. Intervention can be at any and all of these levels.

126.People must communicate their feelings while they are happening.

127.Catch them in the moment and point it out to the client.

128.Anger always manifests in avoidance behavior. Poor grooming, over-eating, substance abuse.

129.Best way to treat people is to allow them to talk. Don't give advice.

130.Many clients will come to you for bad habits.

131.If you can't think it, you can't write it down.

132.If you can't write it down, you can't think it.

133.It's not the stress that causes the difficulty, it's how we respond to the stress.

134.Hypnosis Depth wise, you are what you are, you can't change it. It takes at least ten sessions to get maximum depth.

135.As long way you are in the state of receptivity, you don't need to be formally inducted.

136.As therapists, we force clients to take responsibility for themselves. This helps to heal them.

137.Ben Franklin said, "If the illness is psychosomatic, then why not have the cure be psychogenic?"

138.Aversion Therapy does not work for weight loss.

139.Zeigarnik effect: "finished test syndrome." When you finish tasks, it relieves stress.

140.For panic attacks do something physical.

141.Intervention is the treatment plan.

142.Do not make judgments based on what people tell you.

143. Behavior is the structure for thinking.

144. You cannot develop an intervention or treatment plan without assessment.

145. Assessment: How you think about it? How do you feel about it? What are you doing about it?

146. Belief is cognitive thought, feeling is emotions.

147. Obstacles to success:

    People generally are unwilling to look at themselves.

    People generally have vague goals.

    People want to live in chaos.

    People hate change, even good change.

    People hate to be measured.

148. Change people's behavior by having them do something.

149. Get clients on a time and action program for each action they enumerate. Give suggestions under hypnosis for each of the action programs.

150. Clients should develop autosuggestions to accomplish each action item.

151. Actions should be suggestions to overcome obstacles.

152. Self-hypnosis suggestions should be simple and singular.

153. Our job as hypnotherapists is to reinforce through hypnosis our client-developed plan of action to affect modified behavior.

154. Highly imaginative people are usually persistent.

155. Hypnosis is contraindicated for claustrophobia.

156. People **can** lie under hypnosis.

157. Panic attacks: force them to face the fear. Fear *of the fear* is the problem.

158. The fear (phobia) might be a symptom of the problem.

159. Phobias require a minimum of twelve sessions if you use Systematic Desensitization.

160. Eye Movement Desensitization Restructuring (EMDR) breaks opening clogged memories.

161. EMDR: Think of the scene. Rapidly move the eyes. Francine Shapiro discovered it works for post-traumatic stress syndrome among other things.

162. The body can take little doses of anxiety fairly easily, but it can't take the big hit easily. This is why Systematic Desensitizing works.

163. Let yourself have little doses of anxiety your body can handle, so when you get the big fear, you can handle it.

164. How to deliver suggestions to your client:

    1: The key factor is always getting the client to feel good about themselves.

    2: Use the Ego Strengthening Technique just before giving script suggestions.

165. Willingness is an energy.

166. You must work on **only one thing at a time**, or the subconscious mind will throw it all out.

167. To increase performance, rehearse under hypnosis in slow motion. Give suggestions (receptivity).

168. If the speaker is uncomfortable, the audience will be uncomfortable.

169. Don't do hypnosis on individuals in your audience.

170. Ten percent will not like you. Pick one smiling person and talk to him.

171. Talk soft or say nothing to get attention.

172. Fit the talk to the audience.

173. Who, what, where, when, why, how? These are the questions.

174. Tell them what you are going to tell them, tell them, then tell them what you just told them.

175. Believe in what you say. Love your audience; focus on your audience, not yourself.

176. Be yourself. Make yourself and others comfortable. Be interesting, animated and excited, likable, concerned and optimistic. Be a performer, not an actor. Entertain as well as educate.

177. Use simple understandable language. Walk up to the lectern tall, straight and in control.

178. No one knows what you are going to say, so just say it. Add humor, not jokes.

179. As a teacher, if you get sick, give students an assignment. Take care of yourself mentally and physically.

180. Bridging techniques: get others in the class to answer questions, rather than answer all of them yourself.

181. People tend to resent those who give advice, so just lead them to their own conclusion. It will be the right one.

182. People learn best at the eight or nine year old level.

183. People learn through verbal and demonstration.

184. Acknowledge your limitations, but don't let them stop you.

185. Solutions to problems just come out of nowhere.

186. Emotion is the fuel of fear.

187. Most things you fear in the future **will never happen,** so why spoil your present happiness?

188. Fear is not real. It is of something in the future, and the future is not here yet—and may never come.

189.We are born only with the fear of loud noises and maybe the fear of bright lights. All others we develop, including the fear of falling.

190.We learn fear from personal experience, teachers, parents, siblings and friends.

191.We have to choose to stay in fear.

192.Fear is a thief. It robs us of life and leaves us with nothing except more fear.

193.Unless there is imminent physical danger, there is no need for fear.

194.Recognize that unless you are in physical danger, the fear is irrational.

195.Ultimately, all fear is the fear of death. Loose that, and fear disappears.

196.Since it is inevitable, embrace death, and fear leaves.

197.Confront all fear with courage. Don't retreat—go towards it.

198.Fear shrinks the mind.

199.We can only remain in fear if we are inactive. Do something! Action cures fear!

200.Replacing fear with faith and action leads to hope. A hopeful life is a happy life.

201.Avoid negative thinking; it fuels the fear and makes it grow.

202.Refuse to create fear in your mind, replacing it with faith instead.

203.Fear distorts your reality so you cannot see the reality of what's happening.

204.Fear exaggerates imagined difficulty and consequences.

205.Fear blocks self-confidence.

206.Respond to fear with self-control.

207.The enlightenment of Buddha, Jesus and Mohammed and many other Masters were all based around living life fearlessly, in action and faith!

208. The Past is gone, Tomorrow may never come. Now is all we have!

209. Stay in the Present forever. Experience life now. The future may never come and the future is where fear is focused.

210. The key to overcoming fear and increasing confidence is thinking **realistically**, NOT thinking positively.

211. **Inane positive thinking can generate false confidence**. Realistic assessment and thinking leads to reality-based choices, which gets rid of fear. So, accept it and go beyond it to what's real. Fear isn't real!

212. The past is not you anymore. Now, go on with what you want.

213. Stop doing what hurts you!

About the Author

Dr. Charles William Skillas is an NGH Board Certified Hypnotherapist practicing in metropolitan Atlanta, Georgia and is a National Guild of Hypnotists (NGH) Certified Instructor in Hypnotherapy. Dr. Skillas is also a Fellow of the NGH (FNGH) and has practiced energy healing since 1981 and Hypnotherapy since 1985. He is a member of the Business and Metaphysical Teaching Faculty of St. Johns University and a Faculty Member for The National Board of Hypnotherapy and Hypnotic Anesthesiology.

He is certified in: Advanced and Clinical Hypnotherapy, Hypnotherapy Instruction, Transformational Counseling, Cell Command Therapy, Spirit Releasement Therapy, Neuro-Linguistic Programming, Hypnotic Pain Control, Emergency Hypnosis and Past Life Regression Therapy. His memberships include: The National Guild of Hypnotists, The National Board of Hypnotherapists and Hypnotic Anesthesiologists, The National Federation of Neuro-Linguistic Psychology and The National Federation of Hypnotists. He is also a Licensed Professional Engineer listed in Who's Who in America and is President of the Georgia Chapter of the National Guild of Hypnotists.

Dr. Skillas also earned a Ph.D. in Engineering and has many years of experience in the Aerospace/Defense Industry as: Chief Engineer, General Manager, Vice President of Marketing, and consultant to the Department of Defense and Major Defense Companies of the Western World in Anti Submarine Warfare, Submarine Torpedo Defense, and Mine Countermeasures. He was honored by the US Congress for serving as expert witness and for writing the legislation which created the National Oceanographic and Atmospheric Administration (NOAA). He was Chairman of the NH/ME Bi-State Commission on Oceanography. His business background is an important asset in helping distressed working people solve their real-world problems.

Life@DrSkillas.com   www.DrSkillas.com

0-595-32777-X